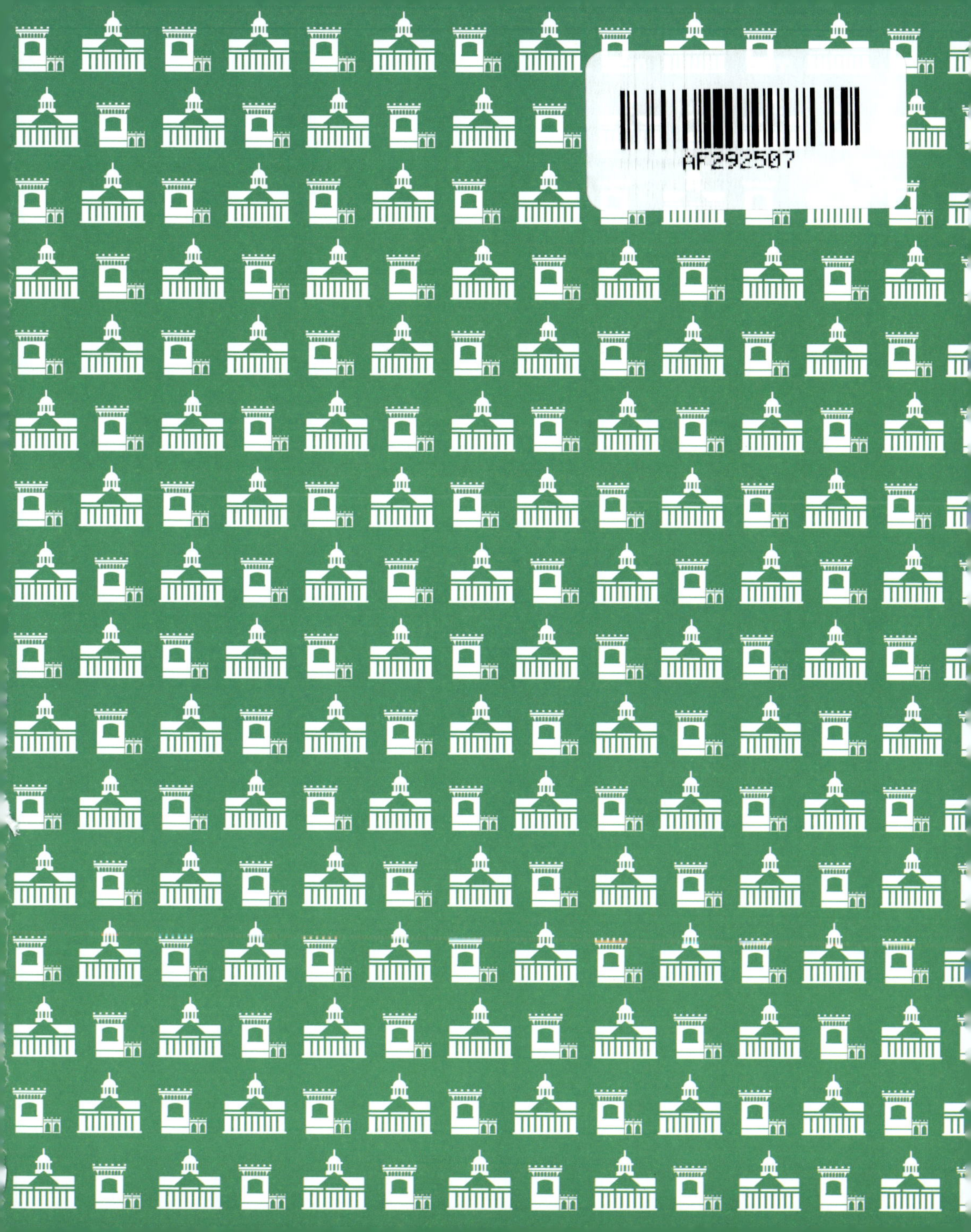

AF292507

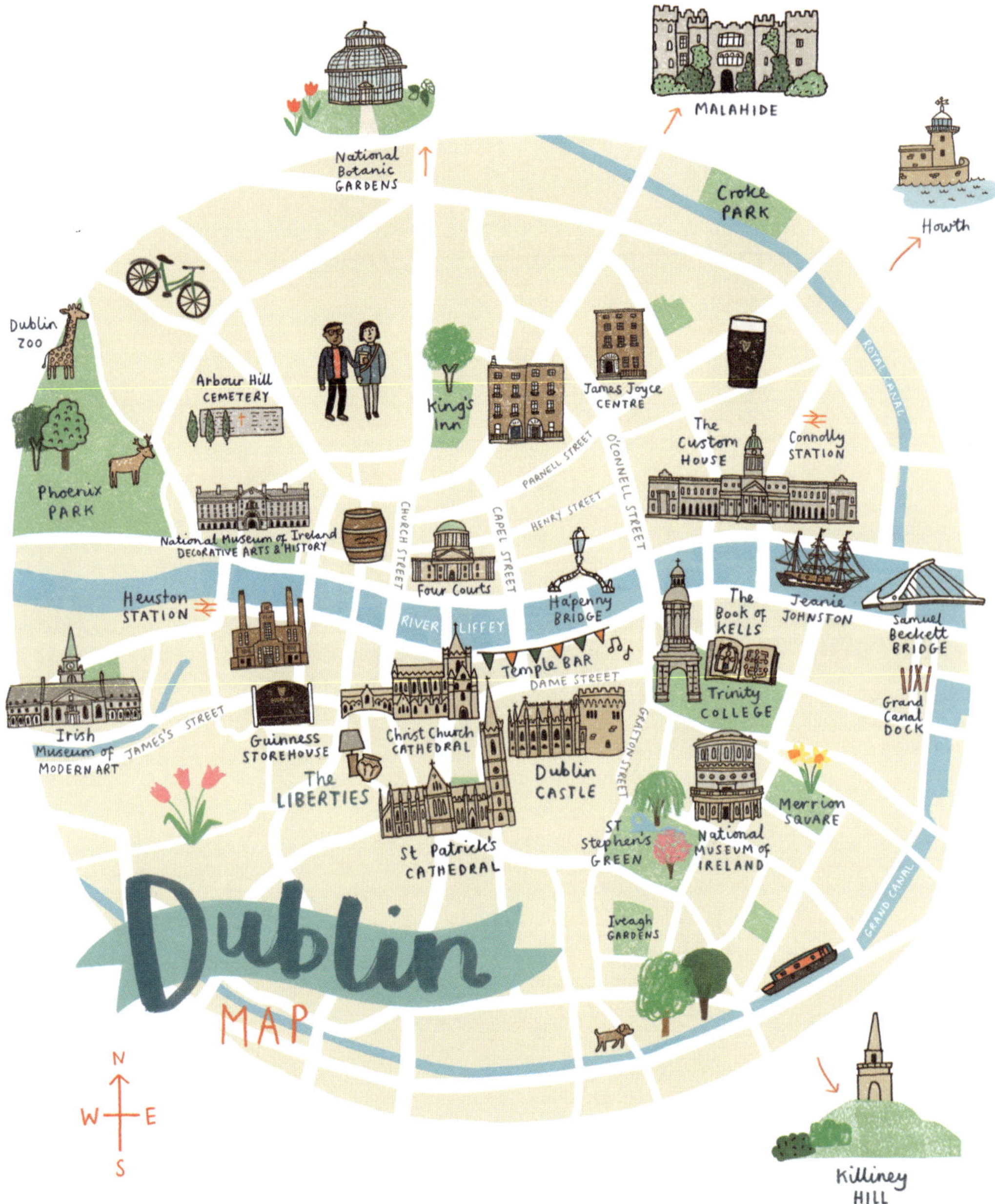

National Botanic GARDENS
MALAHIDE
Howth
Croke PARK
Dublin ZOO
Arbour Hill CEMETERY
King's Inn
James Joyce CENTRE
PARNELL STREET
O'CONNELL STREET
The Custom HOUSE
Connolly STATION
Phoenix PARK
National Museum of Ireland DECORATIVE ARTS & HISTORY
CHURCH STREET
Four Courts
CAPEL STREET
HENRY STREET
ROYAL CANAL
Heuston STATION
RIVER LIFFEY
Ha'penny BRIDGE
Temple BAR
DAME STREET
The Book of KELLS
Jeanie JOHNSTON
Samuel Beckett BRIDGE
Irish Museum of MODERN ART
JAMES'S STREET
Guinness STOREHOUSE
Christ Church CATHEDRAL
Dublin CASTLE
GRAFTON STREET
Trinity COLLEGE
Grand Canal DOCK
The LIBERTIES
St Patrick's CATHEDRAL
St Stephen's GREEN
National MUSEUM OF IRELAND
Merrion SQUARE
GRAND CANAL
Iveagh GARDENS
Dublin
MAP
N W E S
Killiney HILL

Absolutely beautiful.

Dublin City architecture has always had a certain magnetism
and appeal, delineated so beautifully by the diverse images
of our contemporary artists. A must see publication.

Trinity College is an oasis of calm in the heart of
Dublin, one of the world's great centres of learning for
generations of students, myself included.

Me jewel and darling Dublin has another diamond in her crown, this beautiful
collection of images does our great capital justice.

I fell in love with Dublin the day I arrived, fifty years ago,
the only love affair in which I have never wavered!
I so welcome this wonderful celebration of a great city.

We need to see the places we live in through the eyes of artists,
especially cities we trudge through daily with all our baggage,
constantly forgetting to look up and see the beauty.

As a Dubliner born and bred, this is a beautiful prism to
view the city through – its artists' eyes.

Community spirit helped shape this wonderfully creative, vibrant and culturally
diverse Dublin. How appropriate that the city I now call home should be
celebrated through the vision of many of her inspirational artists.

HERBERT PRESS
Bloomsbury Publishing Plc
50 Bedford Square, London, WC1B 3DP, UK
29 Earlsfort Terrace, Dublin 2, Ireland

BLOOMSBURY, HERBERT PRESS and the Herbert Press logo are trademarks of Bloomsbury Publishing Plc

First published in England in 2020 by UIT Cambridge Ltd.
This edition published 2024

A CIP catalogue record for this book is available from the British Library
Library of Congress Cataloguing-in-Publication data has been applied for

ISBN: 978-1-91293-410-2 (hardback) ISBN: 978-1-91293-411-9 (ePub)

3 5 7 9 10 8 6 4 2

Printed and bound in India

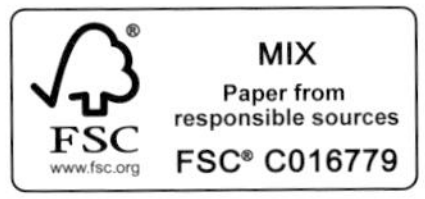

To find out more about our authors and books visit www.bloomsbury.com and sign up for our newsletters

THE DUBLIN ART BOOK

The City Through the Eyes of its Artists®

EDITED BY

EMMA BENNETT

HERBERT PRESS

LONDON · OXFORD · NEW YORK · NEW DELHI · SYDNEY

Acknowledgements

The Dublin Art Book has been made possible by the enthusiasm and talent of the contributing artists and to them I am eternally grateful.

In the inspirational city of Dublin, an illustrious panel of local art professionals helped select images for publication. I am indebted to them for their creative input. They are:

- Oisín Coghlan, Director, Friends of The Earth Ireland

- Joe Drumgoole, Director of Development Relations, MongoDB

- Aoife Flynn, Director, asquared

- Julie Mc Loughlin, Co-Founder, Jando

- Jo Tunmer, Visual Artist

I thank Sheila Stickley, Niall Mansfield, Lauren Downing and Vera Kleinken at UIT for their enthusiasm and continued support for *The City Art Book* Series.

Cheers to the friendly folk who make Dublin such a lovely city to visit, from the jovial bus drivers at the airport to the staff in pubs and coffee shops. Thank you to David Owens, Grafton Street's piano playing street performer for the wonderful music. To Joe and Jo T (Dora The Explorer) for Irish merriment and exploration, thanks.

Usual huge thanks to my family and friends for ongoing support and encouragement. To Brenda Purkiss, Rock Road Library, Kisia and all those who support my work as a visual artist thank you. Naomi Triggol, thanks for years of creative ping-pong. Alison Schuldt and Julia Sadler for proofreading, thank you so much.

CONTENTS

Foreword 6

Preface 7

Around O'Connell Street 10

Over the bridge to south of the River Liffey 28

Trinity College, museums and Merrion Square 34

Grand Canal to Poolbeg Chimneys 50

Around St Stephen's Green 70

St Patrick's Cathedral area 97

The Liberties and on to Rathmines 116

Back north of the river 124

North and South County Dublin 130

Artist Credits 142

FOREWORD

I have travelled the world in the pursuit of Outsider, Naïve or Brut Art, a passion for art from the soul. Early on some asked 'what does ya man know about art?' and they may have been right, but for me art is how it makes me feel. Arriving in Dublin so many years ago, I encountered a much different city than what exists today. Modern Dublin is a tapestry of new cultures, an exuberant artistic space, awash with colour and creativity.

What better way to celebrate Dublin's art culture than through the eyes of 55 inspirational local artists, who have helped mould this city. A unique blend of artists from different generations, cultures and perspectives, that have in so many different ways been able to express just what Dublin means to them.

Through the pages of this book, I feel it is like taking a journey into every nook and cranny of Ireland's magical capital, to feel the 'faces and the places' that have shaped the artists' lives, and to see that portrayed through their own vision. This magnificent body of work allows us to take a journey with the artist, to feel what they may feel, and for an artist to have that power to evoke such an emotion in us, happy or sad, is perhaps their greatest gift. A wonderfully crafted collaboration of styles and expressions that best represents their Dublin, and for all the readers to discover or rediscover just what this exuberant city means to them.

Brent Pope

RTÉ sports analyst, Author, Charity worker, Curator and Art collector

PREFACE

Dublin is an iconic city loved the world over. Visitor or local you will understand why this is. If you have never had the chance to visit, pack your bags immediately! *The Dublin Art Book* offers a fresh perspective on the city, through the eyes of 55 local artists it inspires.

There is little mystery as to why Dublin is adored. Its connection to the Irish Sea via a breath-taking bay and the calm waters of the River Liffey provide a perfect setting. With 21 bridges both old and new over the river, connecting the north and south of the city, Dublin has the feel more of a series of villages rather than a traditional capital. Perhaps it is this village feel, with the friendliness of its locals, that contributes to the warm feeling you experience in Dublin

Georgian squares, converted industrial buildings, modern architectural structures, even a 120-metre stainless steel spire, it's all here in Dublin. Streets named to honour Irish heroes are alive with buskers, performance artists, pop-up art exhibitions, independent shops, cafes and galleries. You'll also find magnificent markets and street sellers. The cobbled corners are home to pubs alive with music, mixed with the sound of laughter and friendly banter.

Dublin is a modern vibrant city with a proud historical past, so it's little wonder it provides such magical inspiration to its artists. *The Dublin Art Book* is the fifth in *The City Art Book* Series (with Cambridge, Oxford, Edinburgh and Liverpool) and represents just some of the talented artists working in and around Dublin. With the help of the map, potter through this city with *The Dublin Art Book* in your hand and stand for a while in the footsteps of an artist.

Emma Bennett
Creator and Editor of *The City Art Book* Series

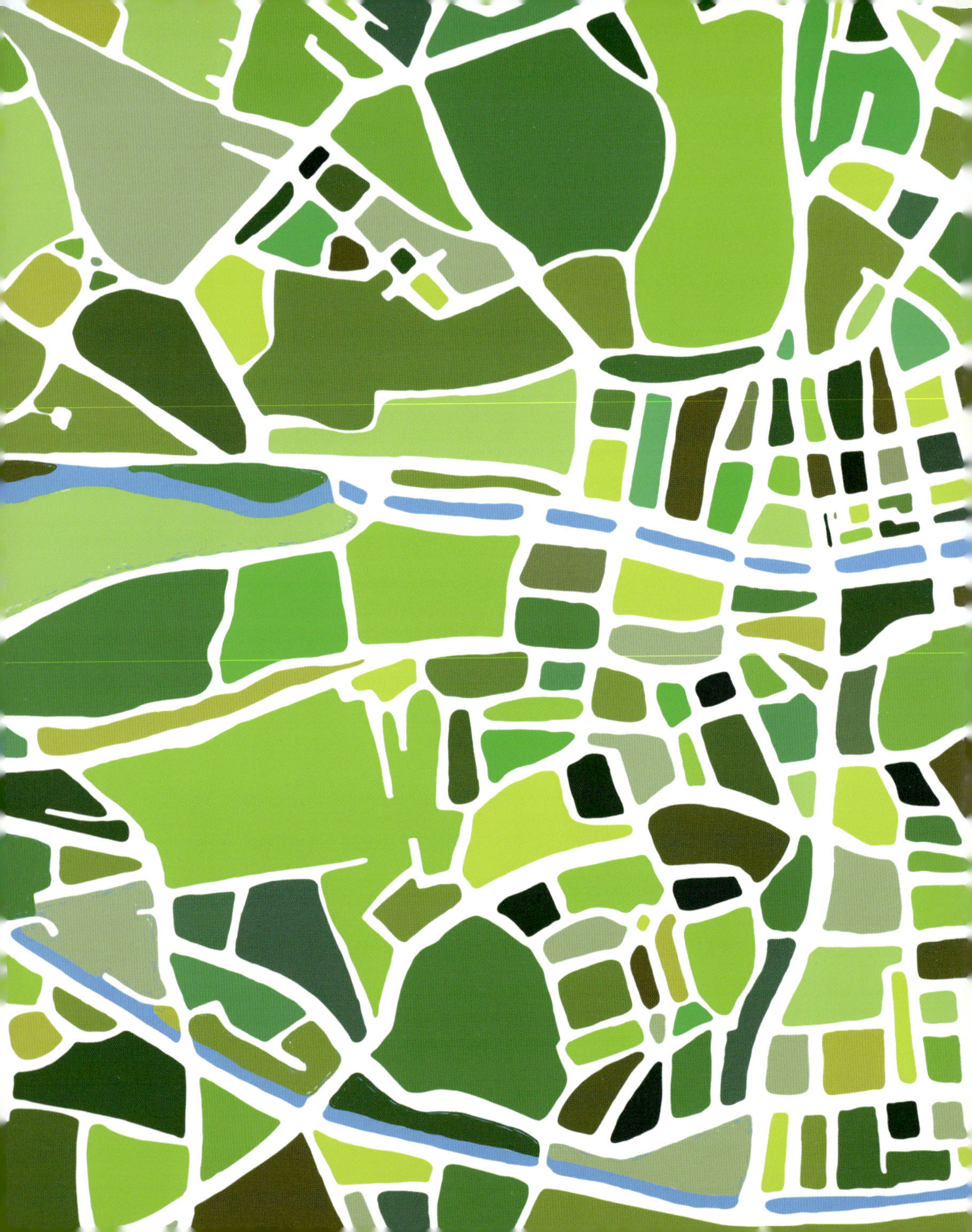

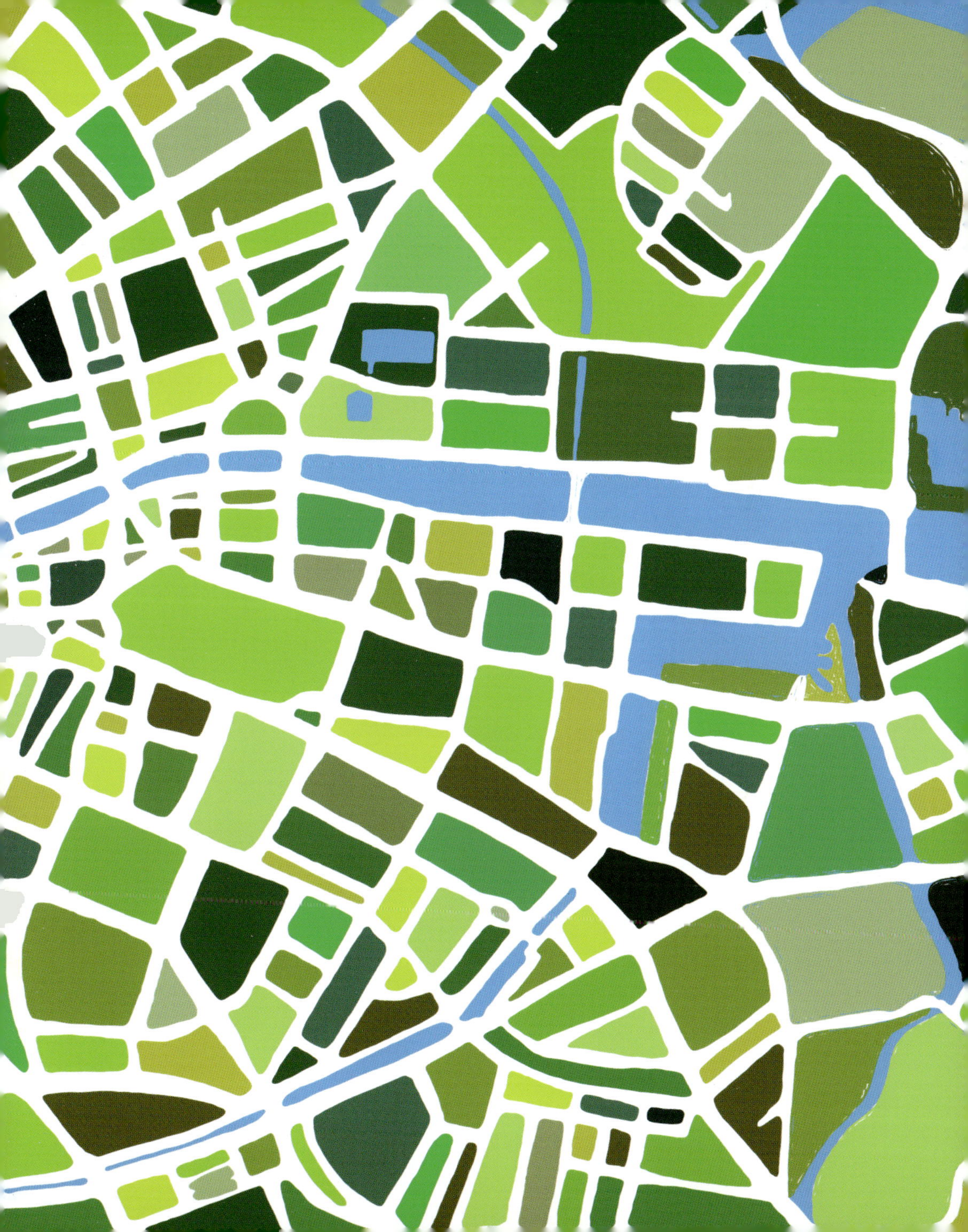

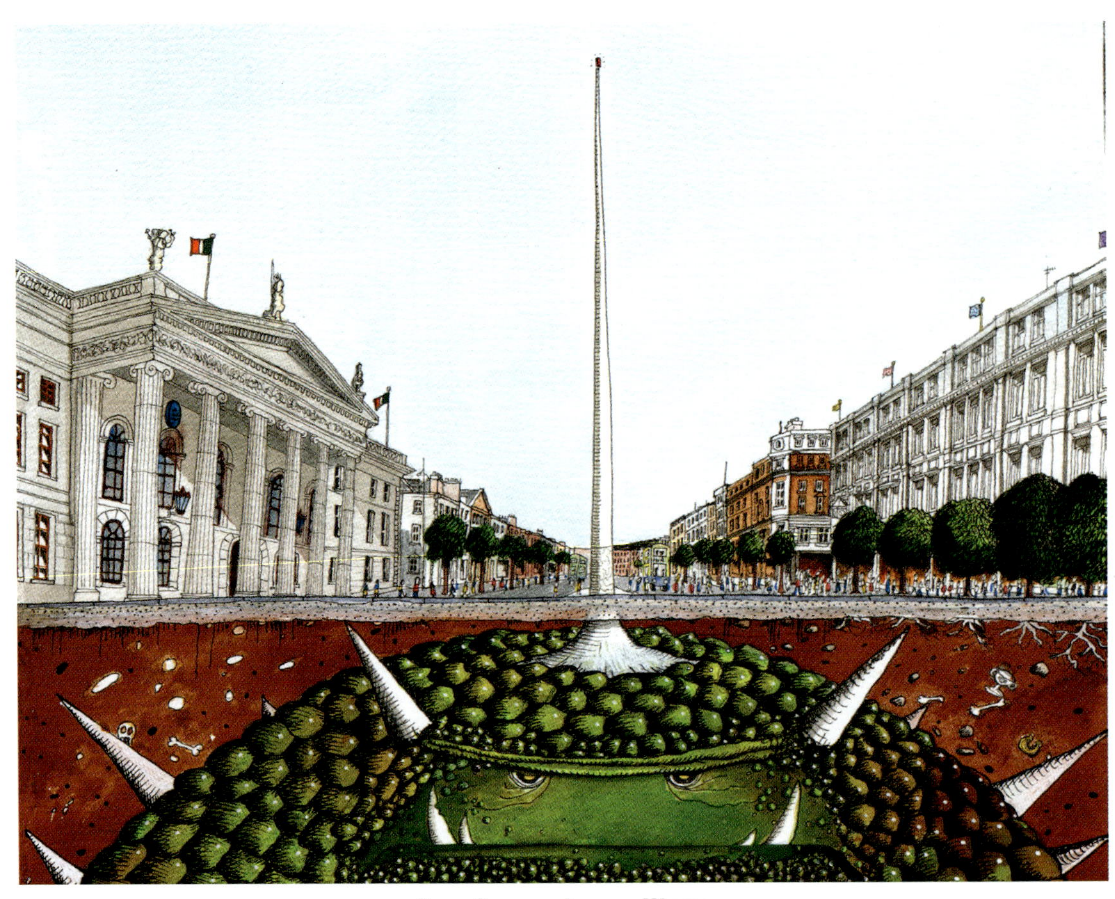

THE SPIRE, ANNIE WEST
PREVIOUS TWO PAGES: MAP OF DUBLIN, RICHARD DALTON

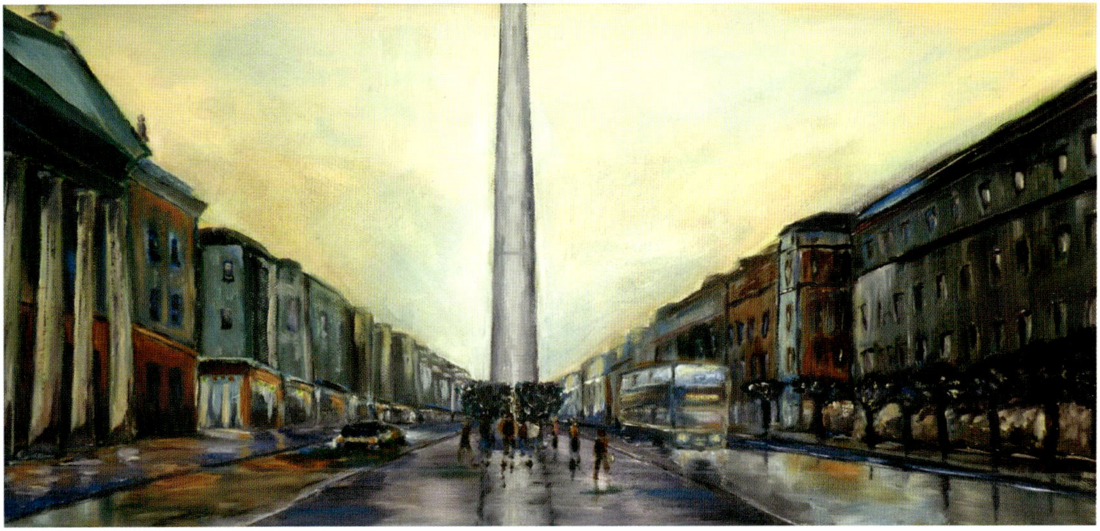

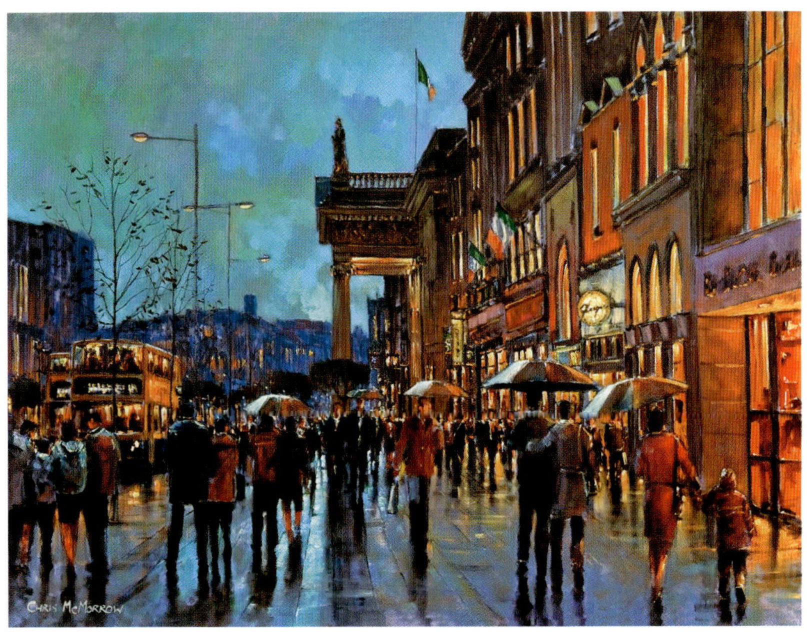

O'CONNELL STREET, MARIE O'CALLAGHAN

O'CONNELL STREET, CHRIS MCMORROW

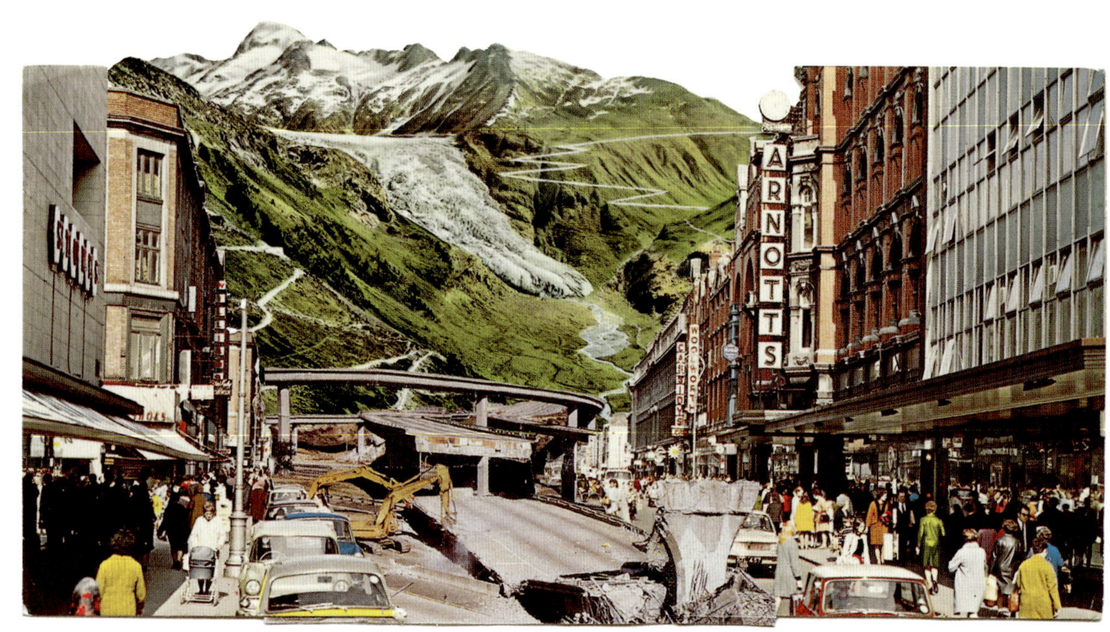

TROUBLE WITH THE GLACIER IN HENRY STREET, SEAN HILLEN

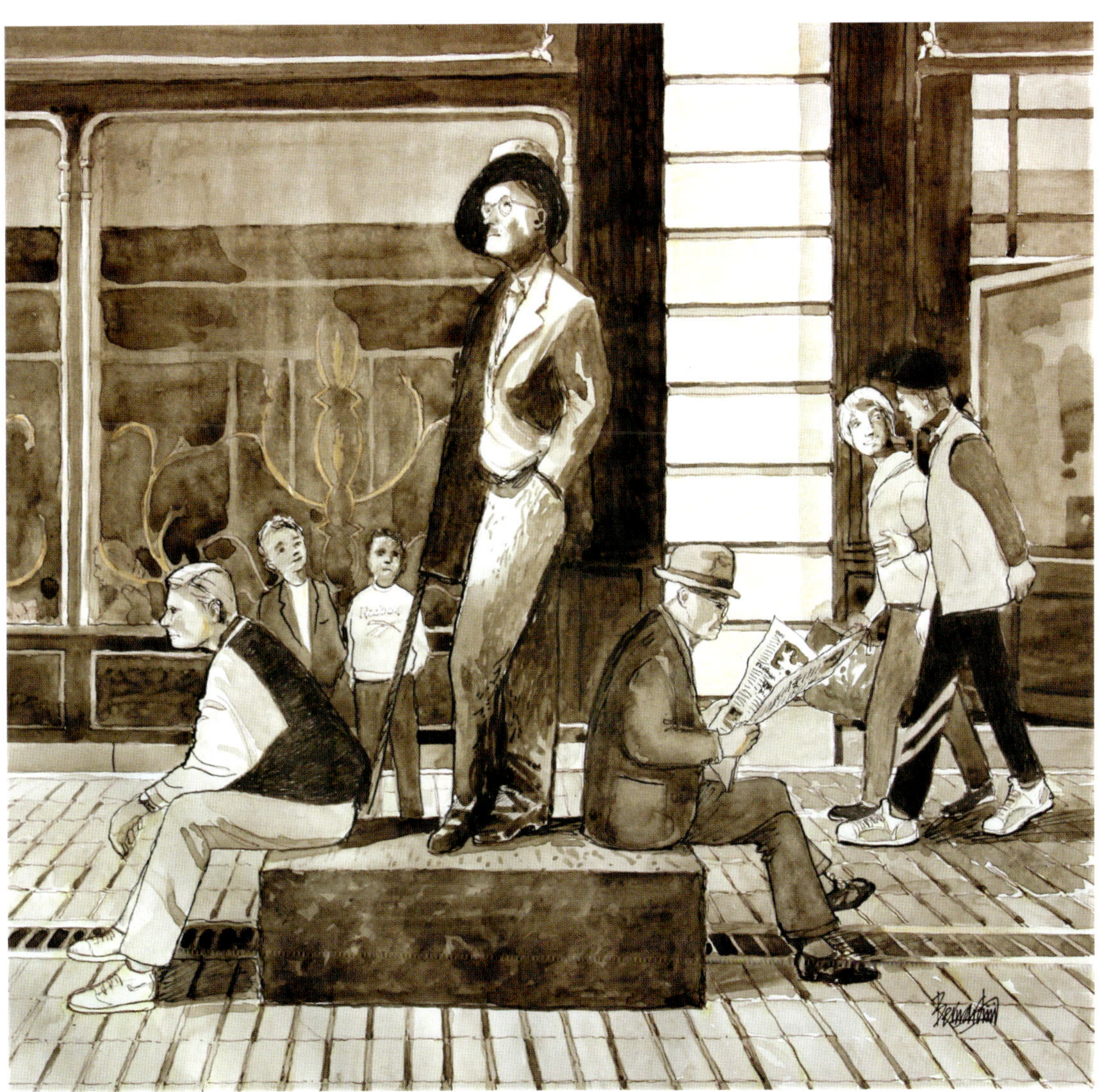

THE JAMES JOYCE STATUE, WALTER BERNARDINI

THE G.P.O.
DUBLIN, IRELAND

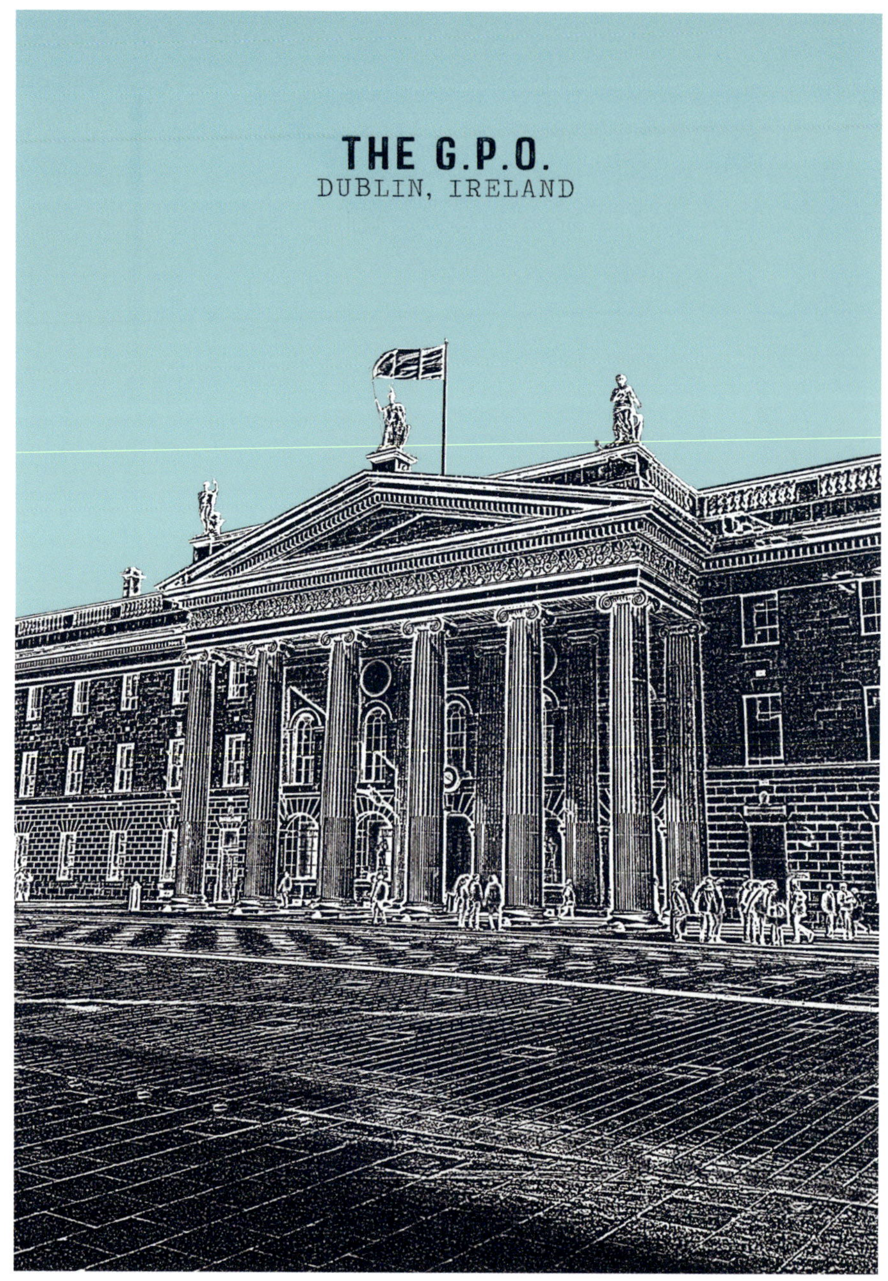

THE GENERAL POST OFFICE, JANDO

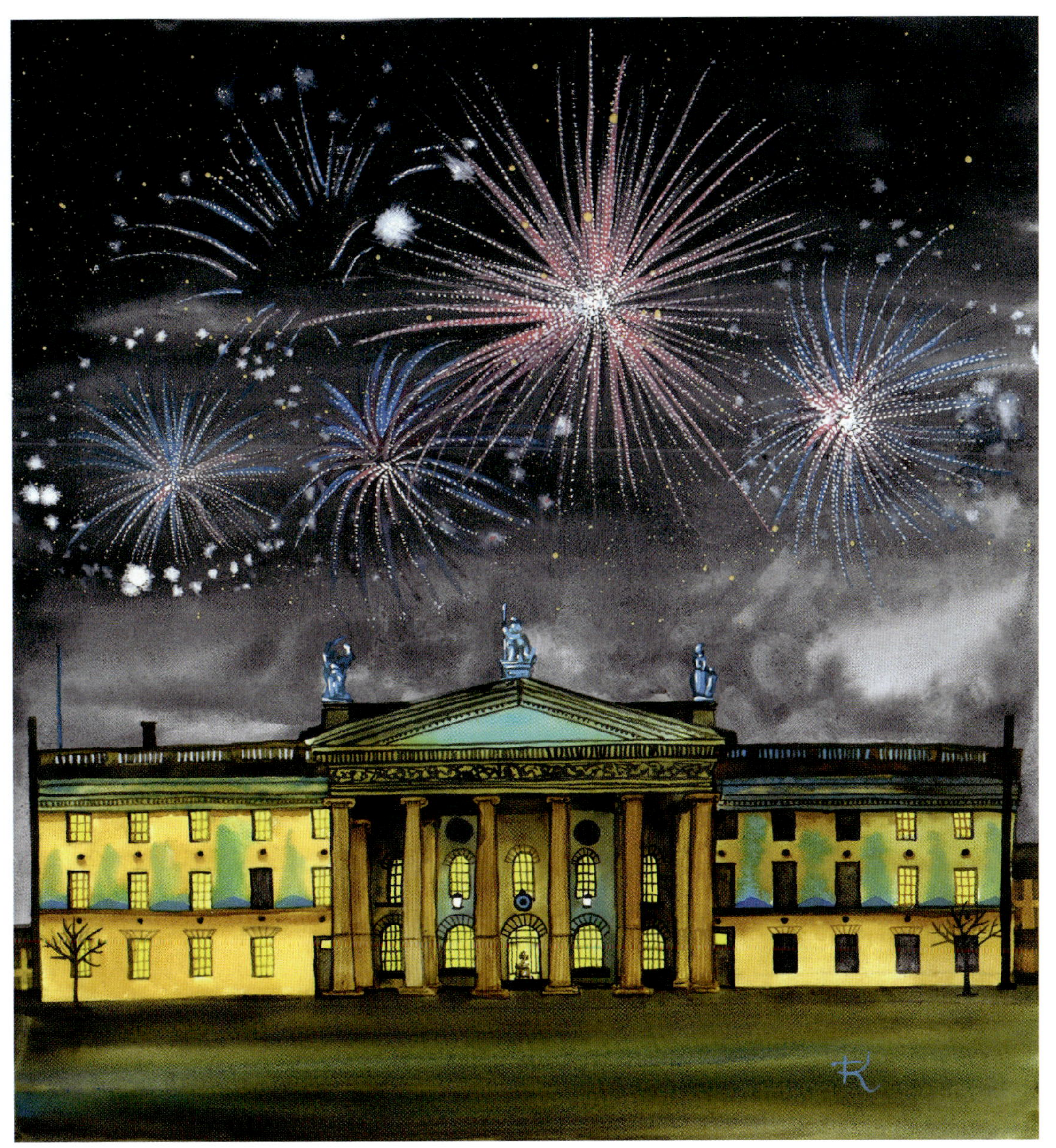

THE GENERAL POST OFFICE, TERRI KELLEHER

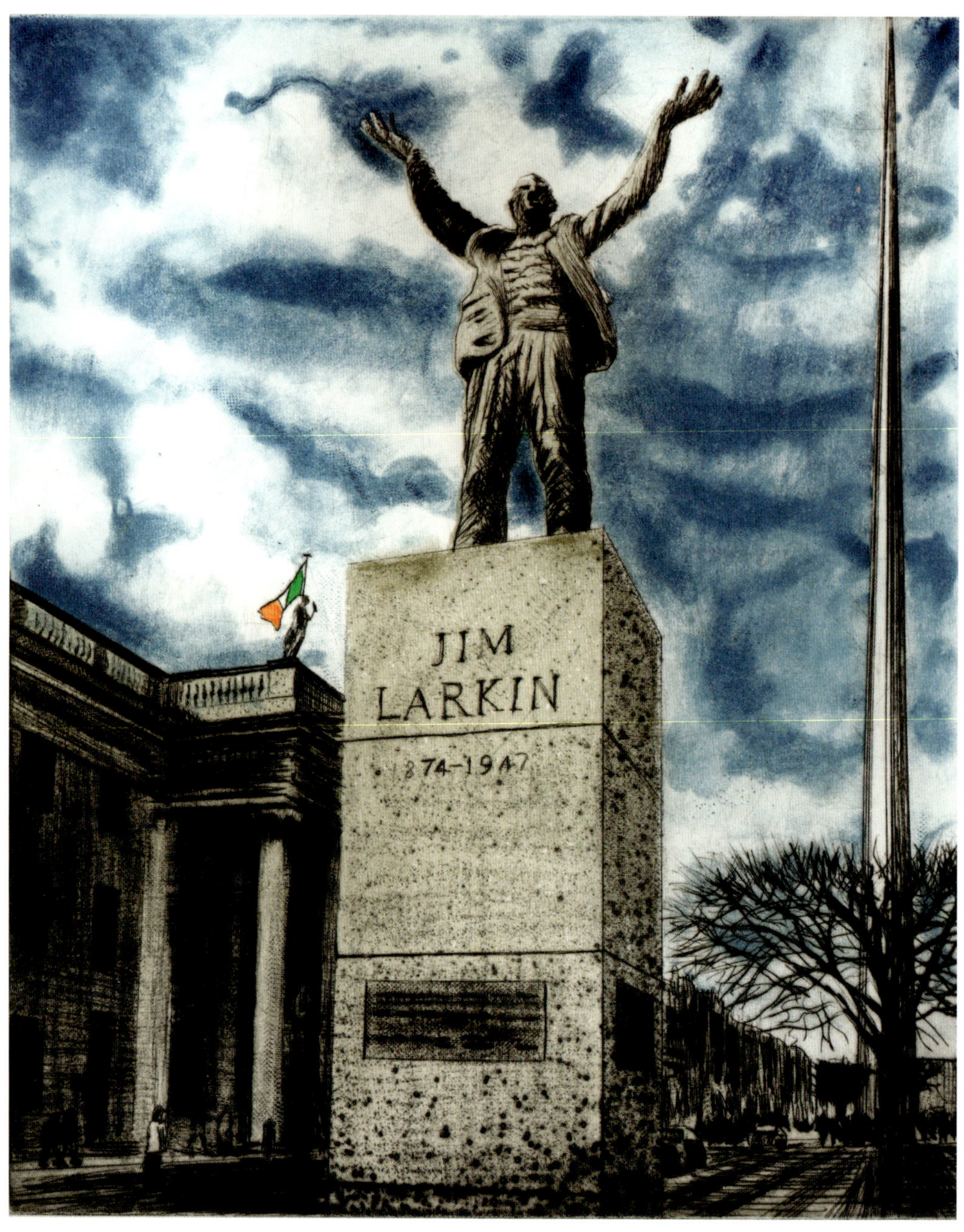

JIM LARKIN STATUE, DERMOT RYAN

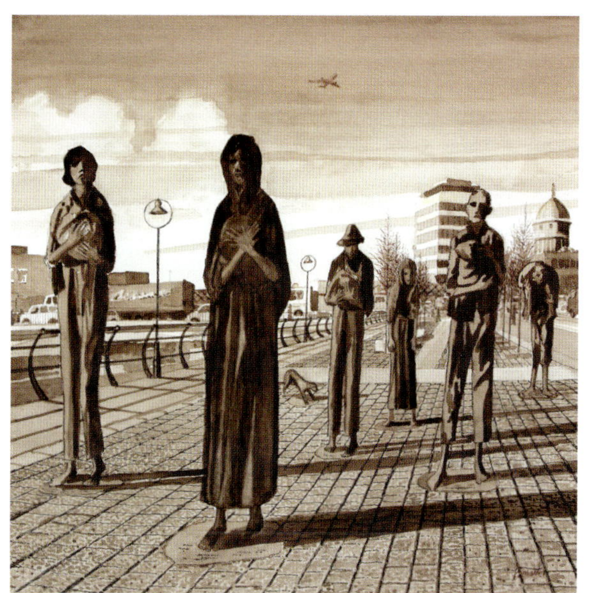

The Famine Memorial, Walter Bernardini

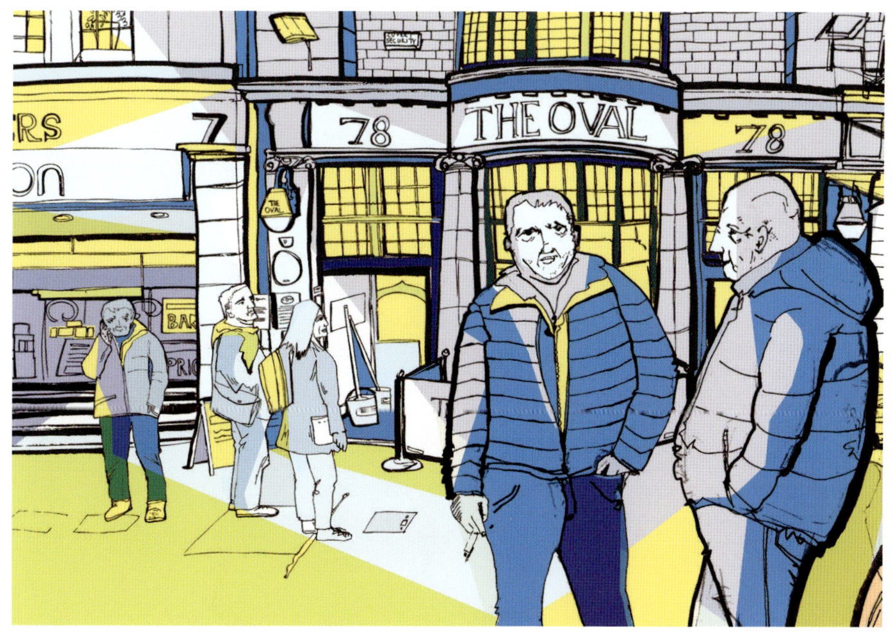

Abbey Street Lower, Eva Kelly

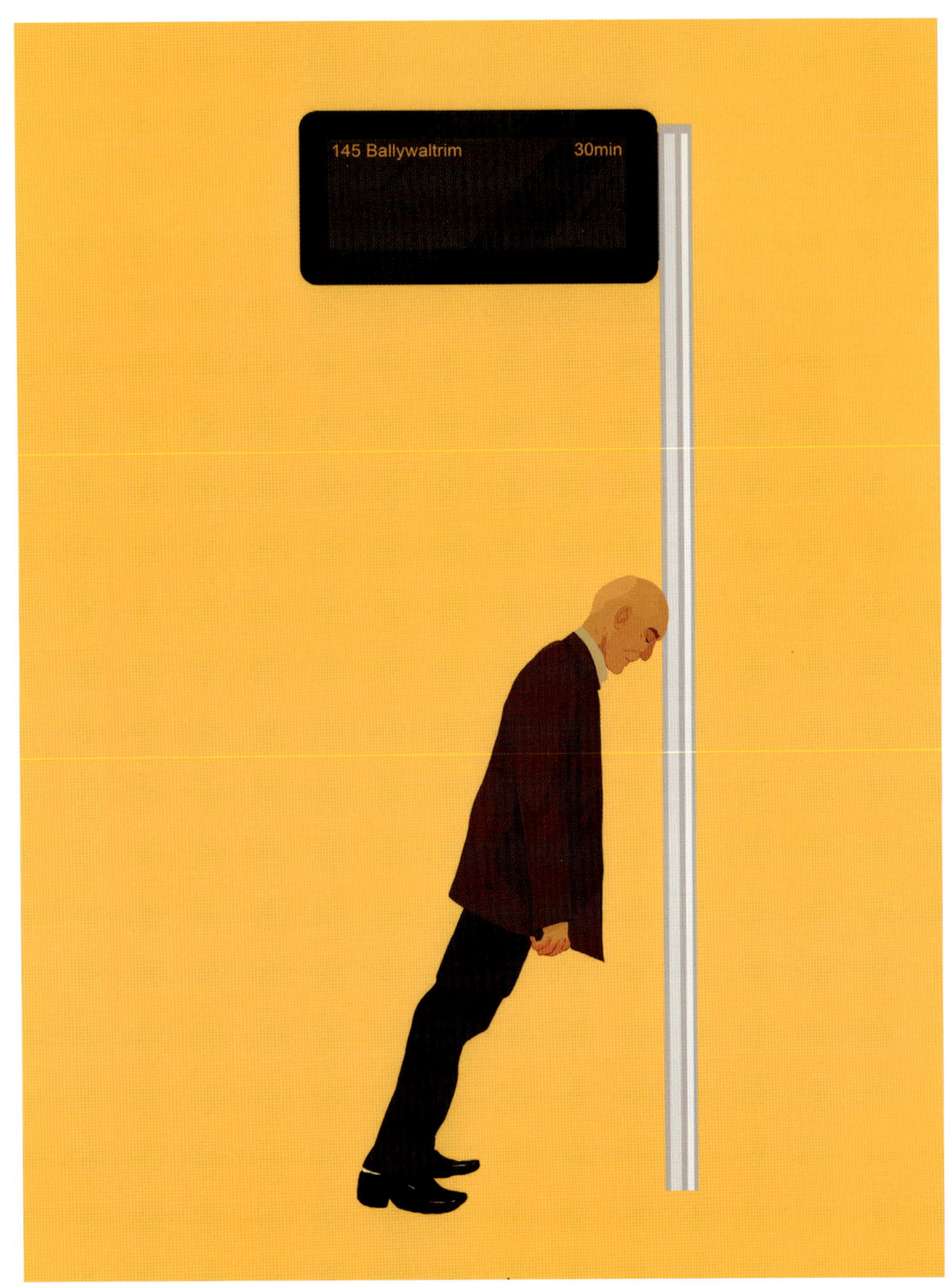

Bus stop, Rob Torrans

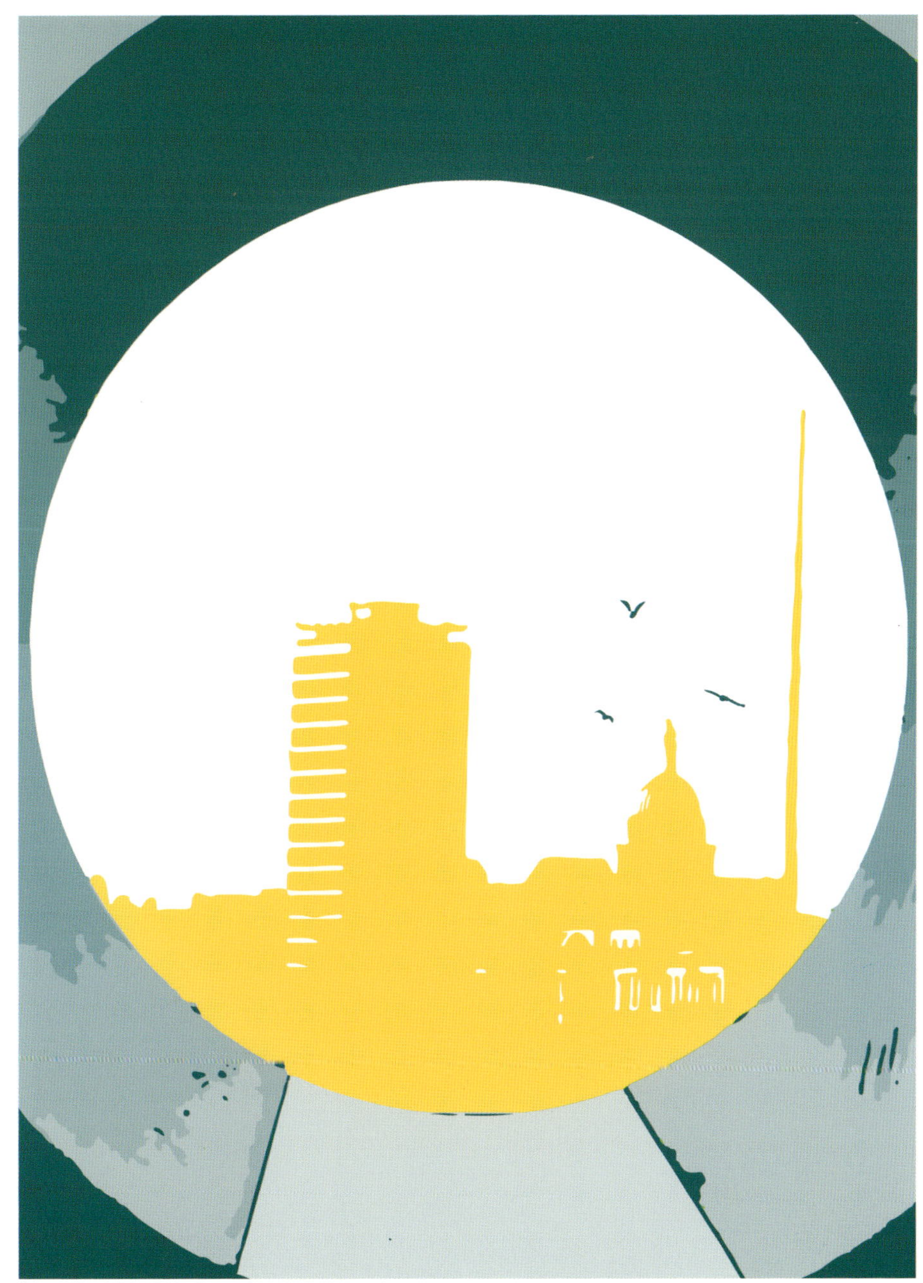

SAMUEL BECKETT BRIDGE, AMY HENNESEY

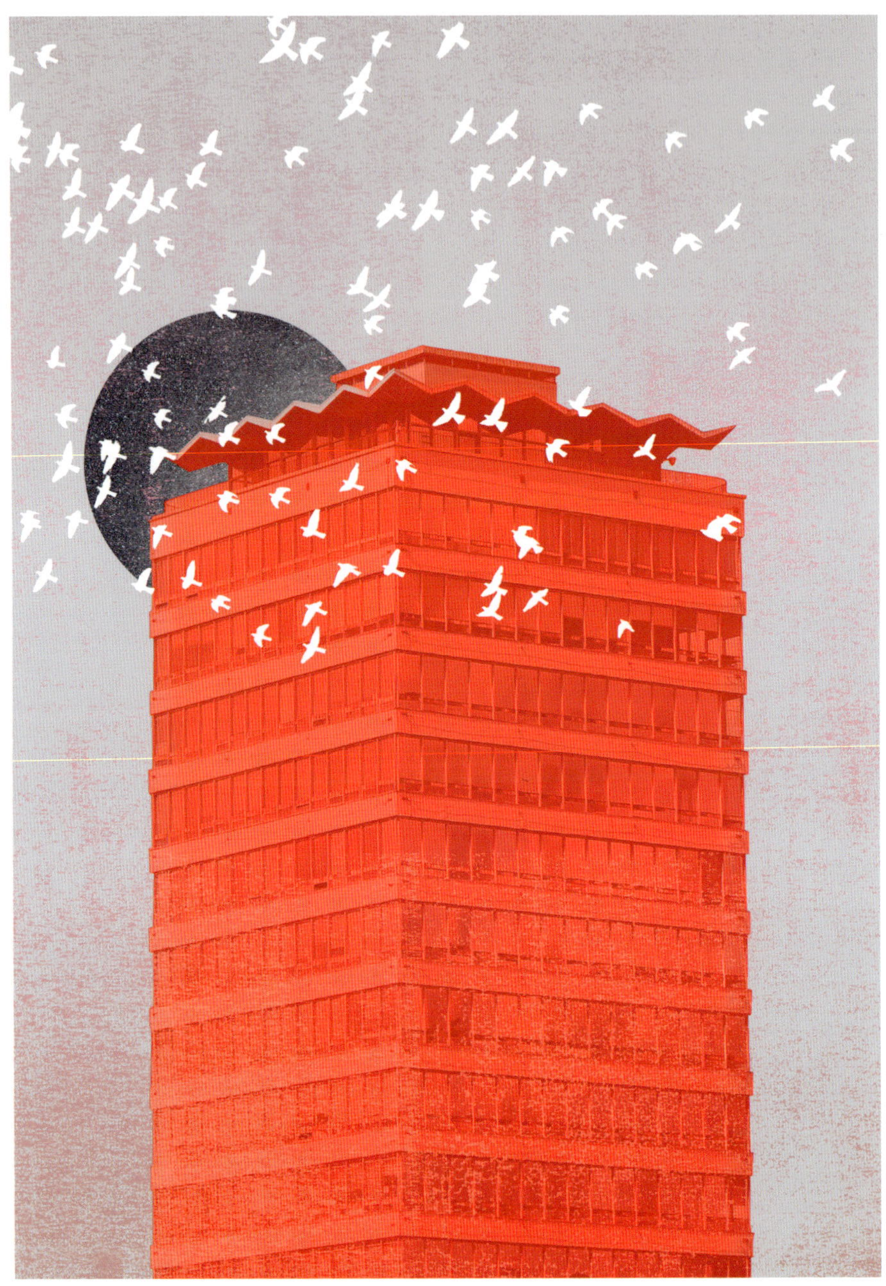

LIBERTY HALL, JANDO

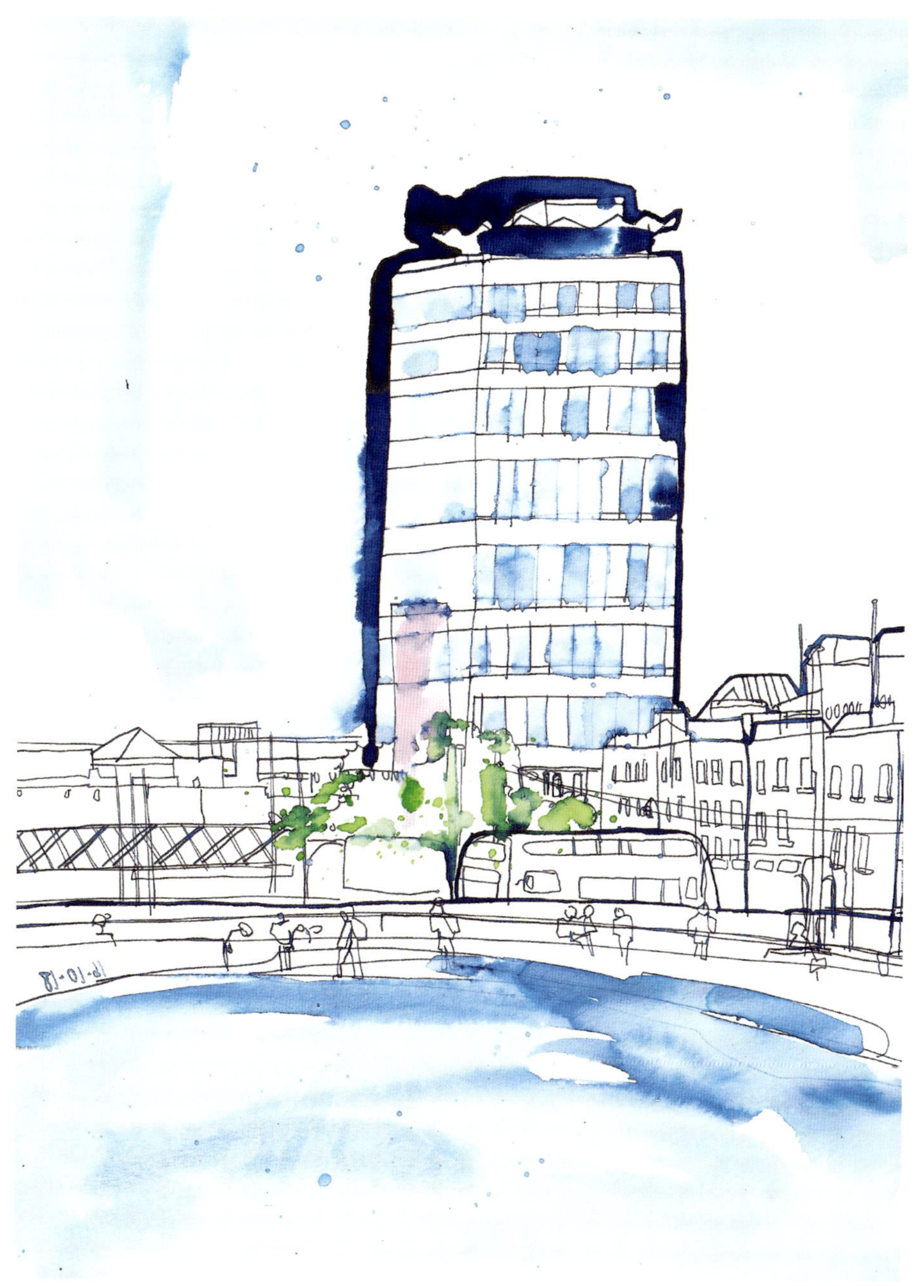

LIBERTY HALL, EVA KELLY

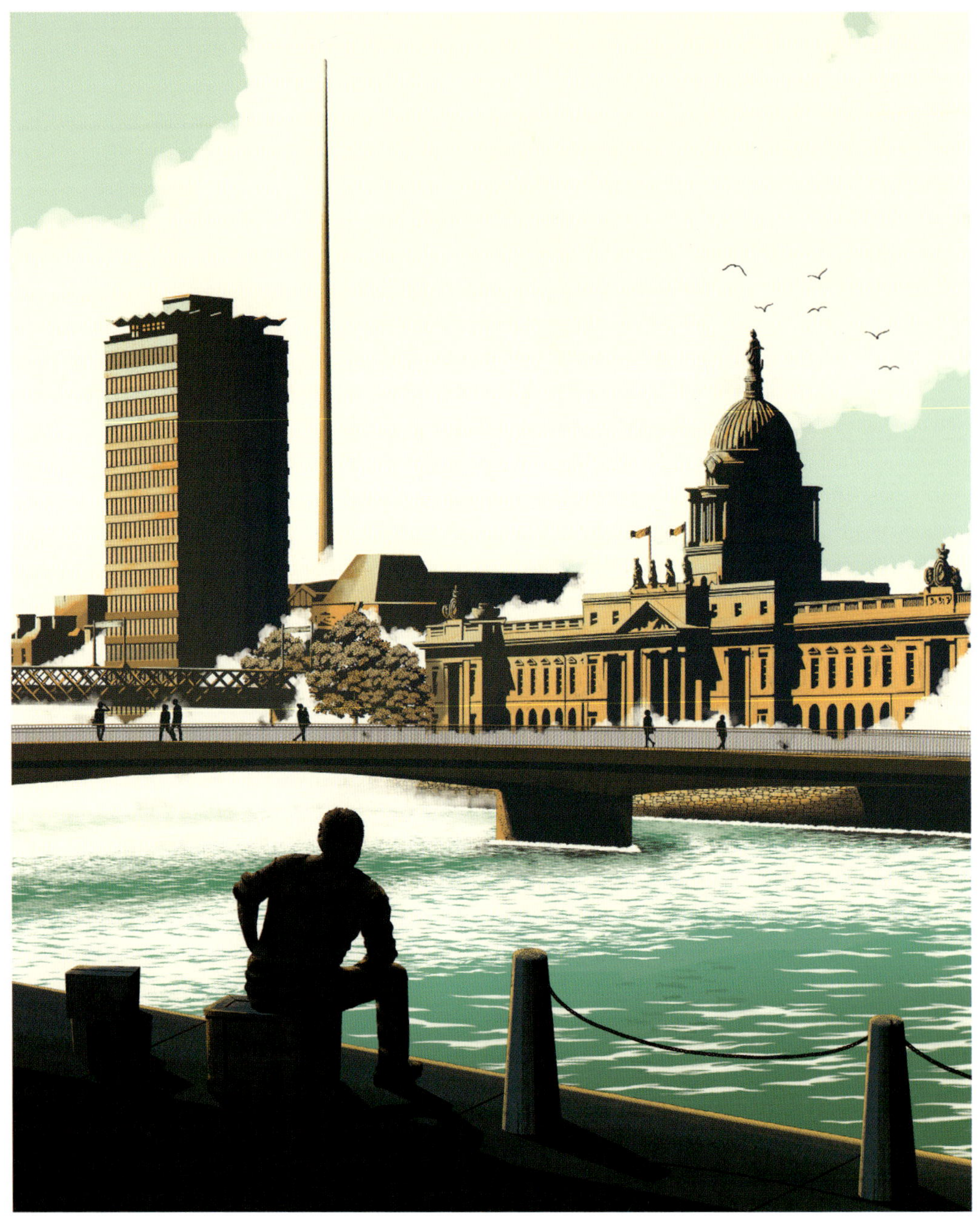

THE CUSTOM HOUSE, CONOR SMYTH

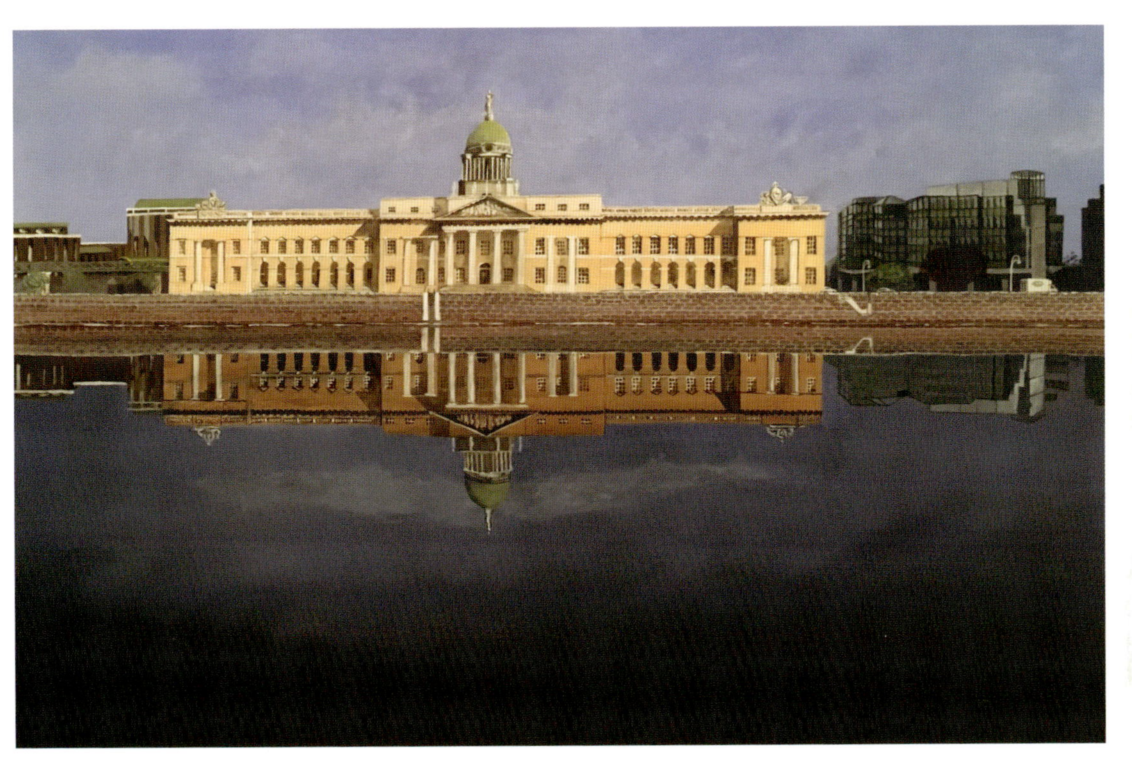

THE CUSTOM HOUSE, BRIAN O'NEILL

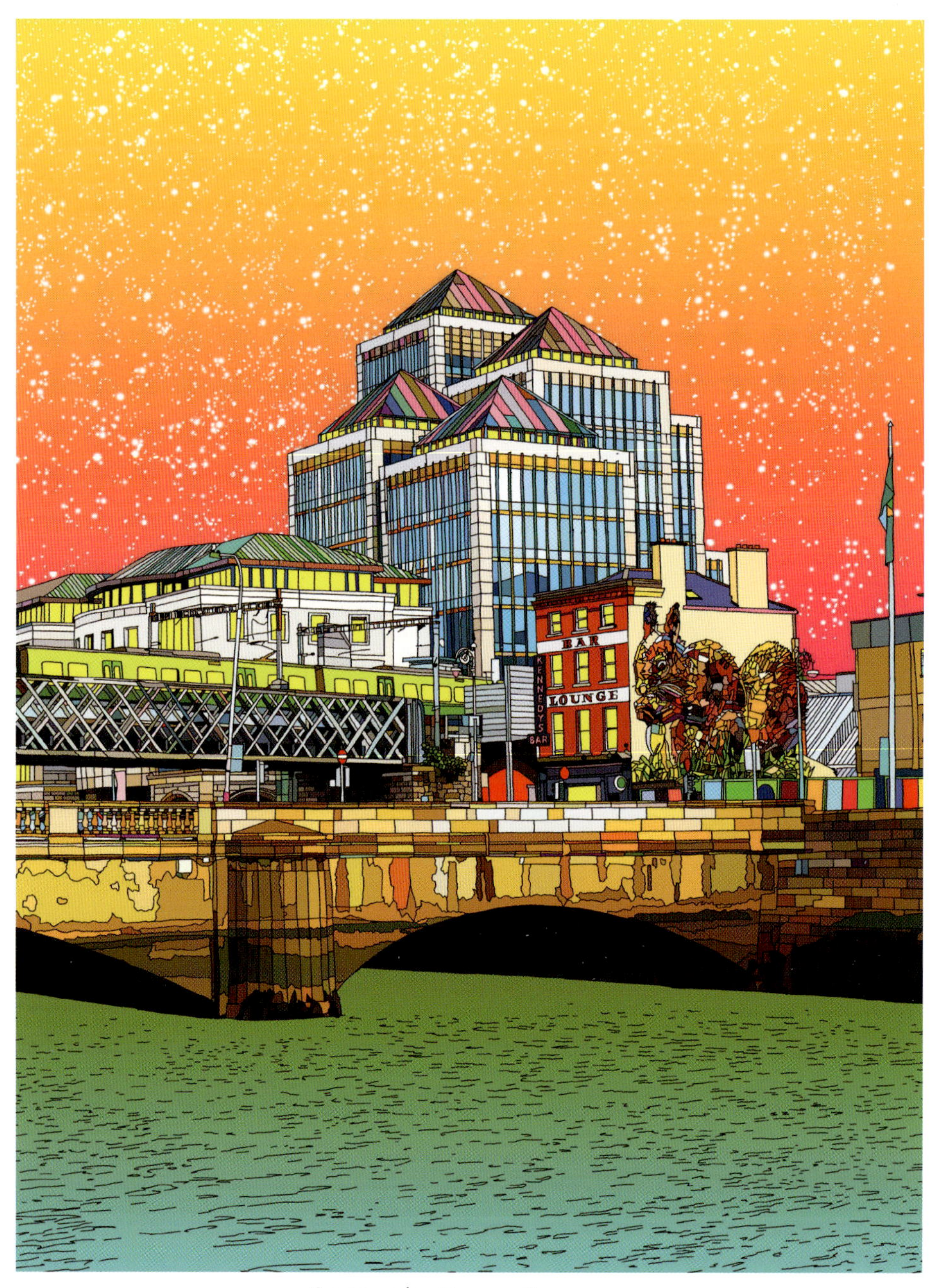

GEORGE'S QUAY, SKETCHY

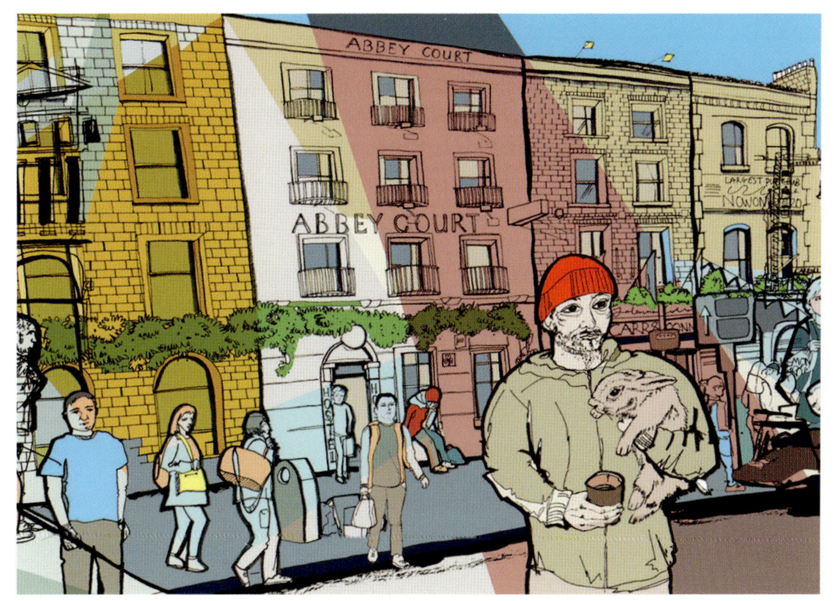

BACHELORS WALK, EVA KELLY

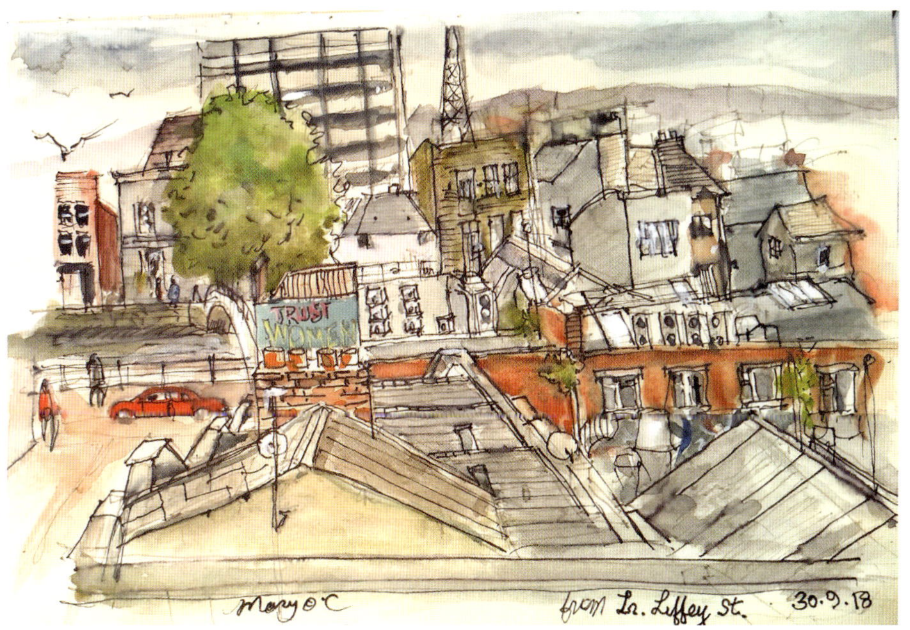

LITTLE LIFFEY STREET, MARY O'CARROLL

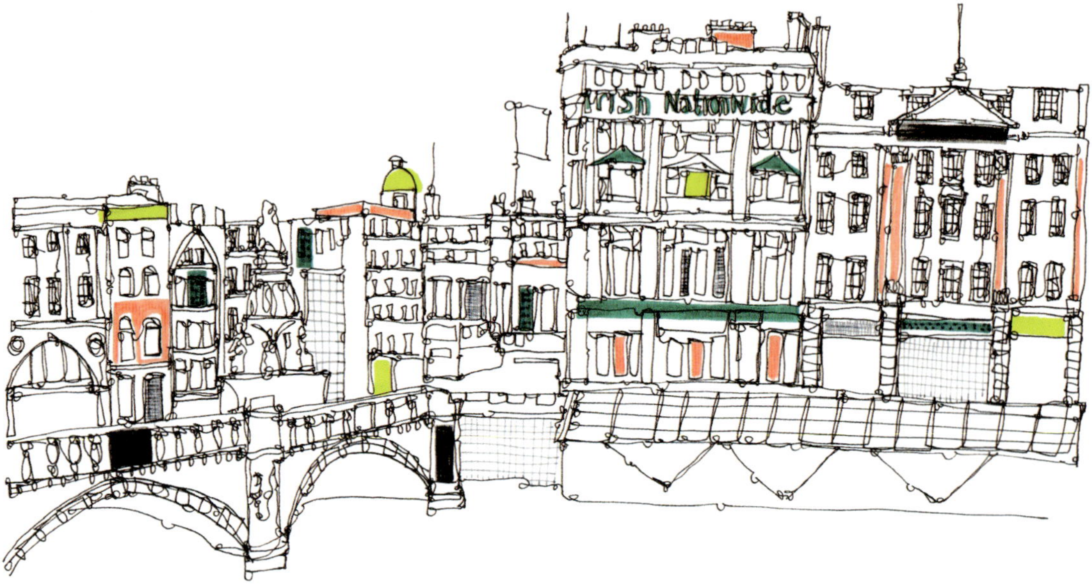

O'CONNELL STREET, RUTH ALLEN

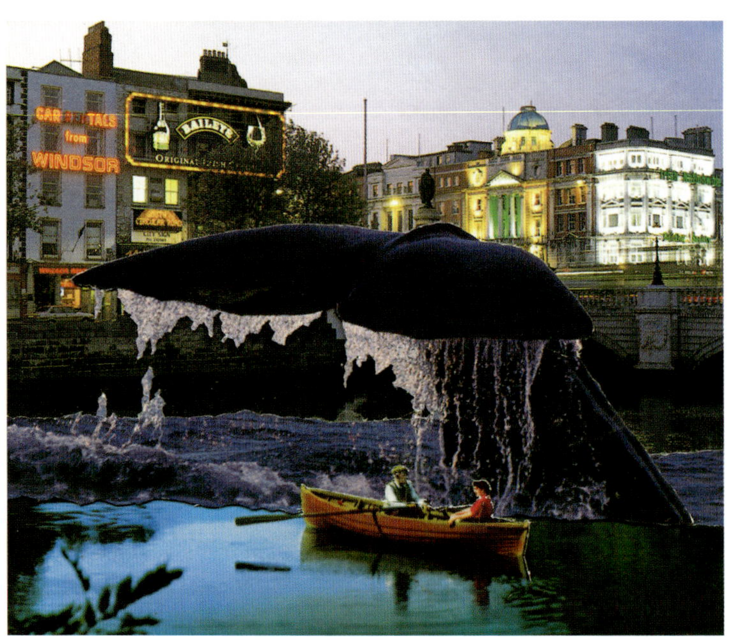

BOATING ON THE LIFFEY, IRELANTIS COLLAGE, SEAN HILLEN

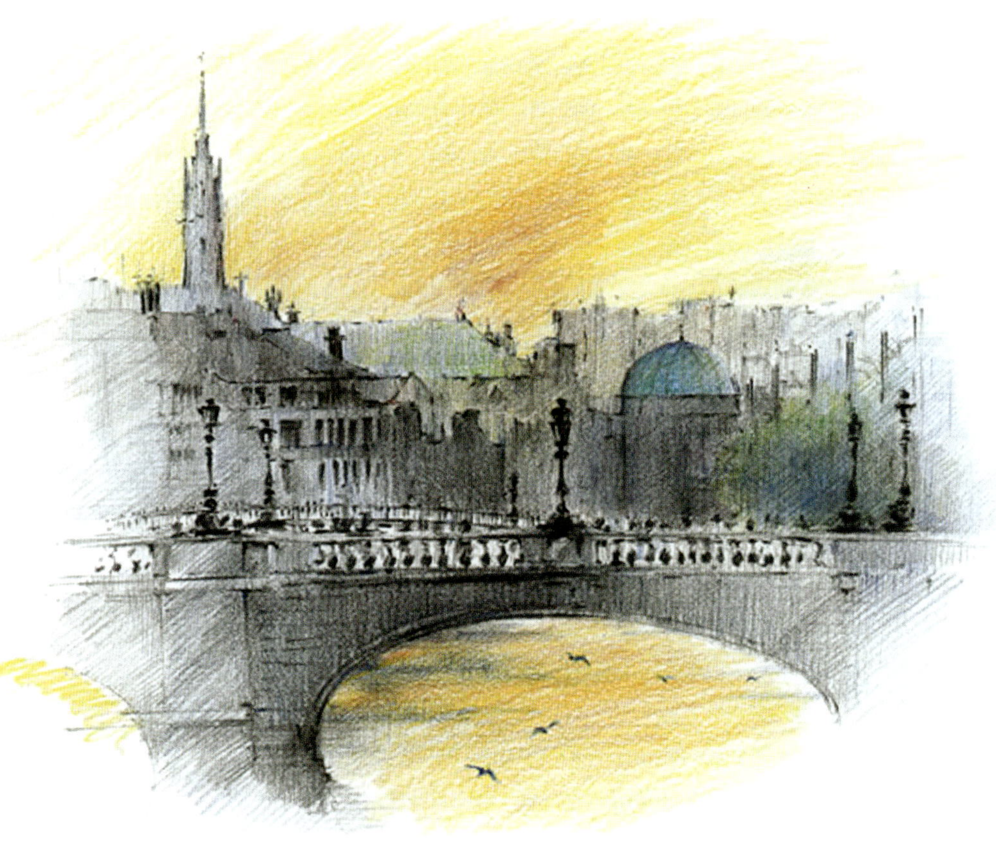

O'connell Bridge, Desmond McCarthy

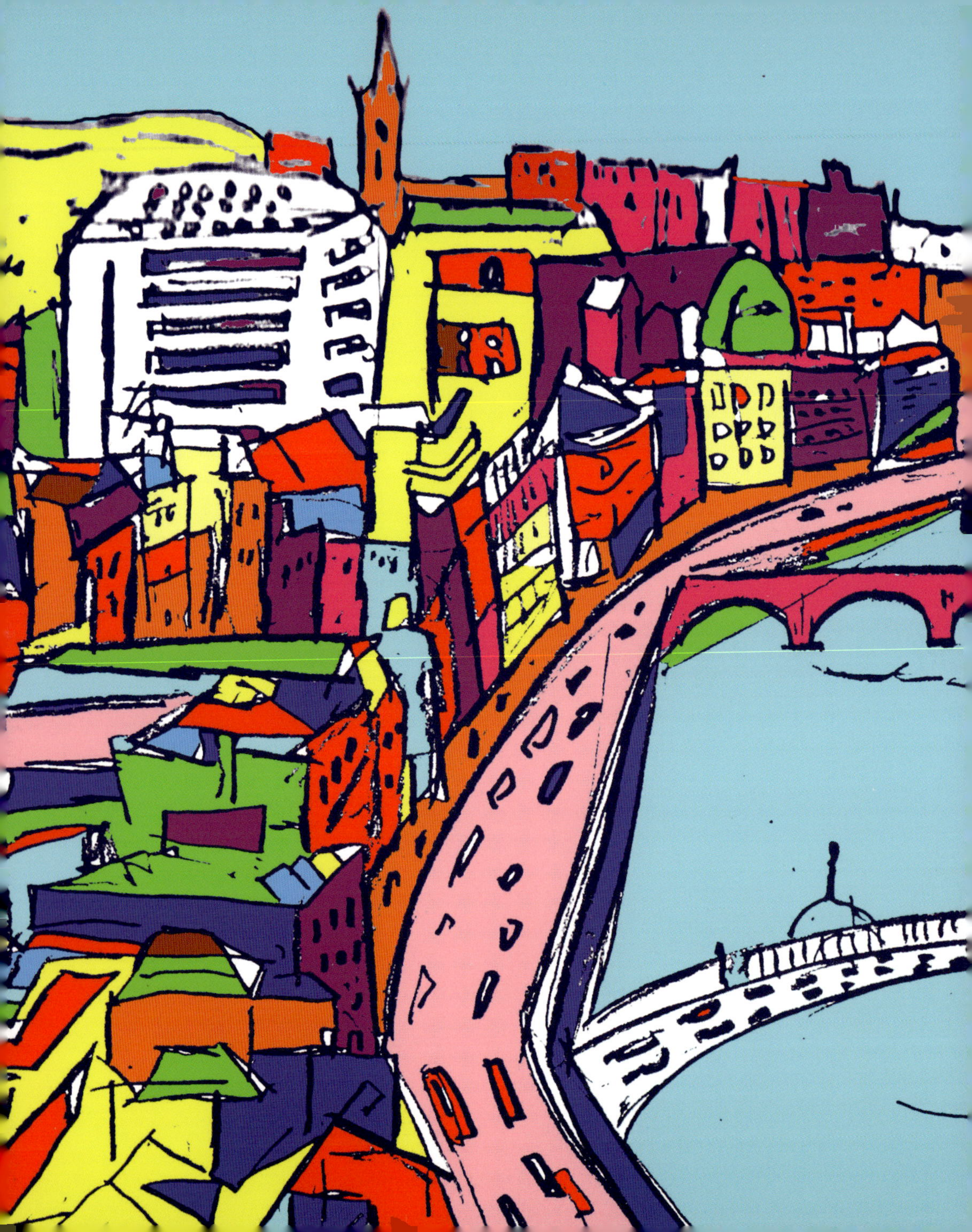

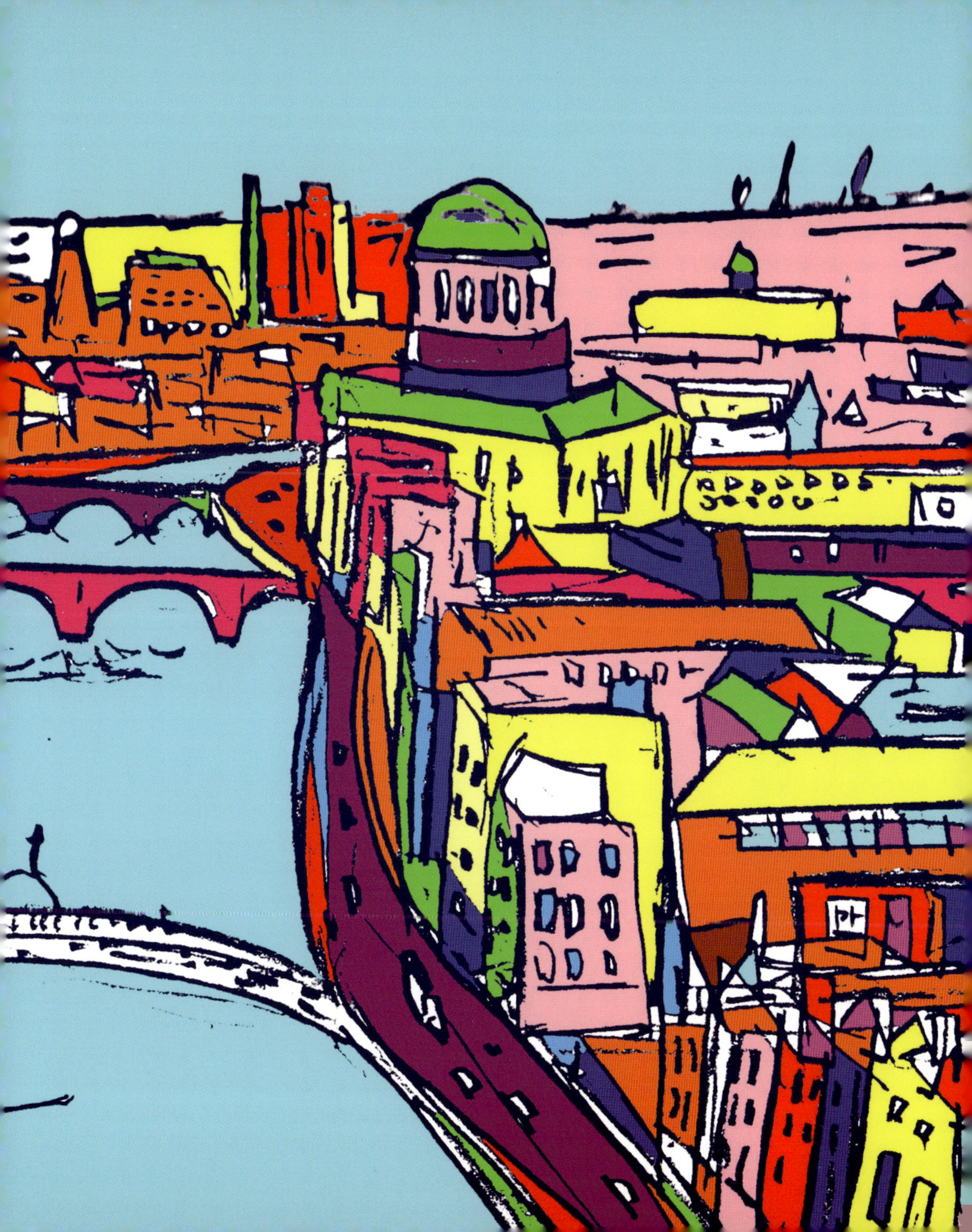

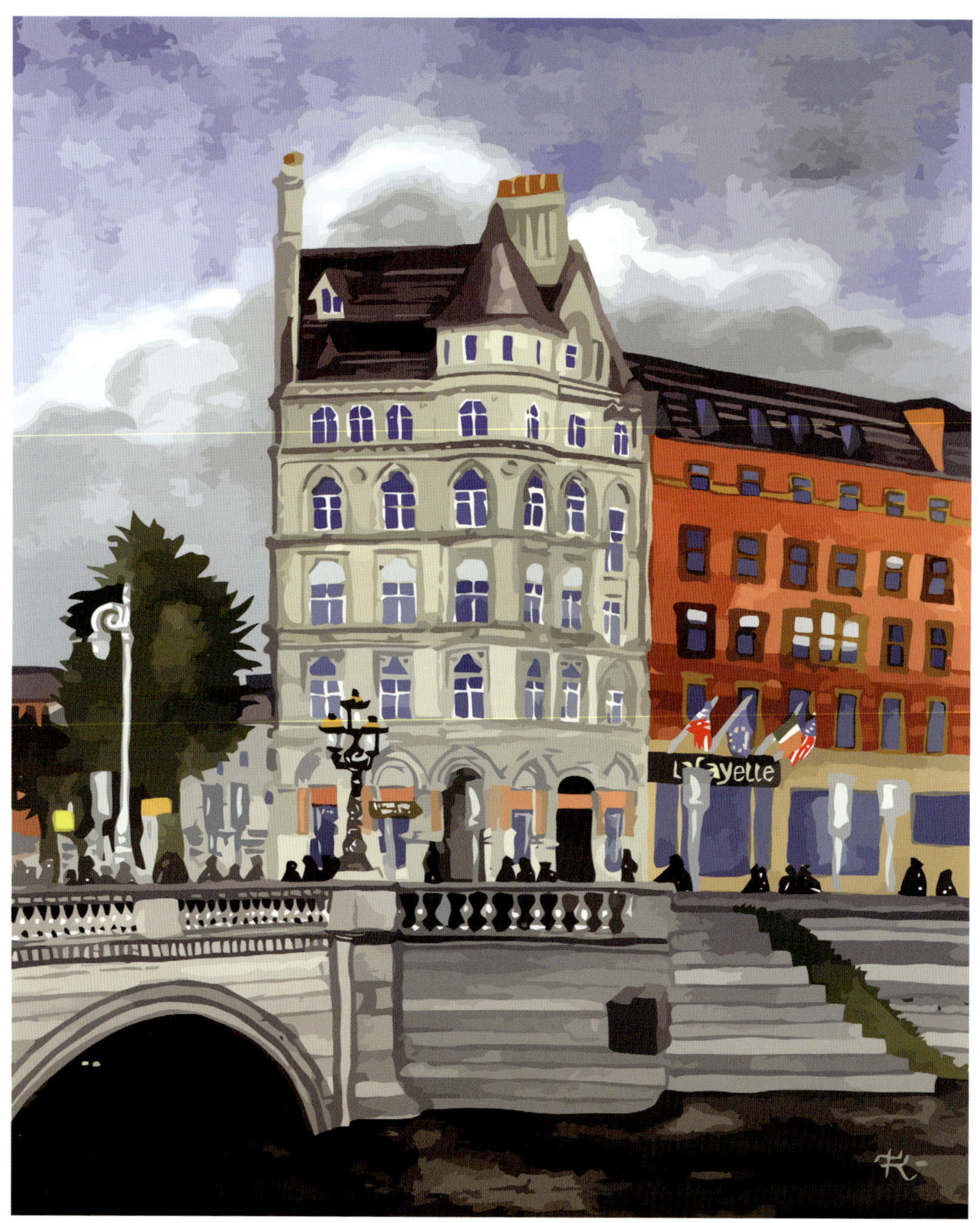

THE LAFAYETTE BUILDING, TERRI KELLEHER
PREVIOUS TWO PAGES: THE LIFFEY, JOHN FRAZER

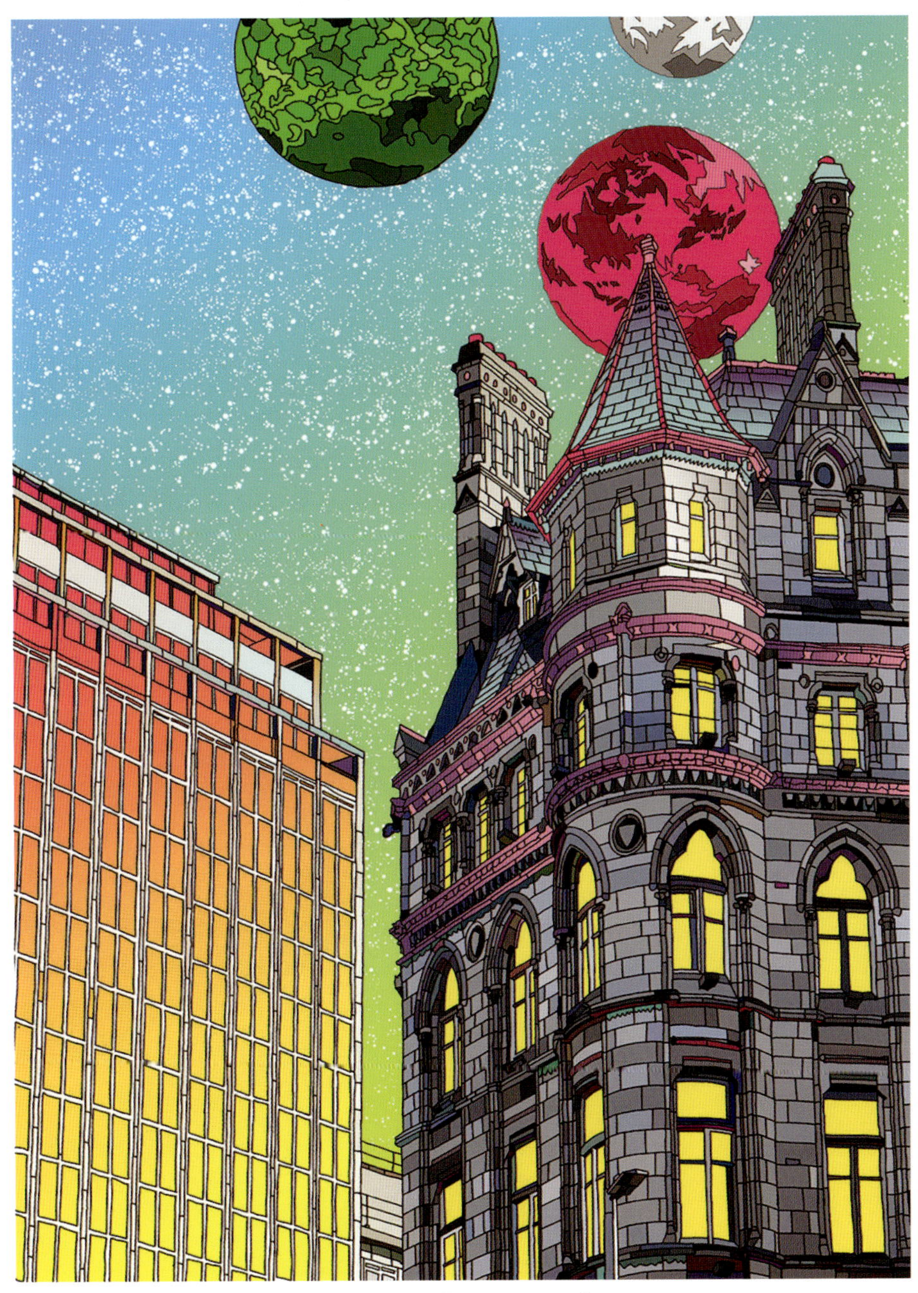

The Lafayette Building, Sketchy

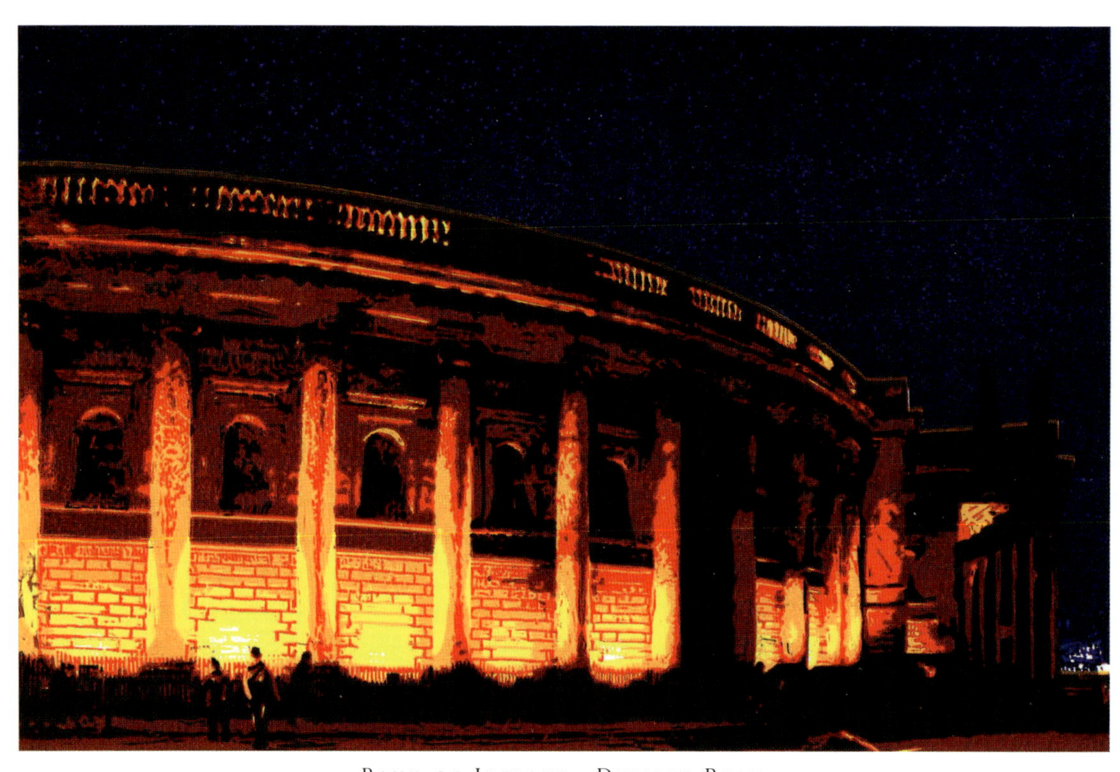

BANK OF IRELAND, DERMOT RYAN

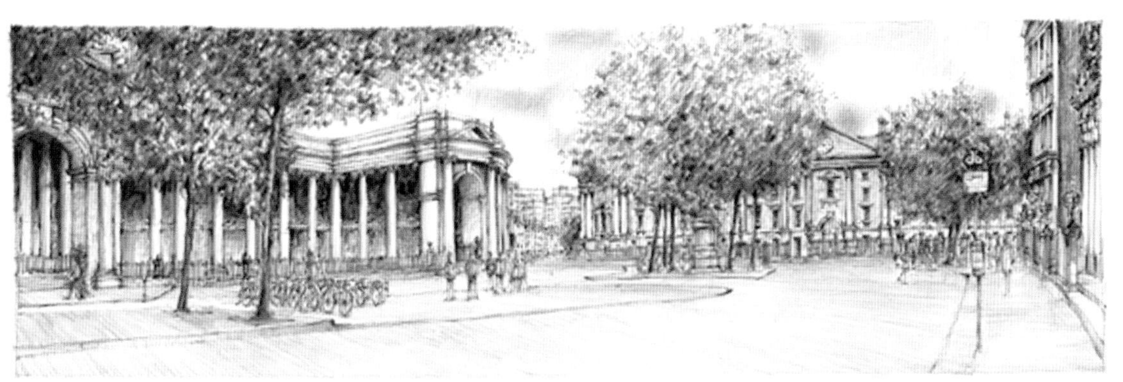

BANK OF IRELAND, DESMOND McCARTHY

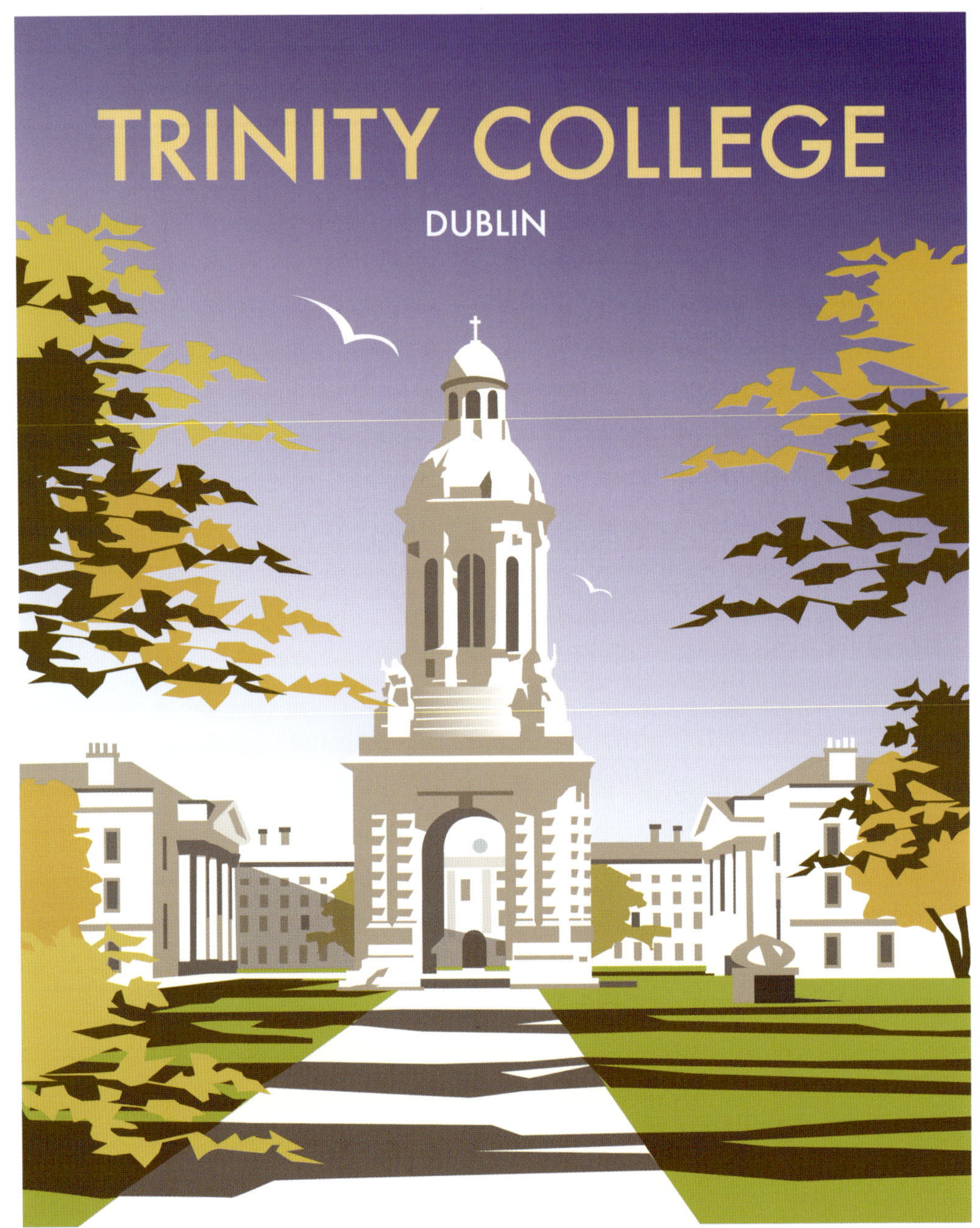

TRINITY COLLEGE, DAVE THOMPSON

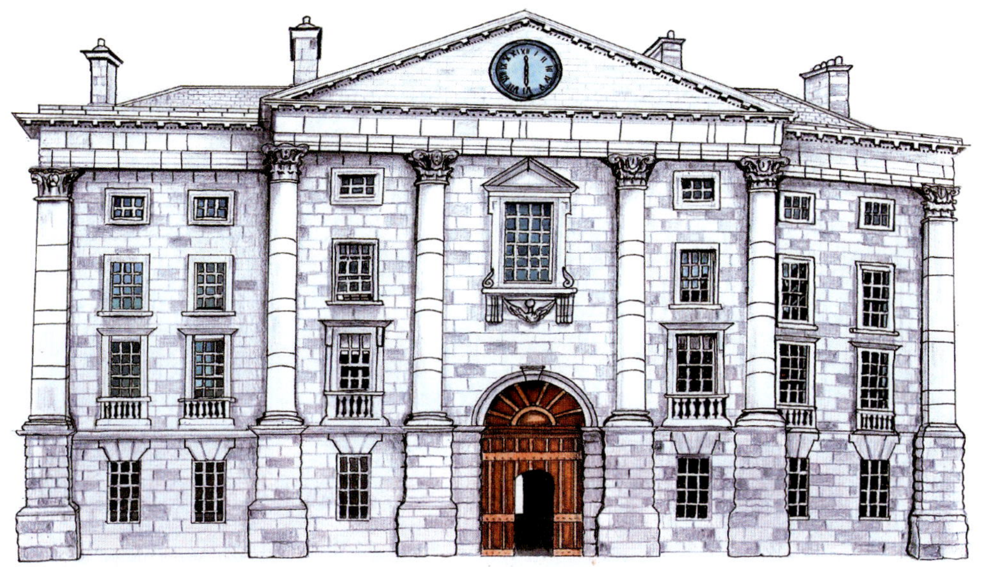

TRINITY COLLEGE, BRIAN O'NEILL

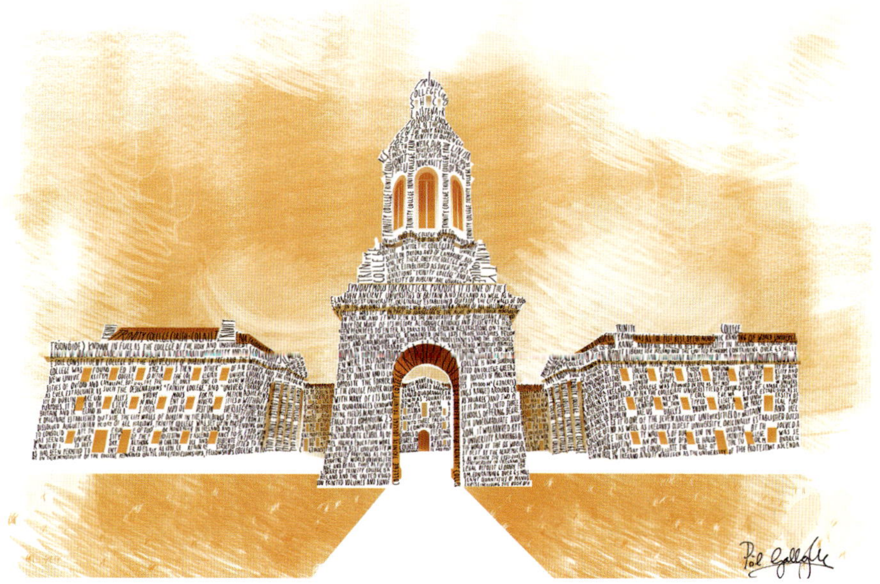

TRINITY COLLEGE, POL GALLAGHER

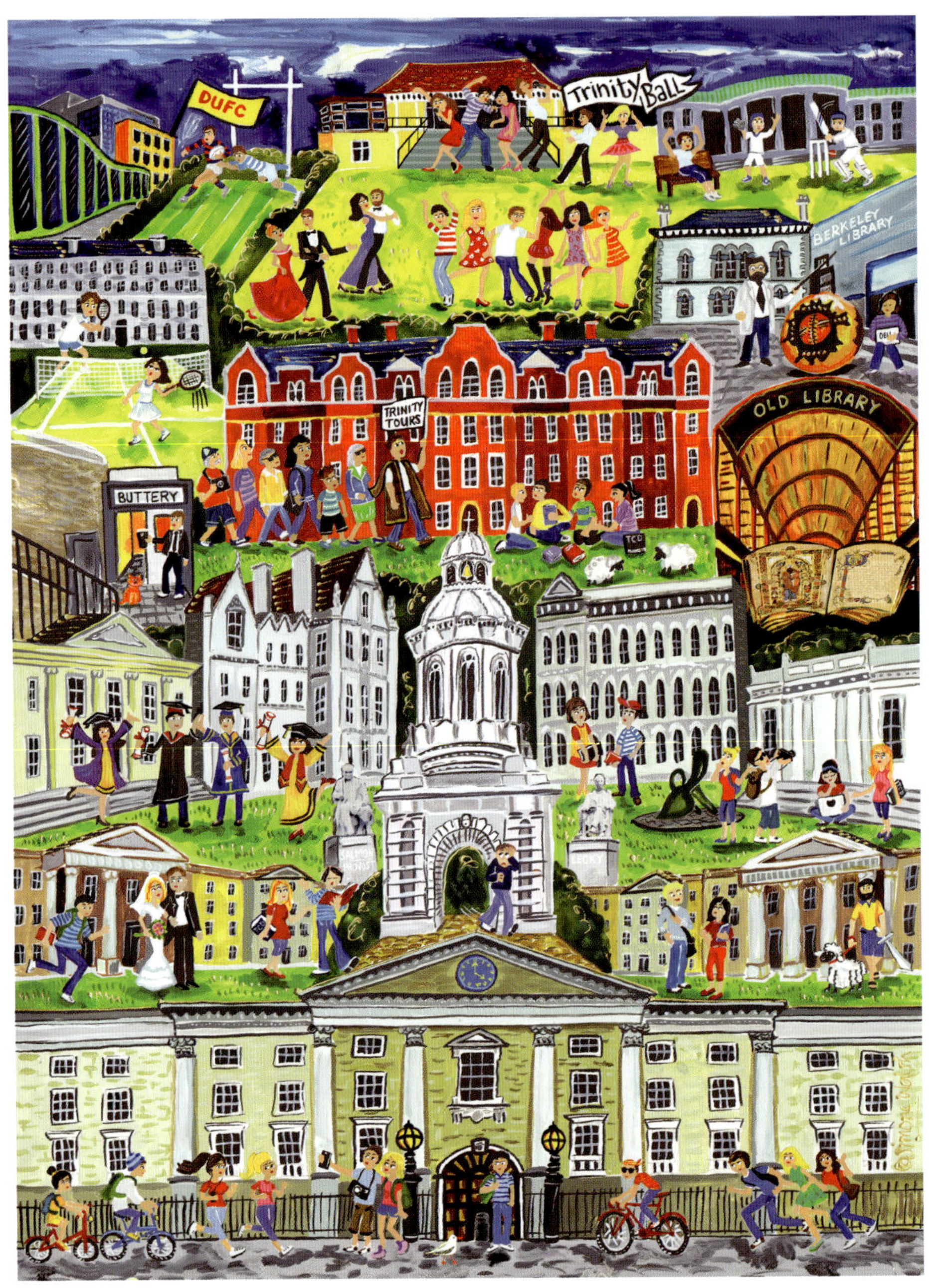

TRINITY COLLEGE, SIMONE WALSH

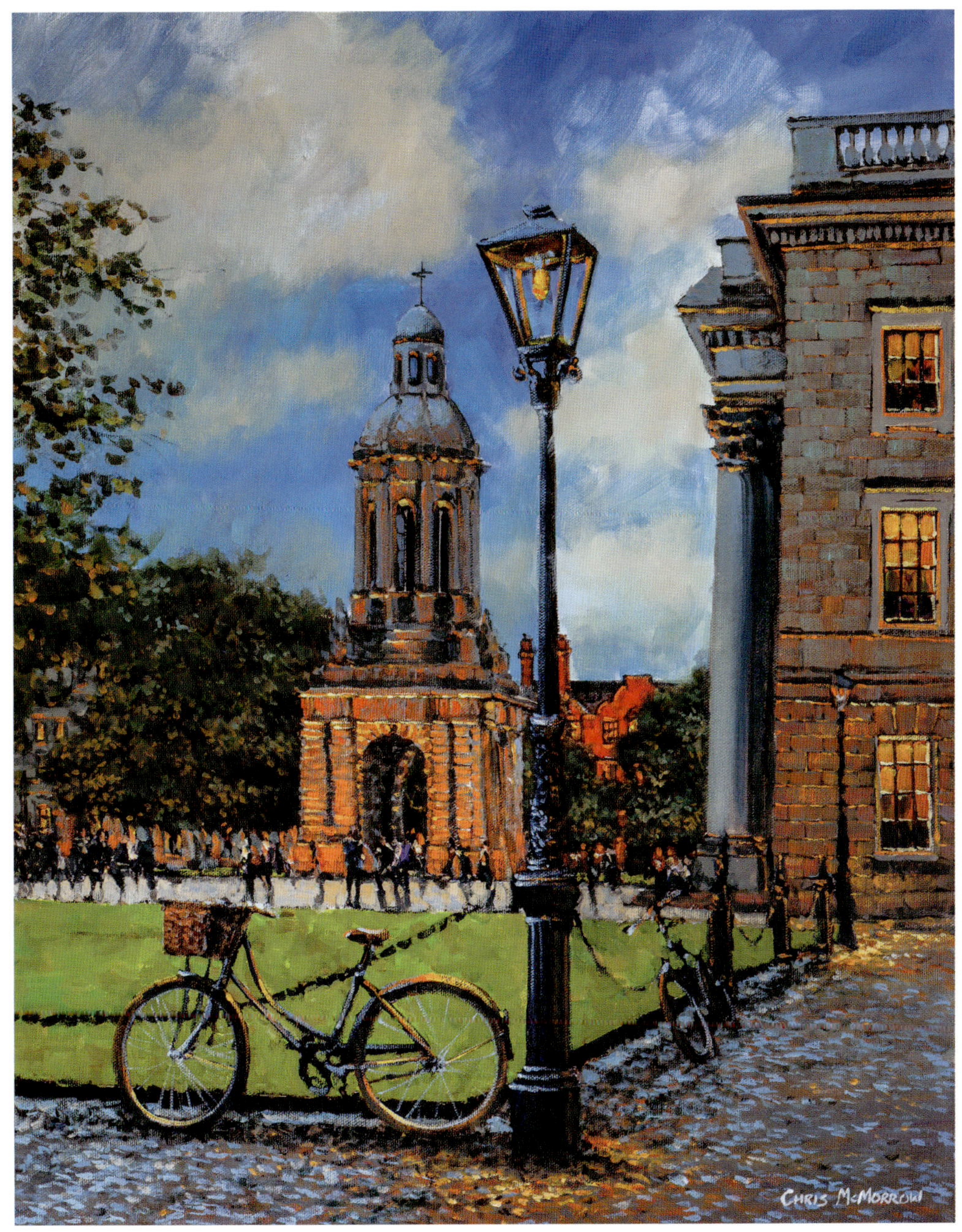

TRINITY COLLEGE, CHRIS McMORROW

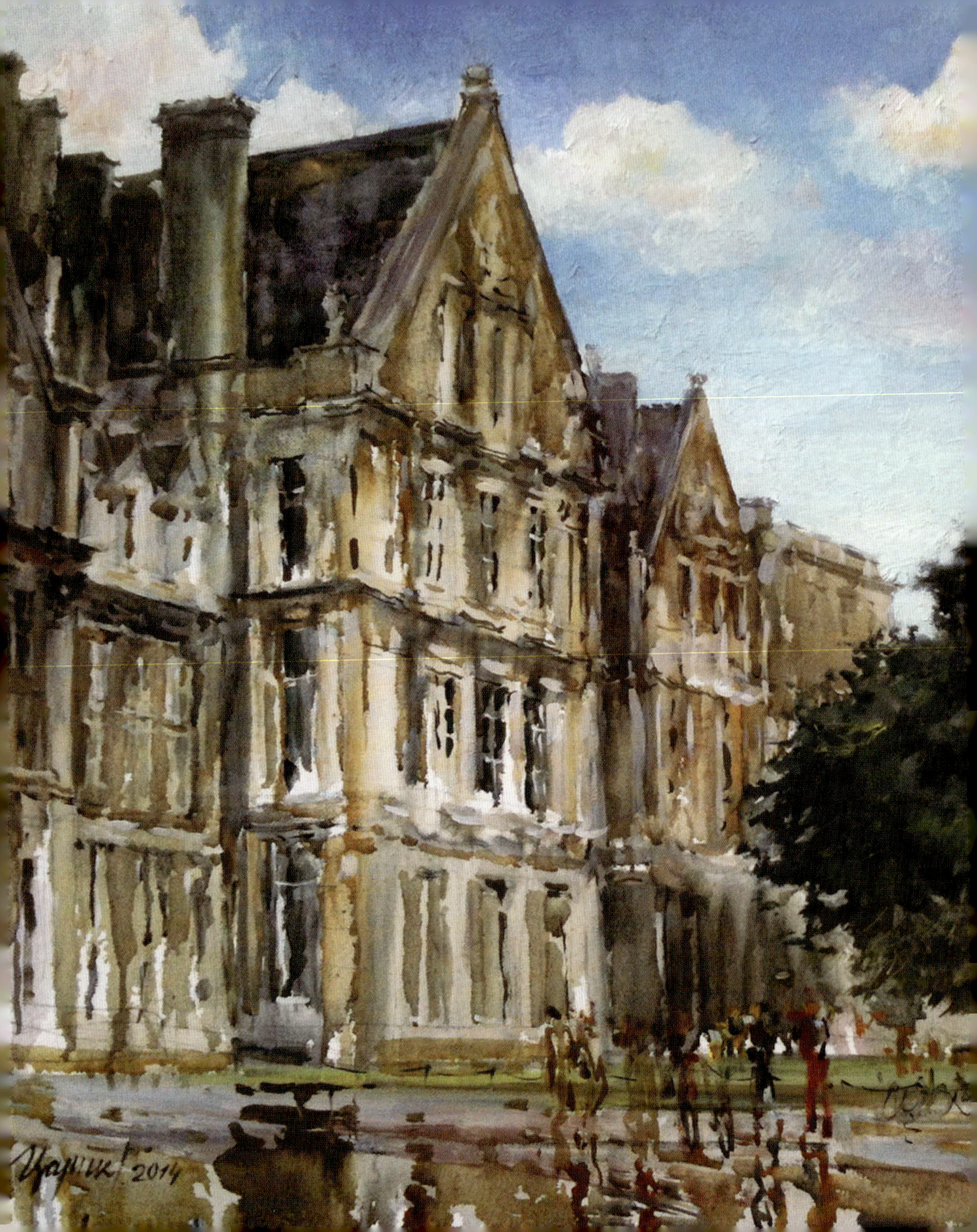
Чарин 2014

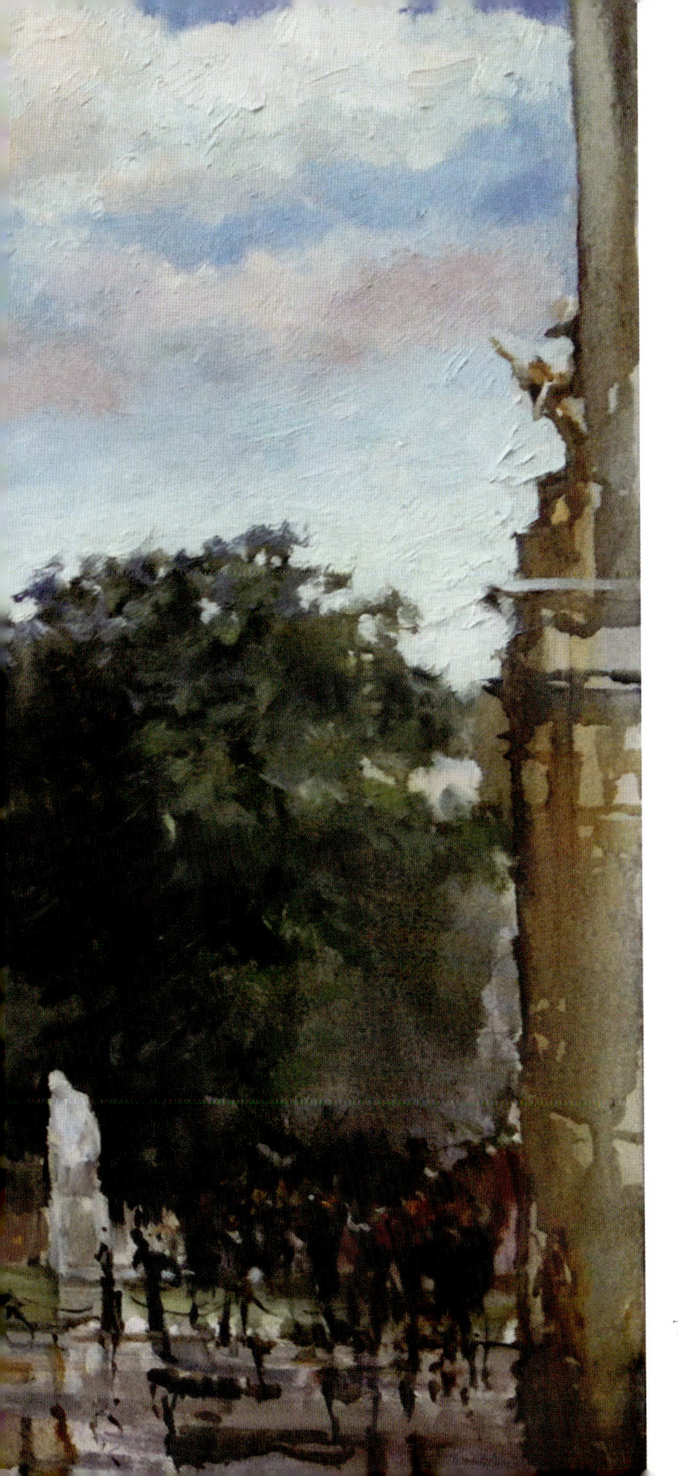

TRINITY COLLEGE, TETYANA TSARYK

TRINITY COLLEGE LIBRARY, EMMA BENNETT

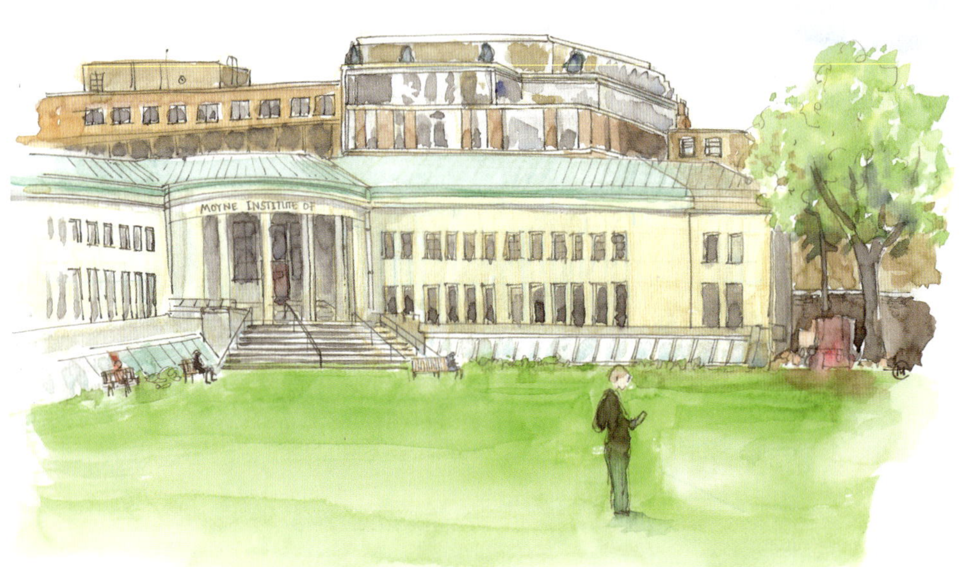

THE MOYNE INSTITUTE, TRINITY COLLEGE, EMMA MONTONEN

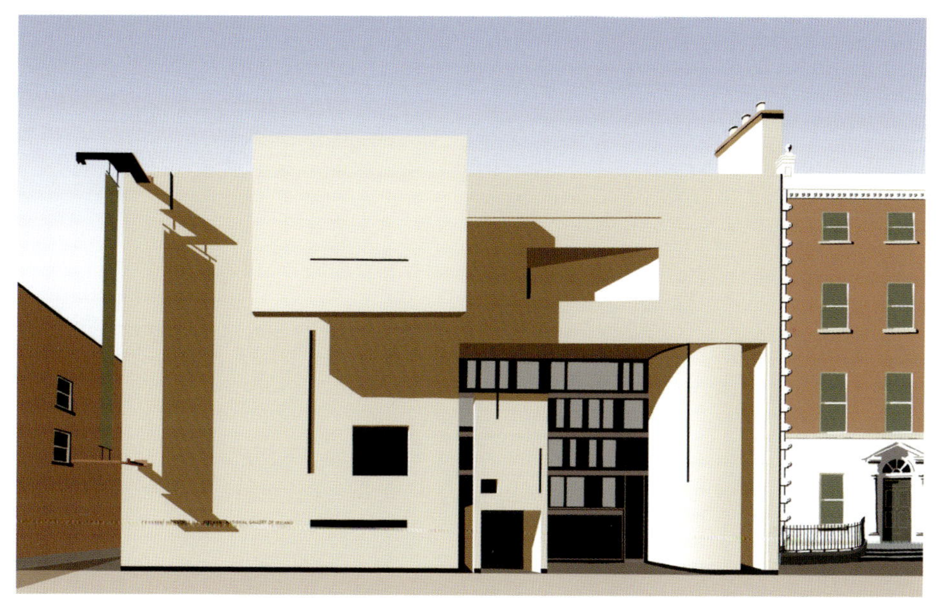

NATIONAL GALLERY OF IRELAND, RICHARD O'NEILL

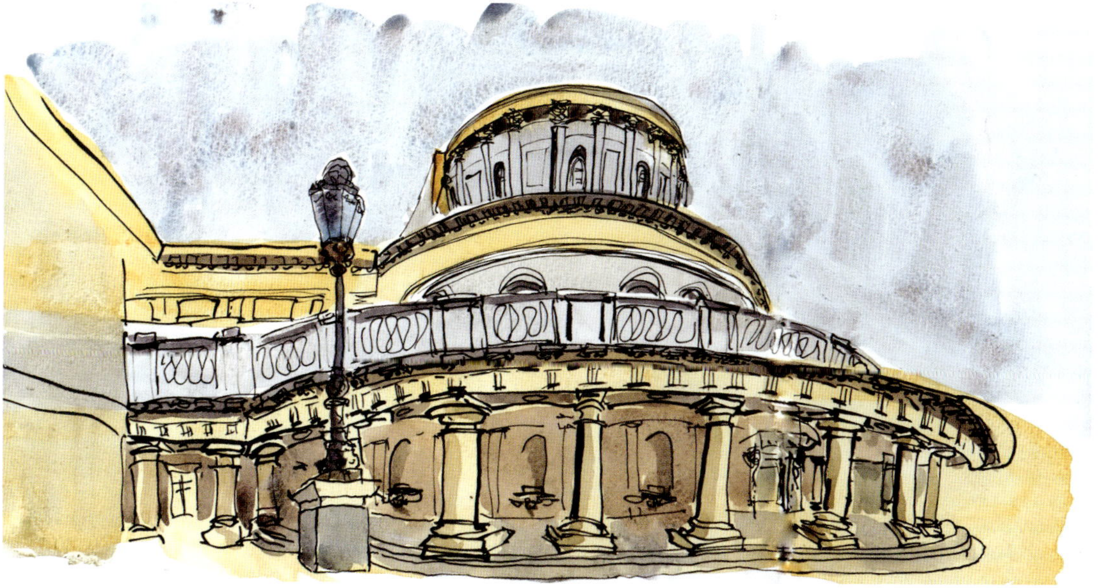

NATIONAL MUSEUM OF IRELAND, MARIE-HÉLÈNE BROHAN DELHAYE

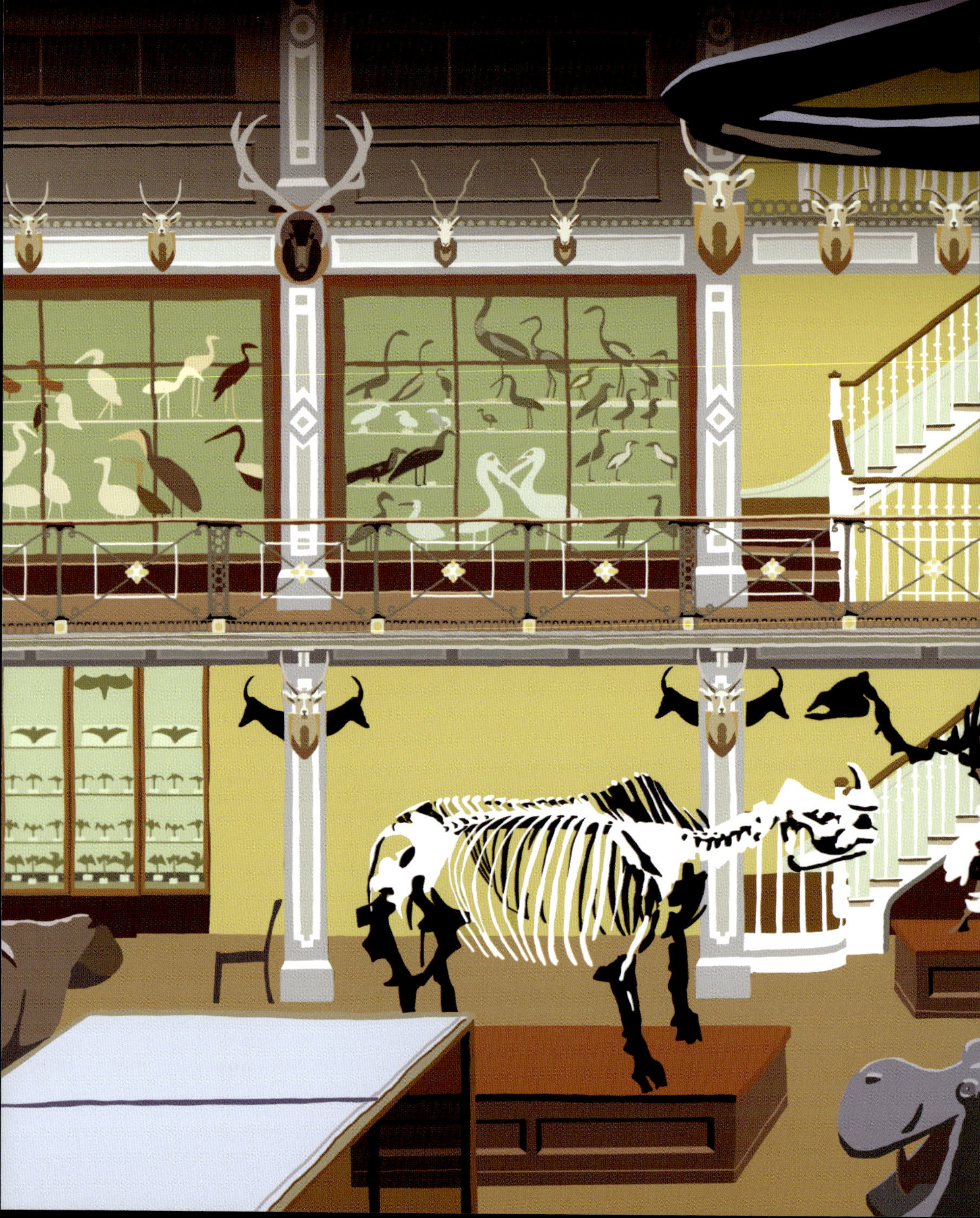

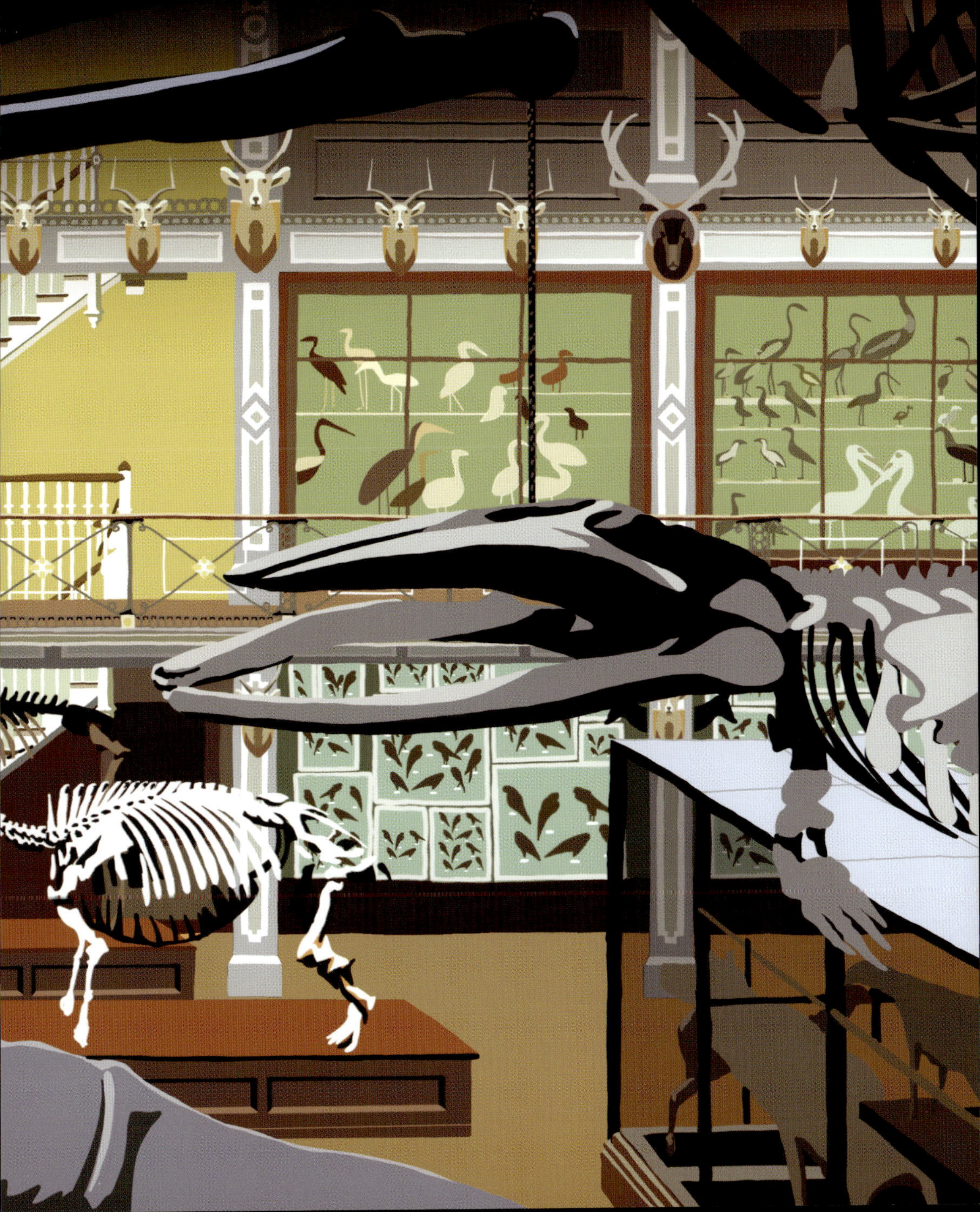

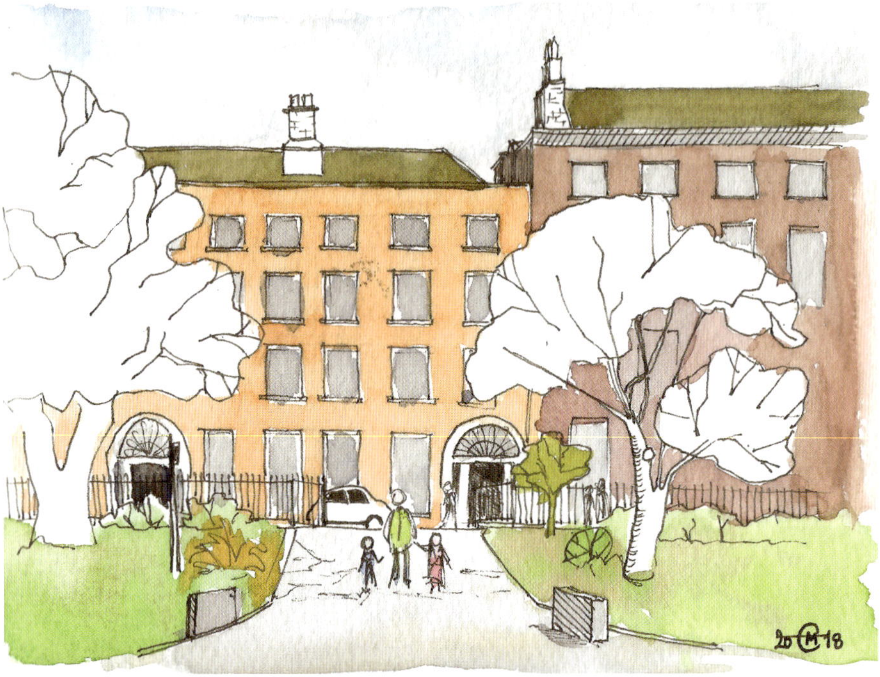

MERRION SQUARE, EMMA MONTONEN

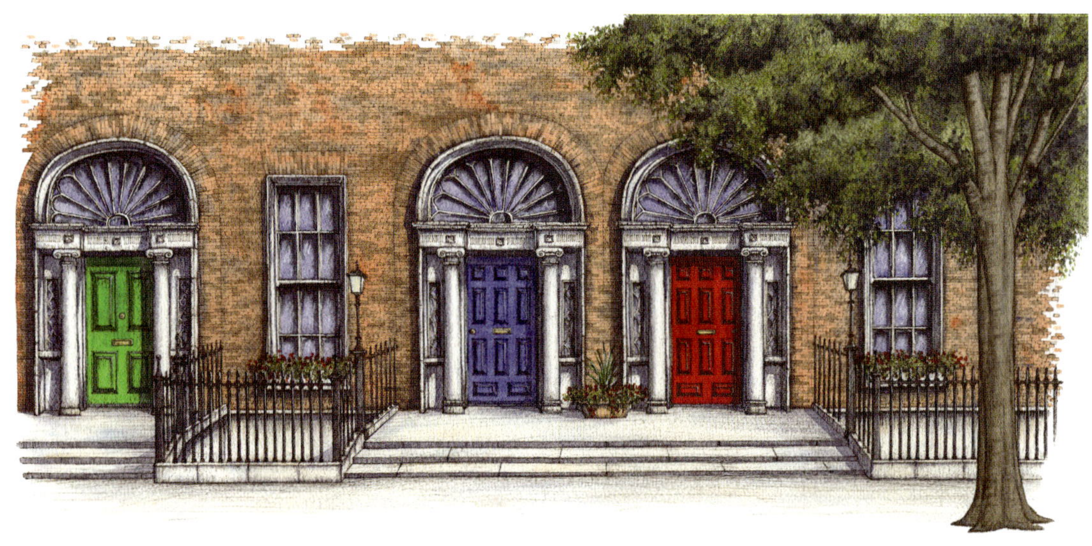

GEORGIAN DOORS, JIM SCULLY
PREVIOUS TWO PAGES: NATURAL HISTORY MUSEUM, RICHARD O'NEILL

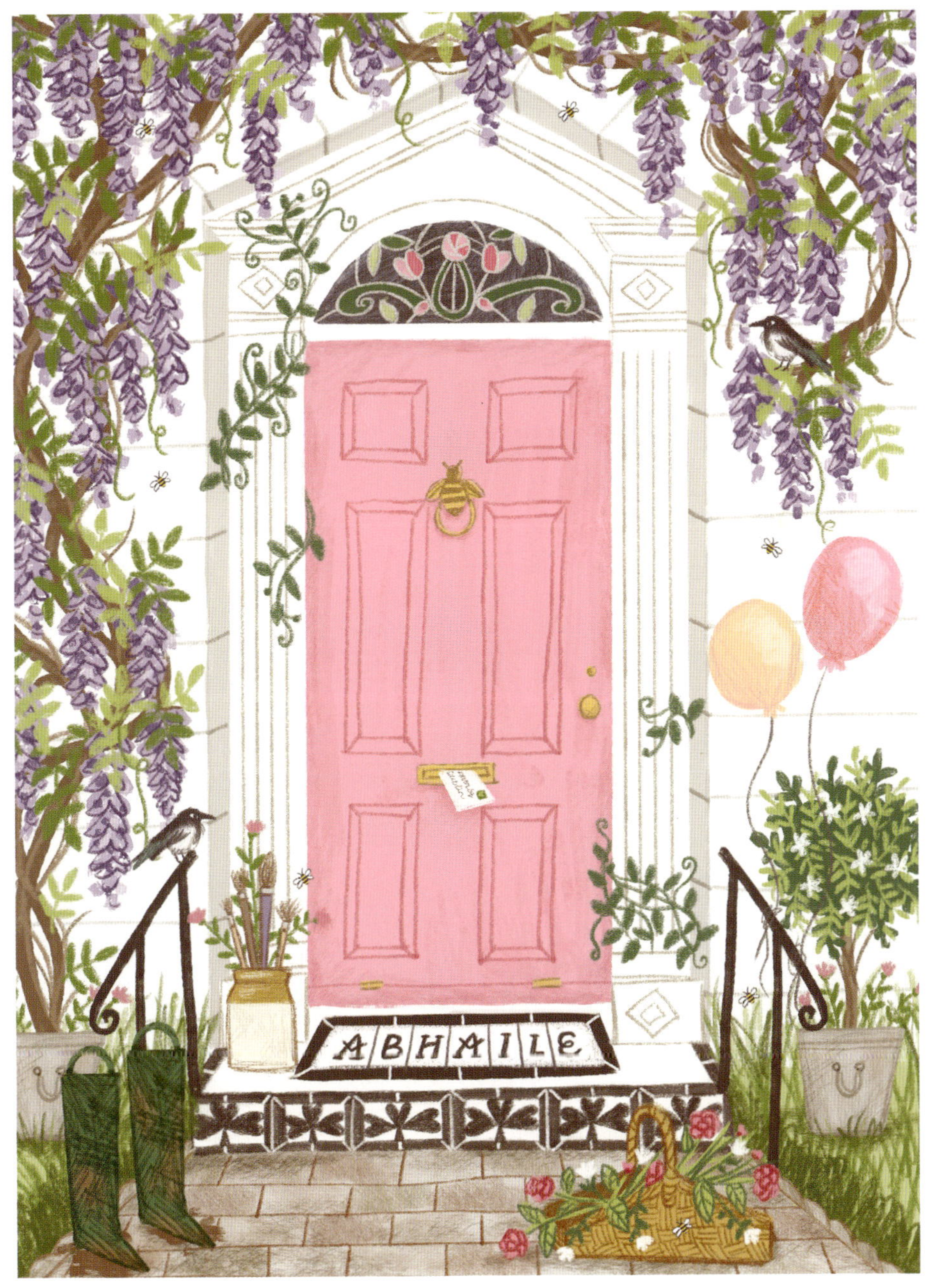

BUMBLEBEES AND BLOOMS, RACHEL CORCORAN

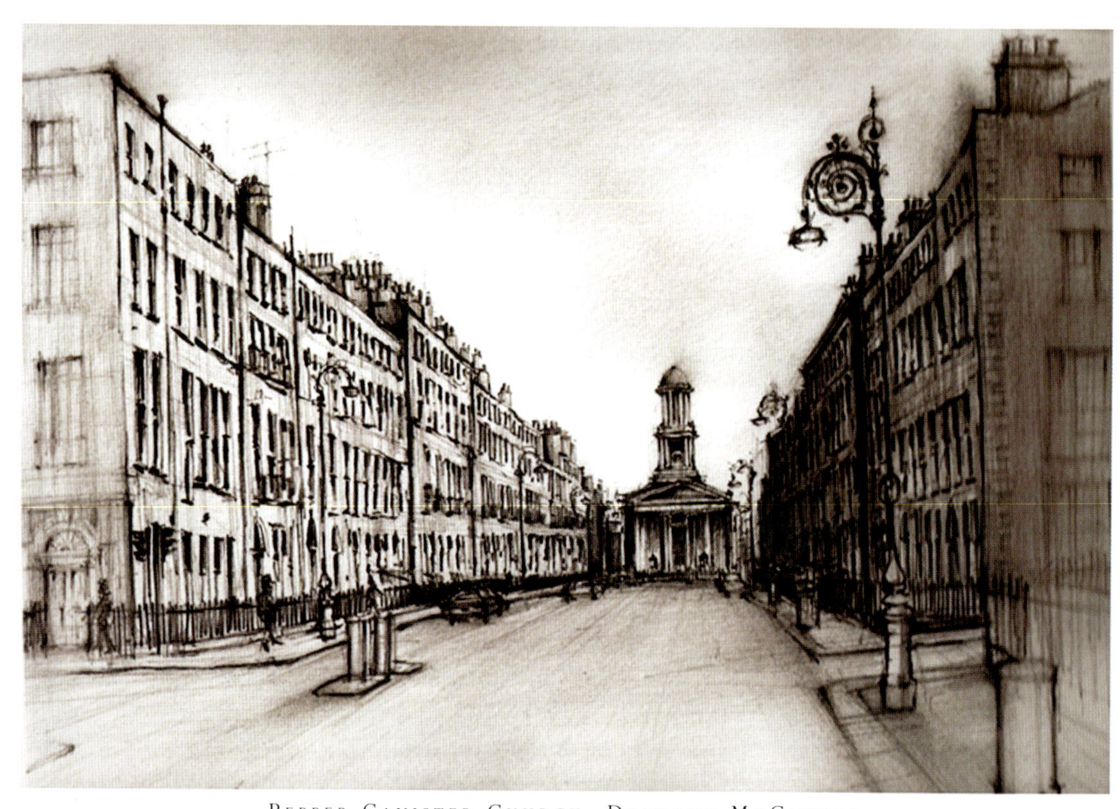

PEPPER CANISTER CHURCH, DESMOND MCCARTHY

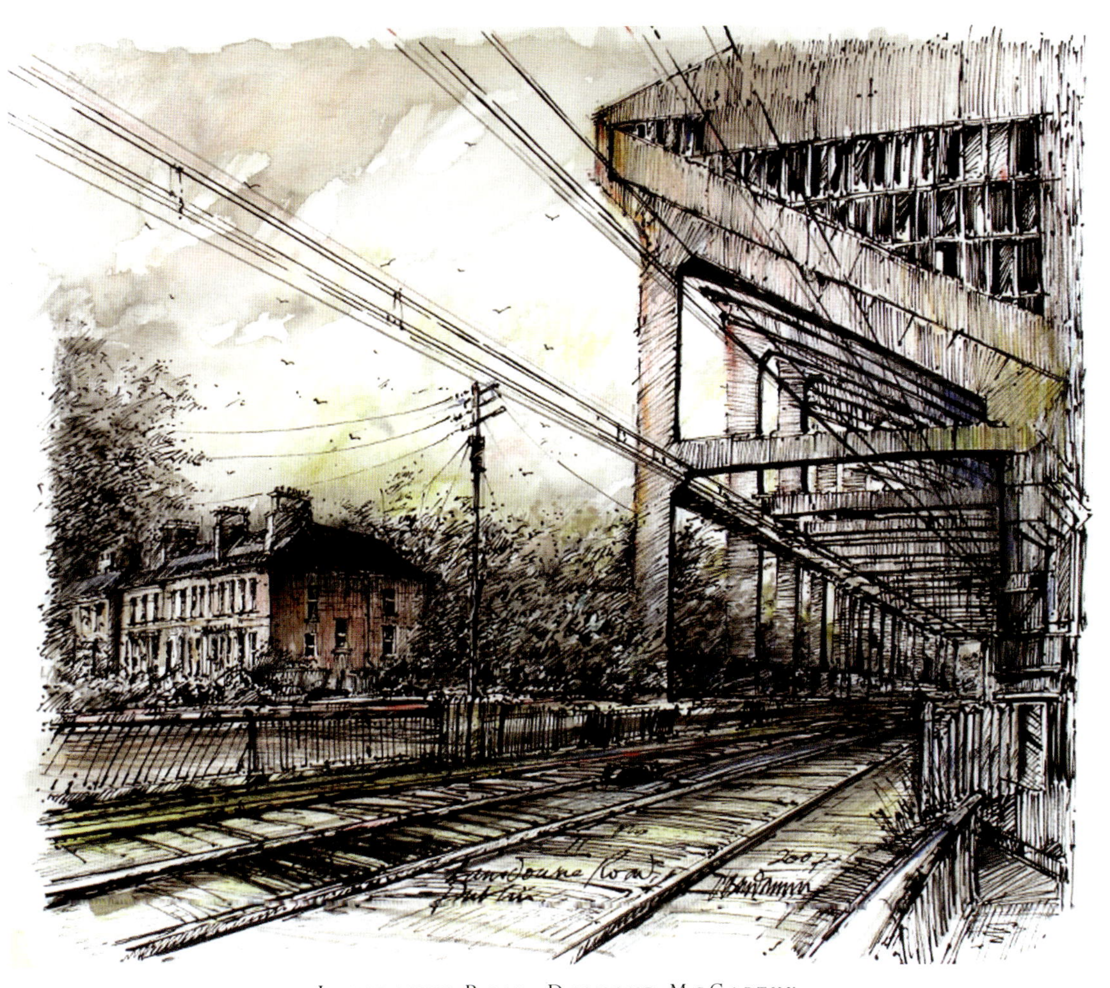

LANSDOWNE ROAD, DESMOND McCARTHY

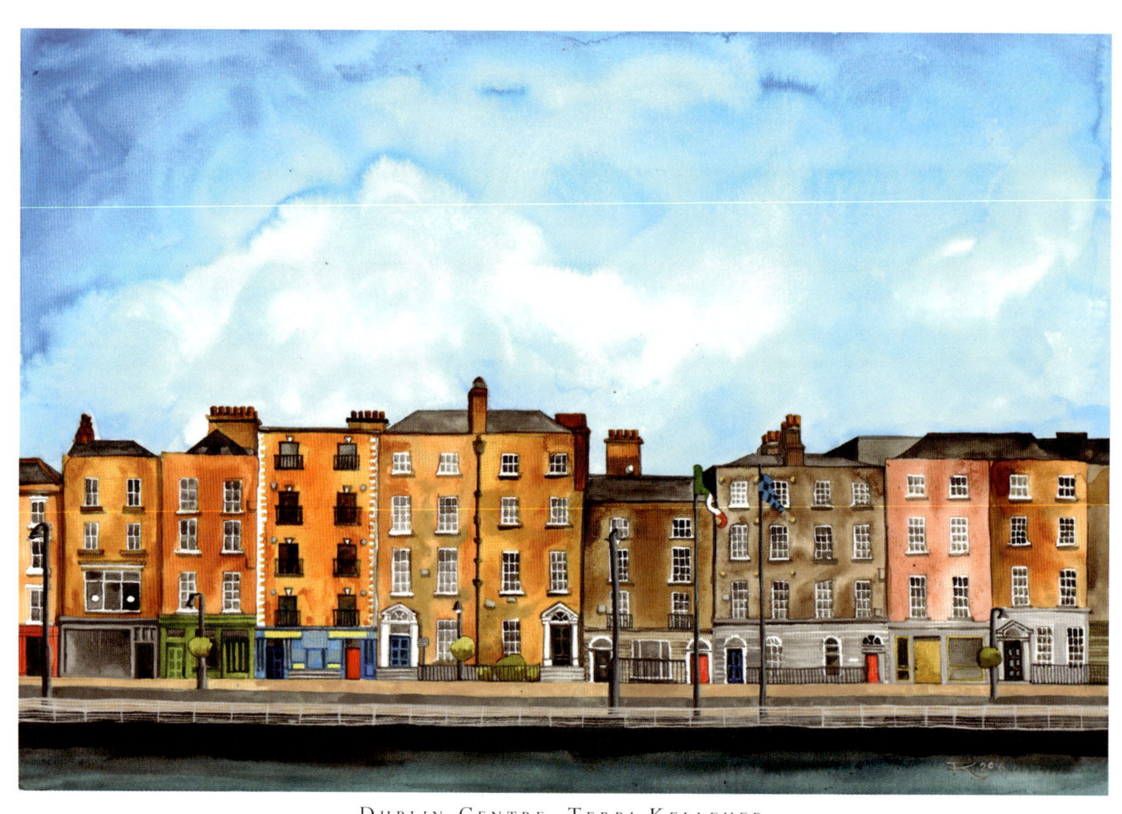

DUBLIN CENTRE, TERRI KELLEHER

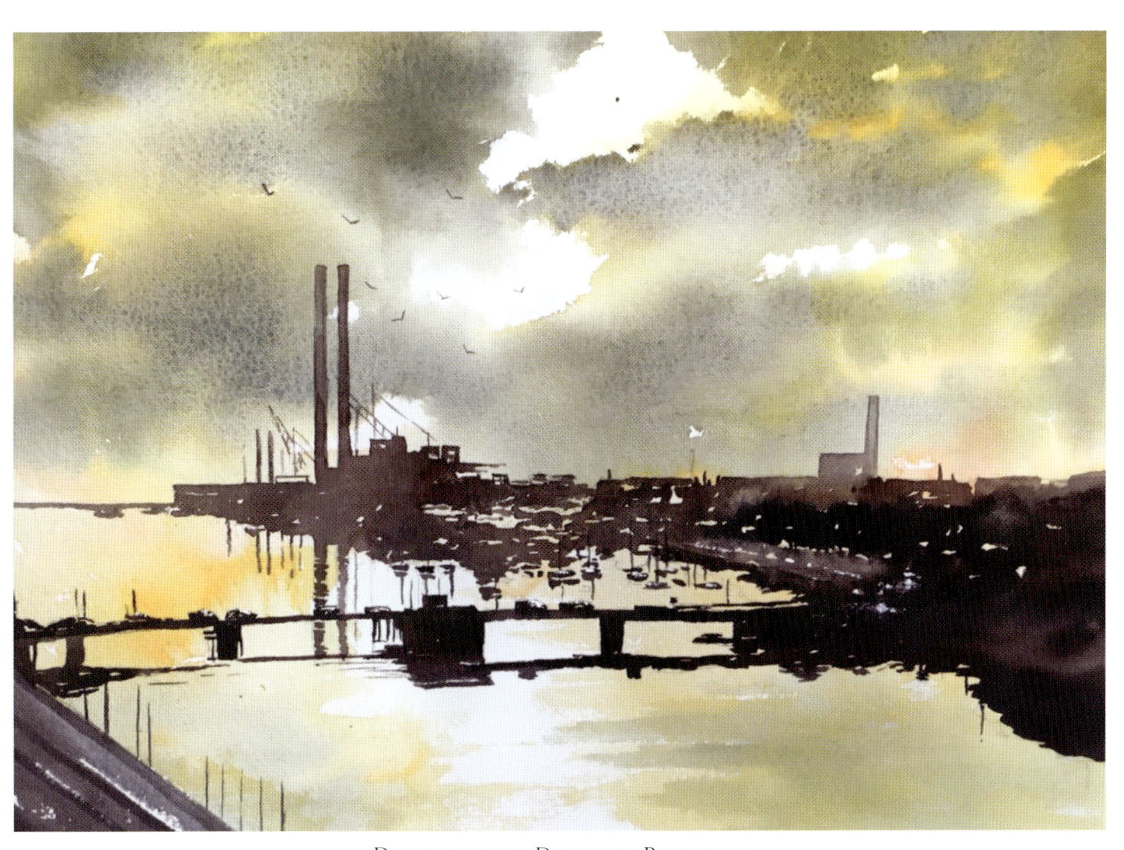

DOCKLANDS, DERMOT BRENNAN

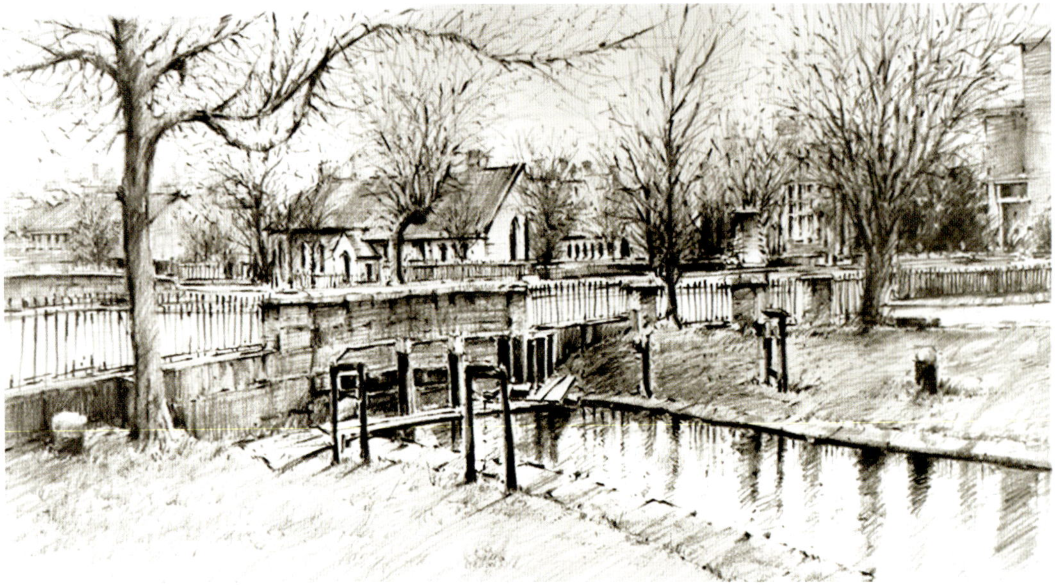

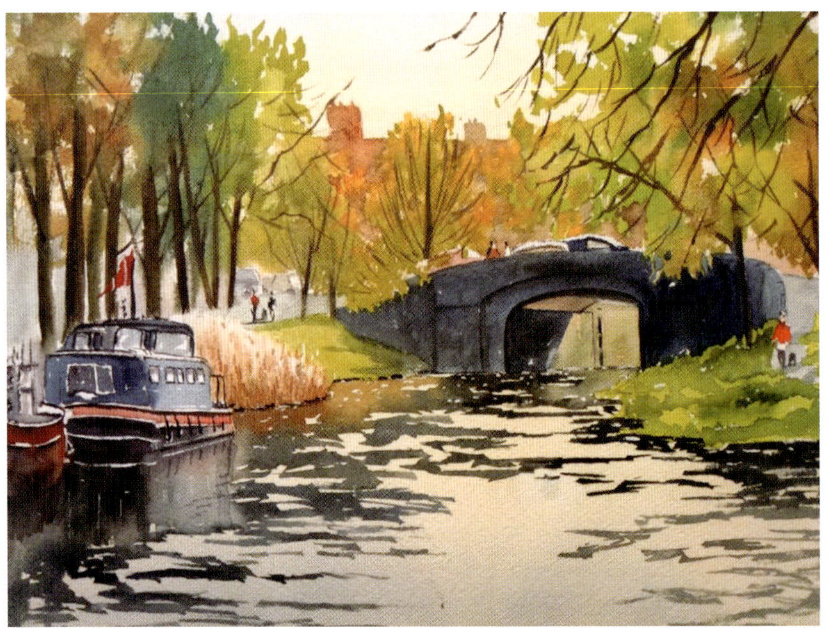

SCHOOLHOUSE AND MOUNT STREET BRIDGE, DESMOND McCARTHY

GRAND CANAL, DERMOT BRENNAN

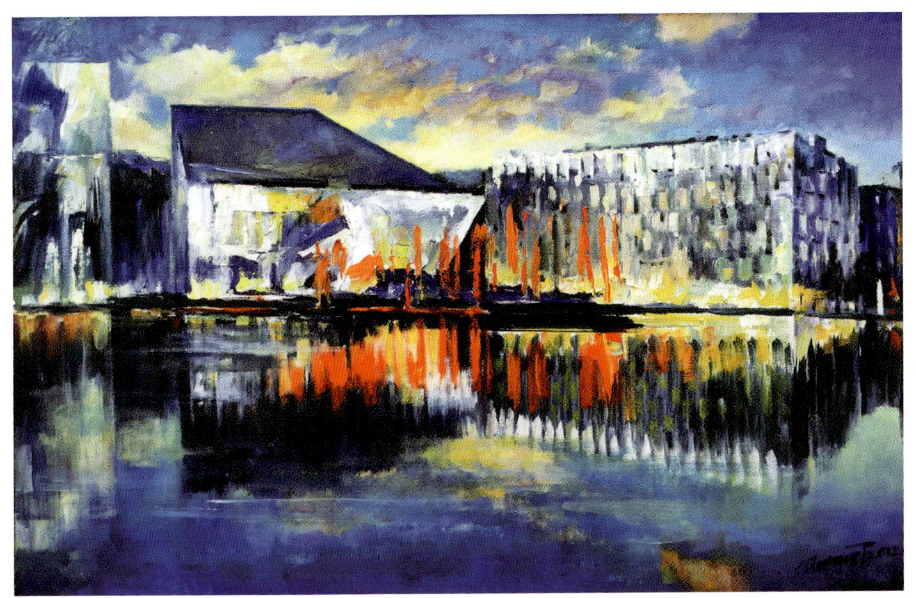

B O R D G Á I S E N E R G Y T H E A T R E , T E T Y A N A T S A R Y K

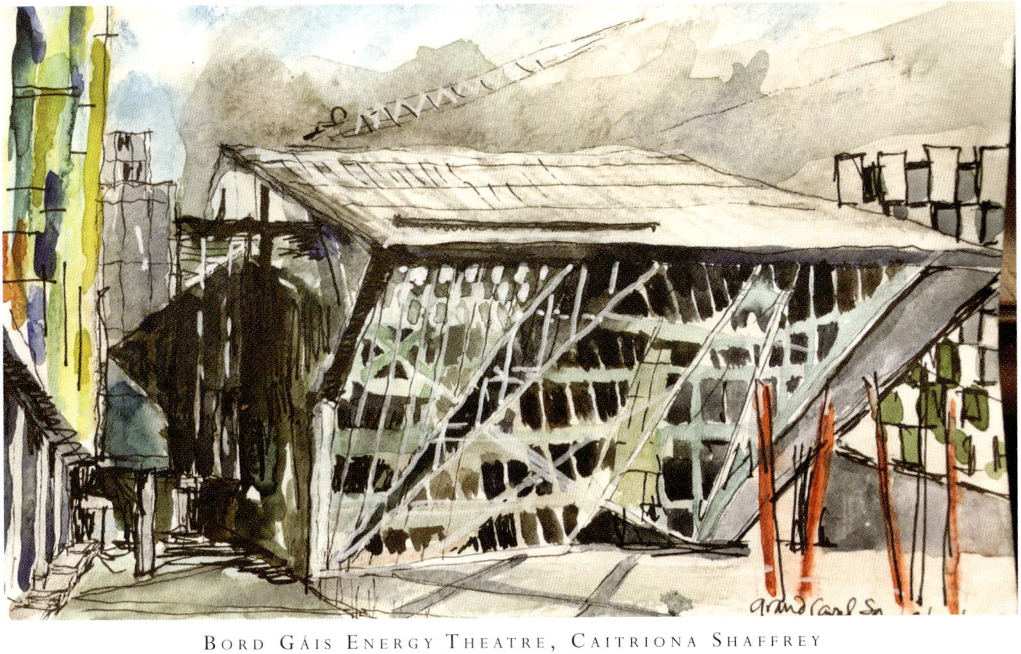

B O R D G Á I S E N E R G Y T H E A T R E , C A I T R I O N A S H A F F R E Y

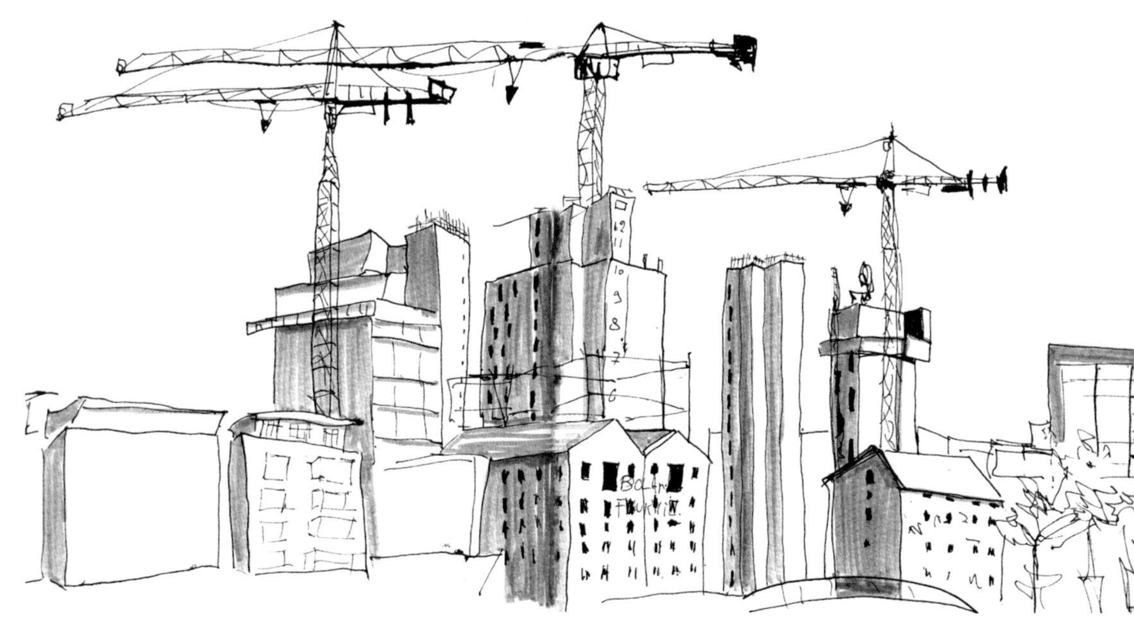

GRAND CANAL DOCK, MARIE-HÉLÈNE BROHAN DELHAYE

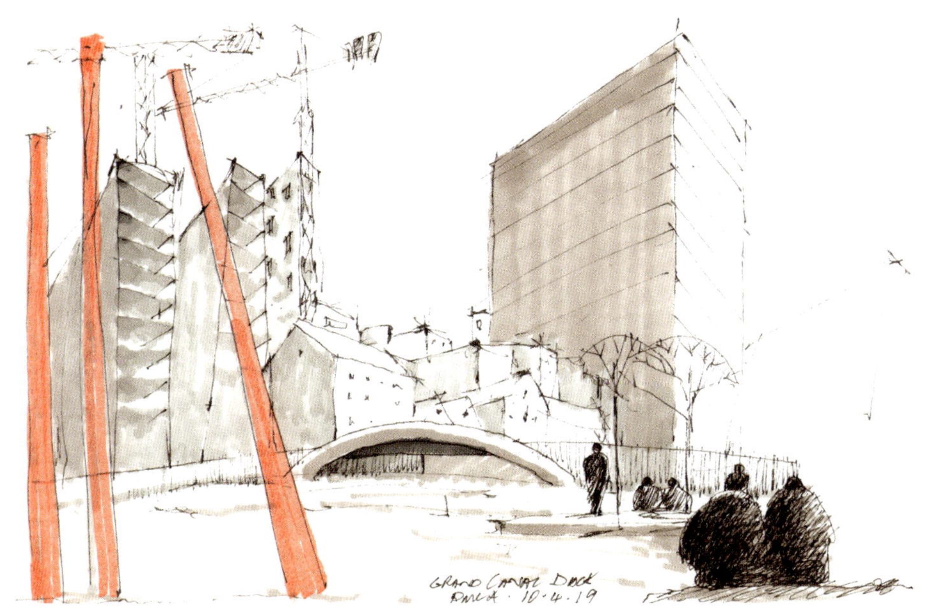

GRAND CANAL DOCK, PATRICK McAFEE

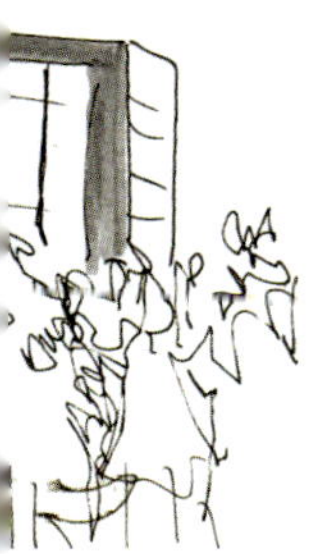

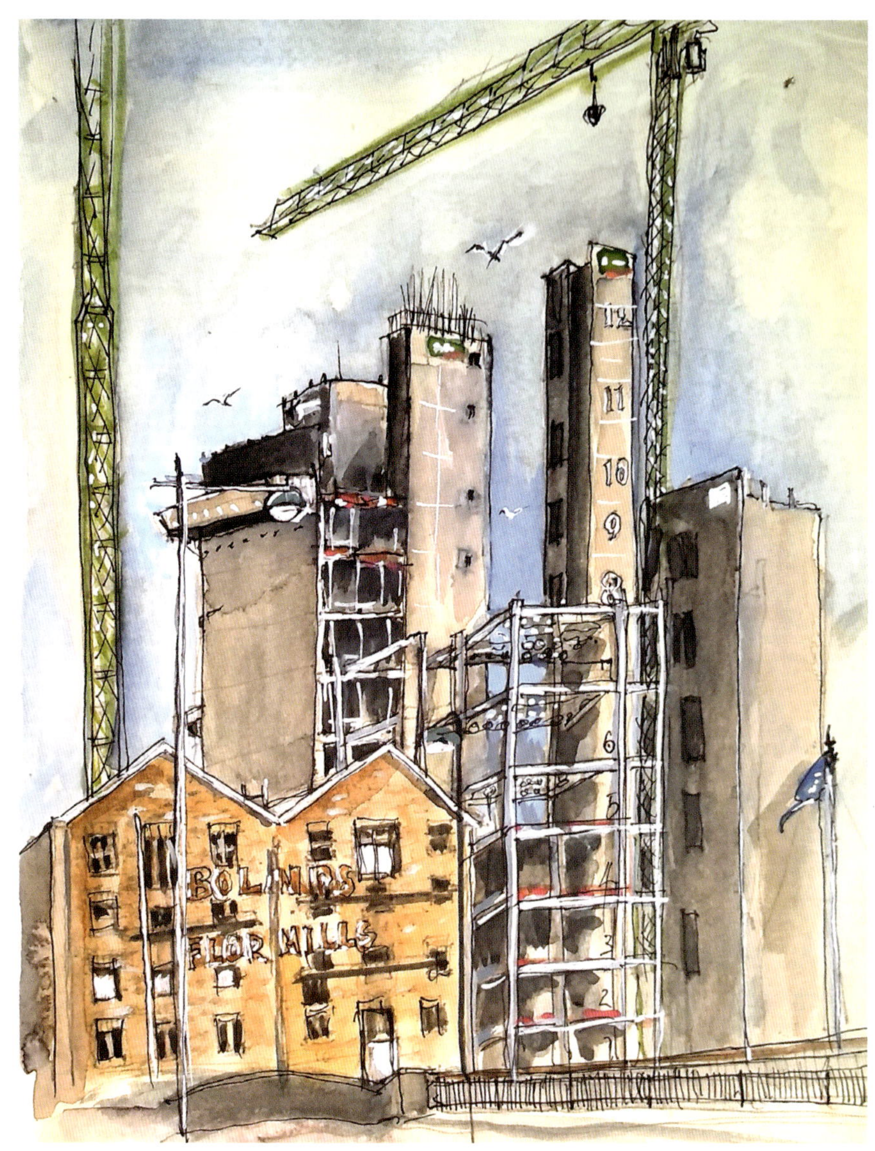

BOLAND'S MILLS, GRAND CANAL DOCK, MARY O'CARROLL

GRAND CANAL DOCK
DUBLIN, IRELAND

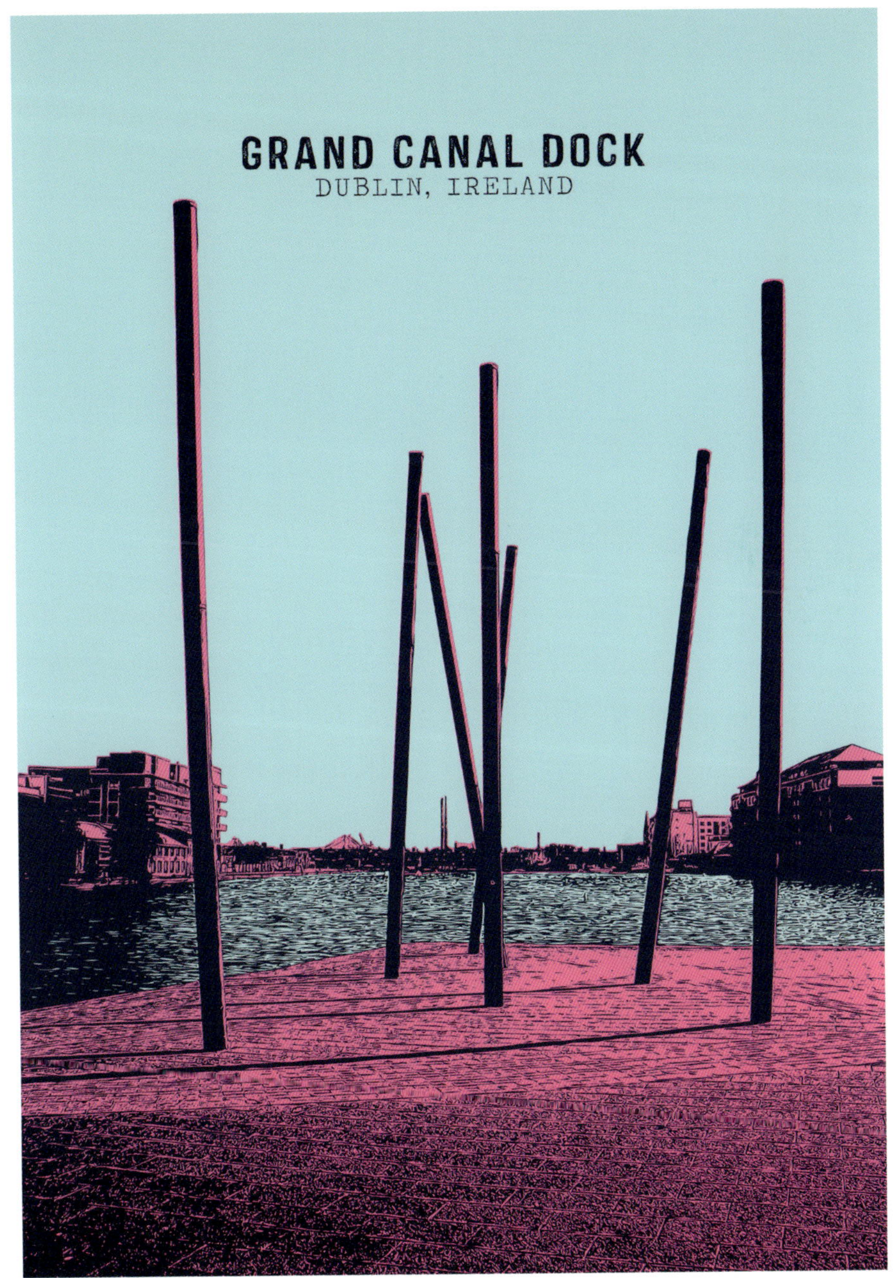

GRAND CANAL DOCK, JANDO

POOLBEG CHIMNEYS
DUBLIN, IRELAND

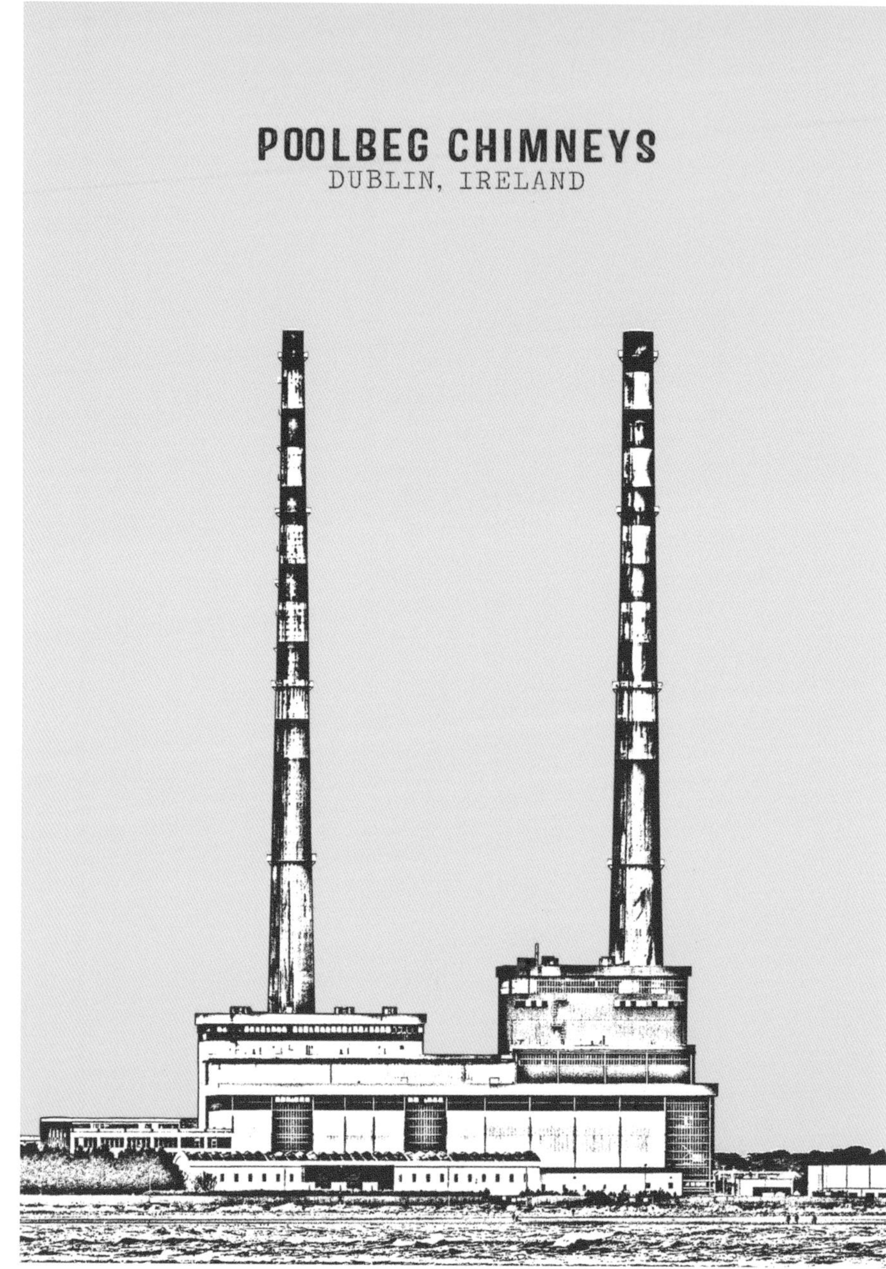

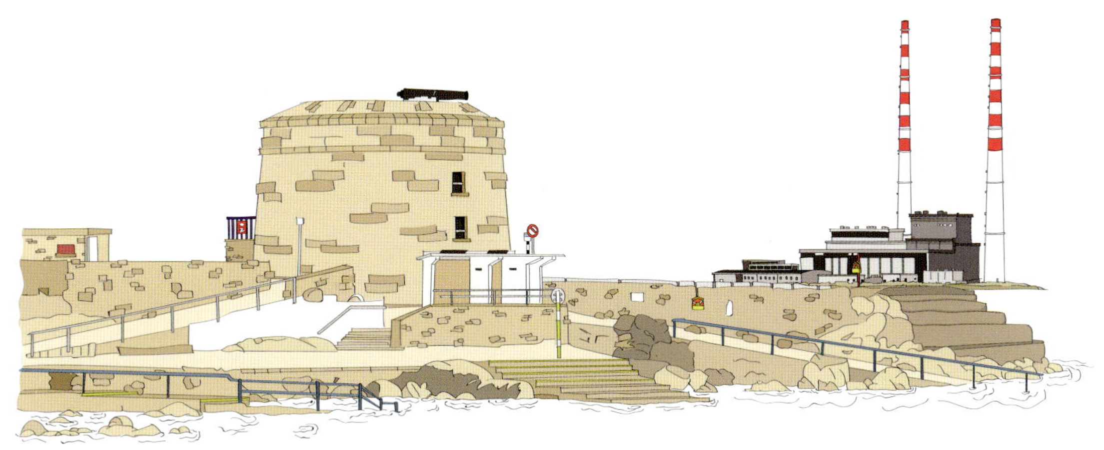

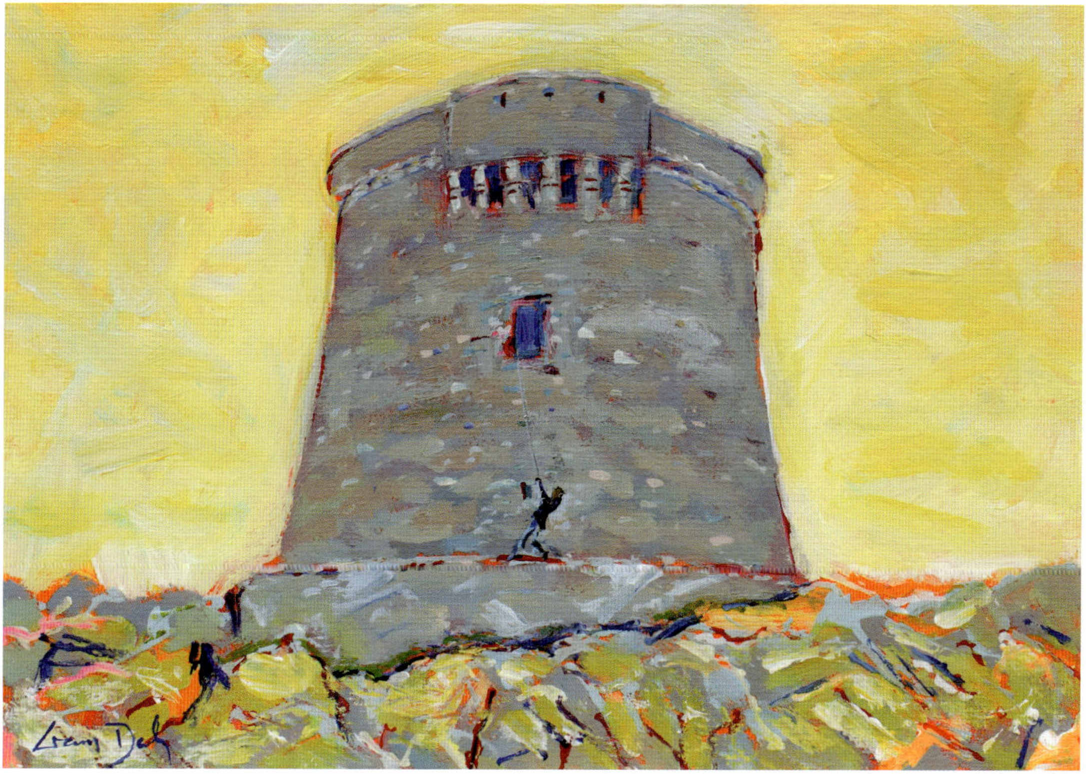

MARTELLO TOWER, IRELAND'S EYE, LIAM DALY

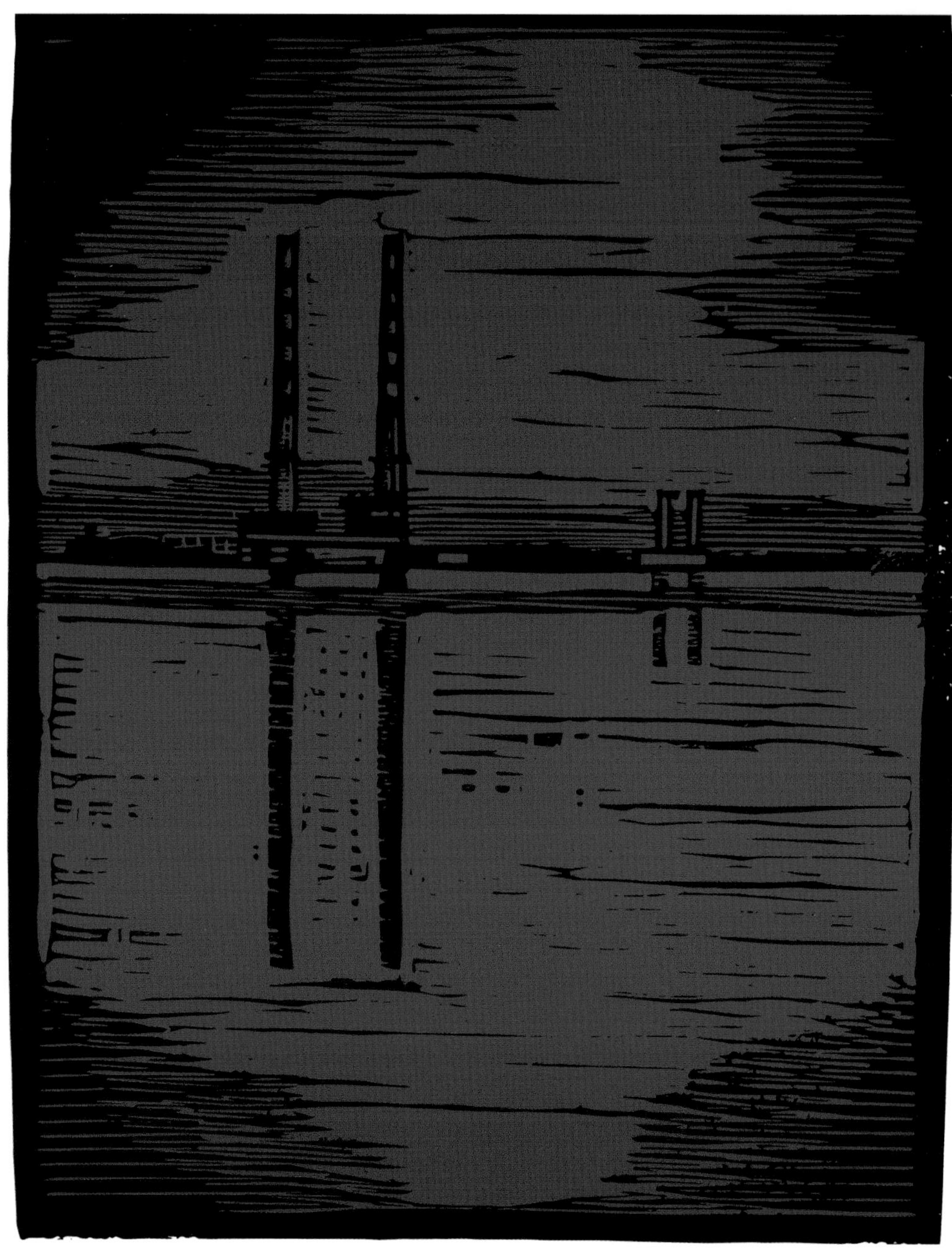

POOLBEG CHIMNEYS, JONATHAN BRENNAN

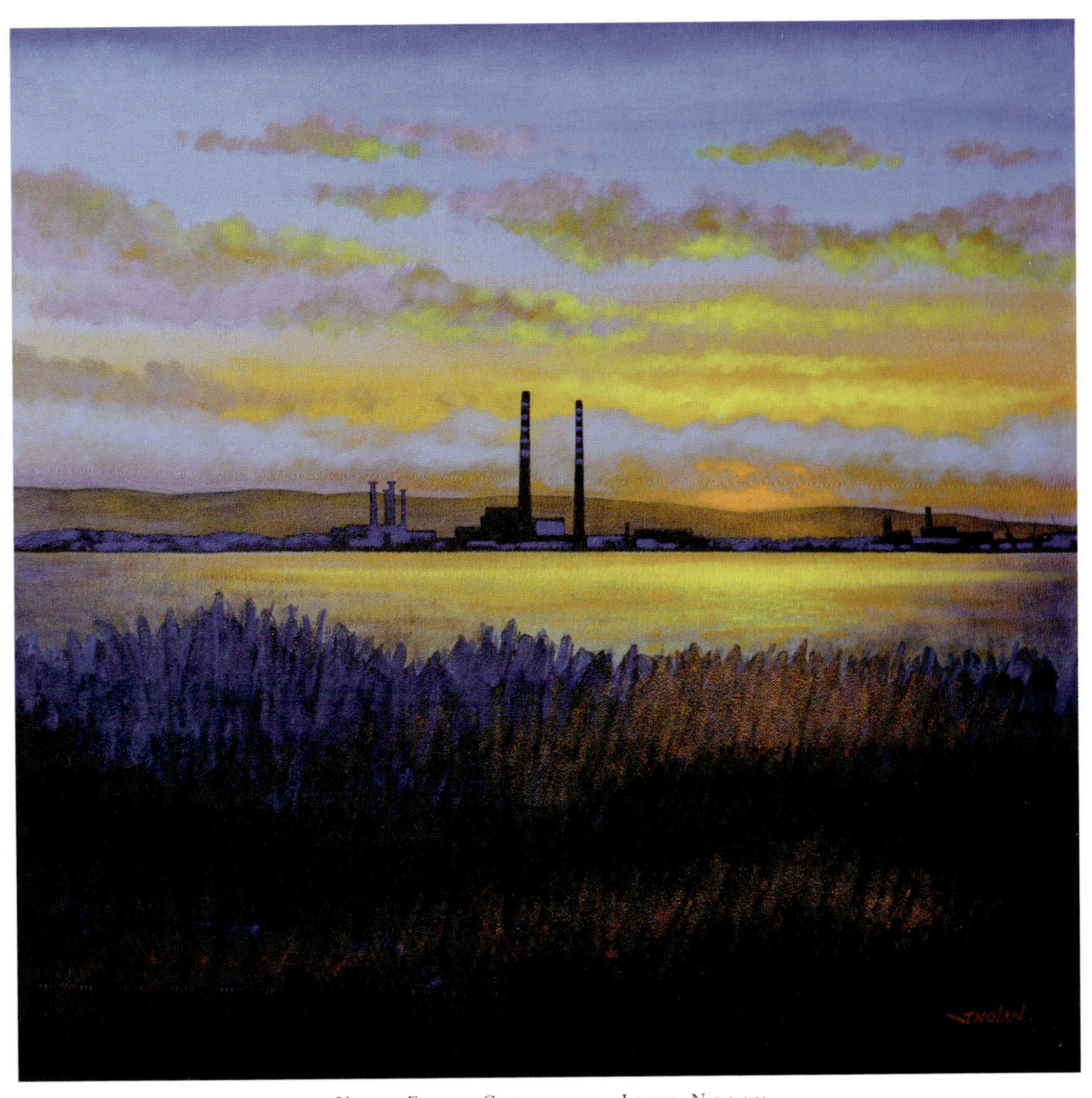

VIEW FROM CLONTARF, JOHN NOLAN

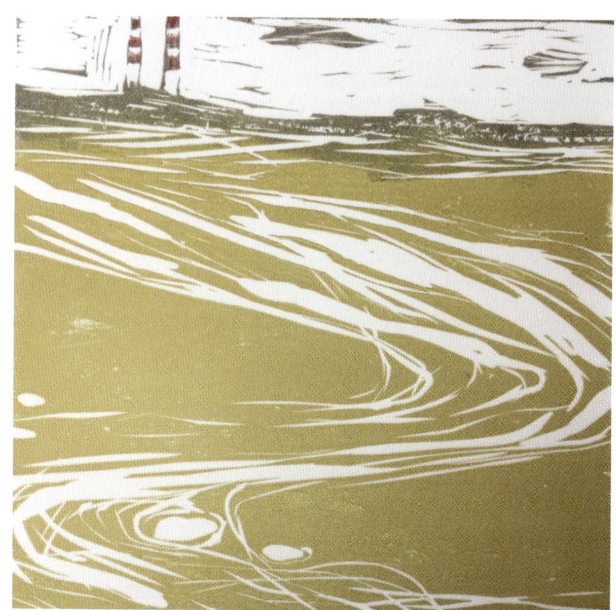

POOLBEG, MARTA WAKULA-MAC

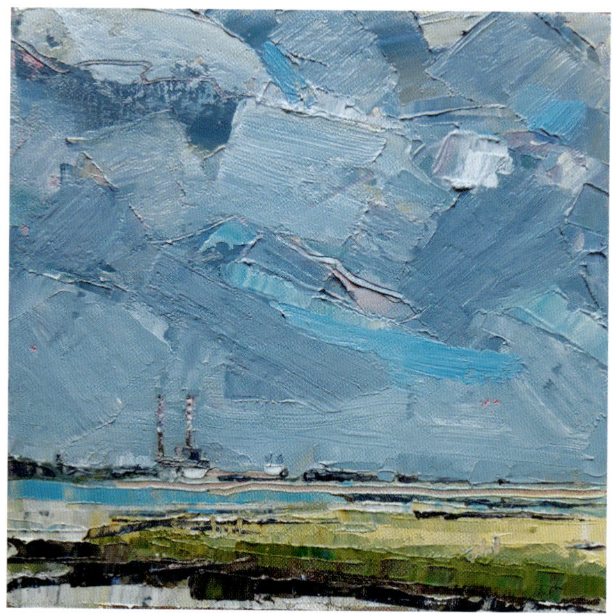

SANDYMOUNT, ISOBEL HENIHAN

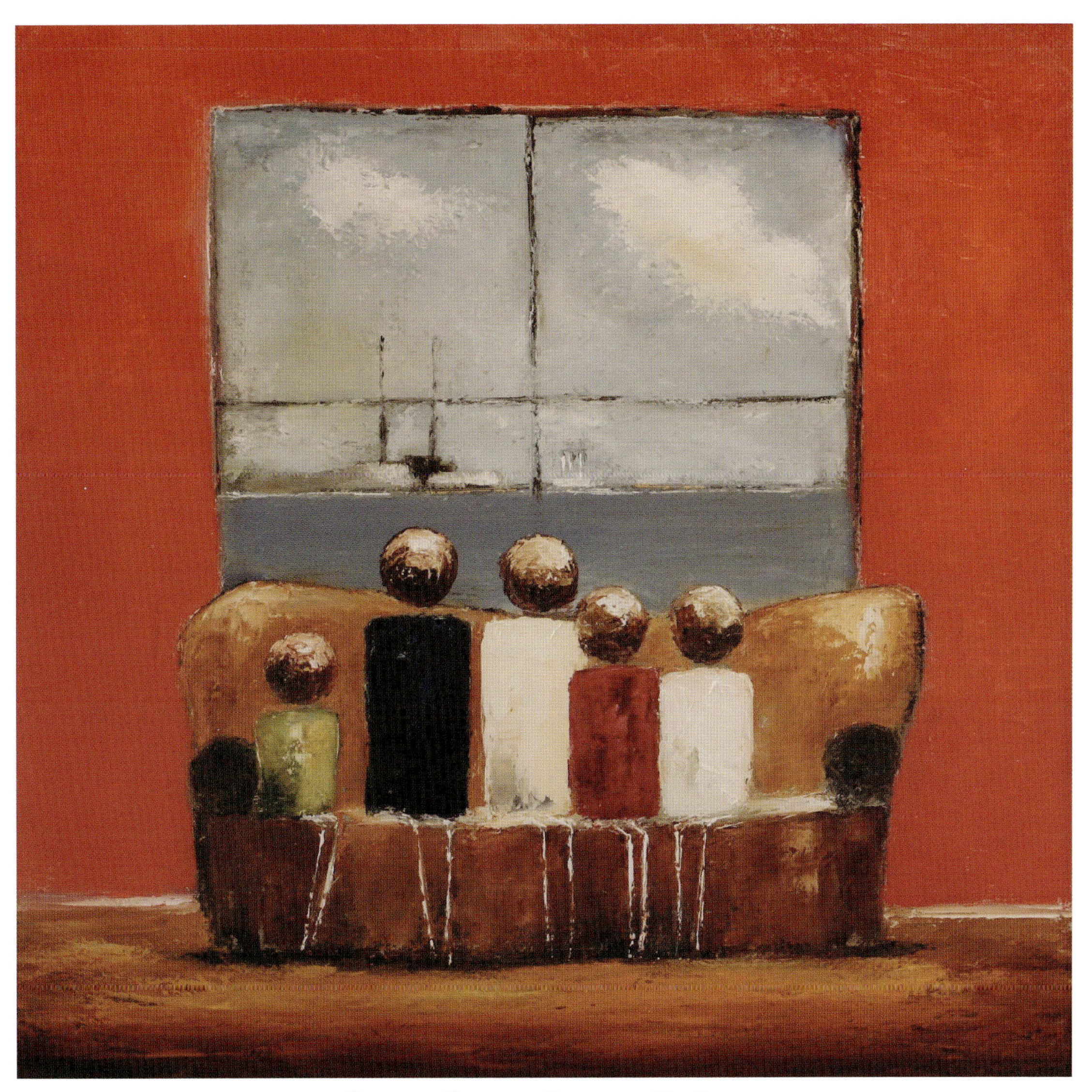

On the Couch, Padraig McCaul

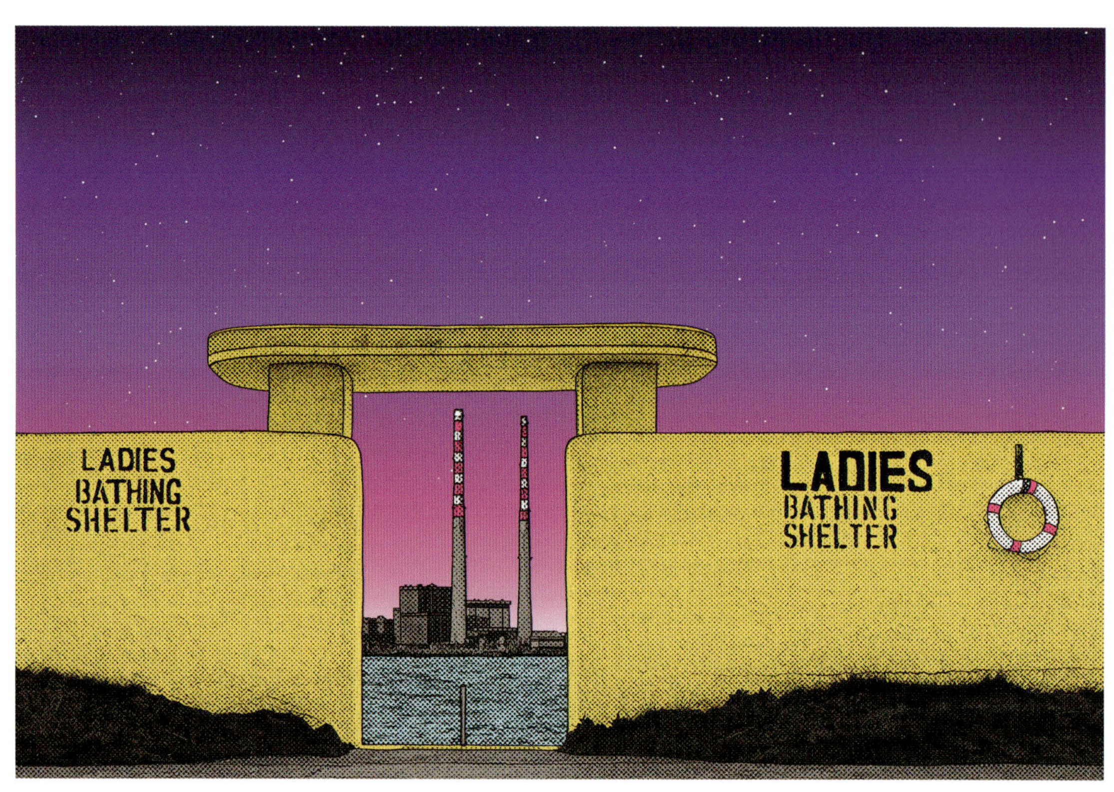

WOMEN'S BATHING SHELTER, BULL ISLAND, JANDO

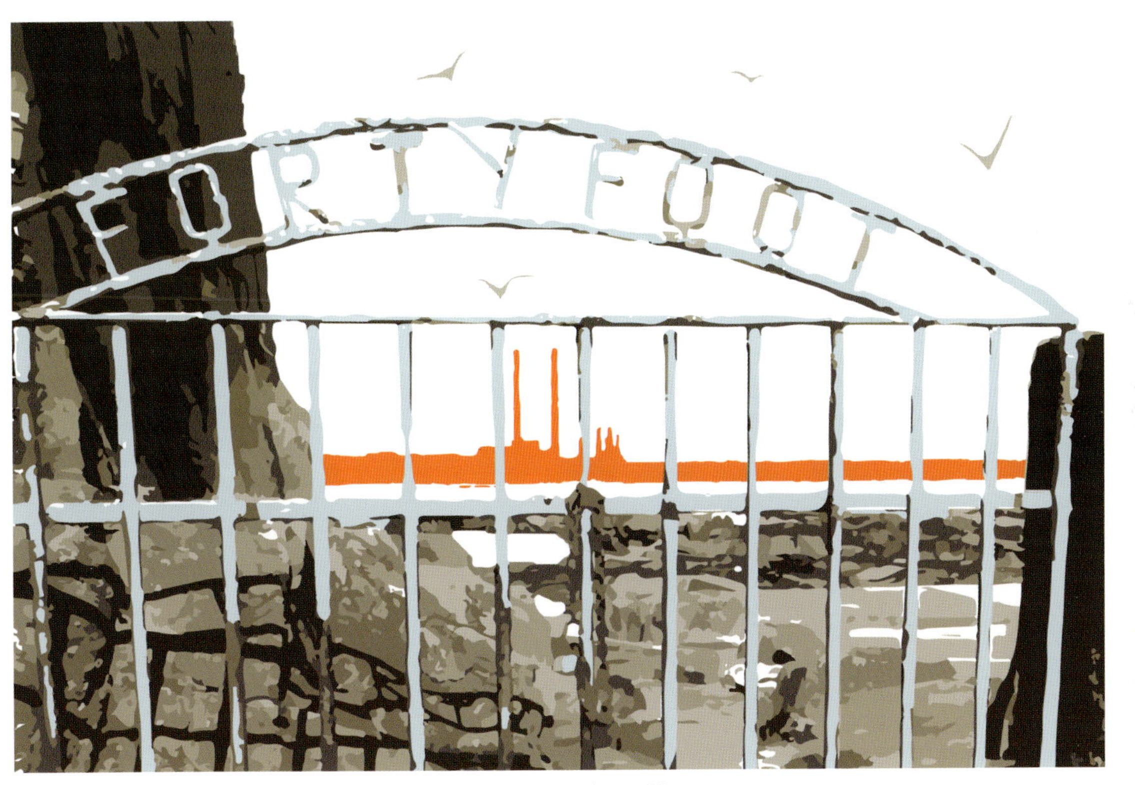

THE FORTY FOOT, AMY HENNESEY

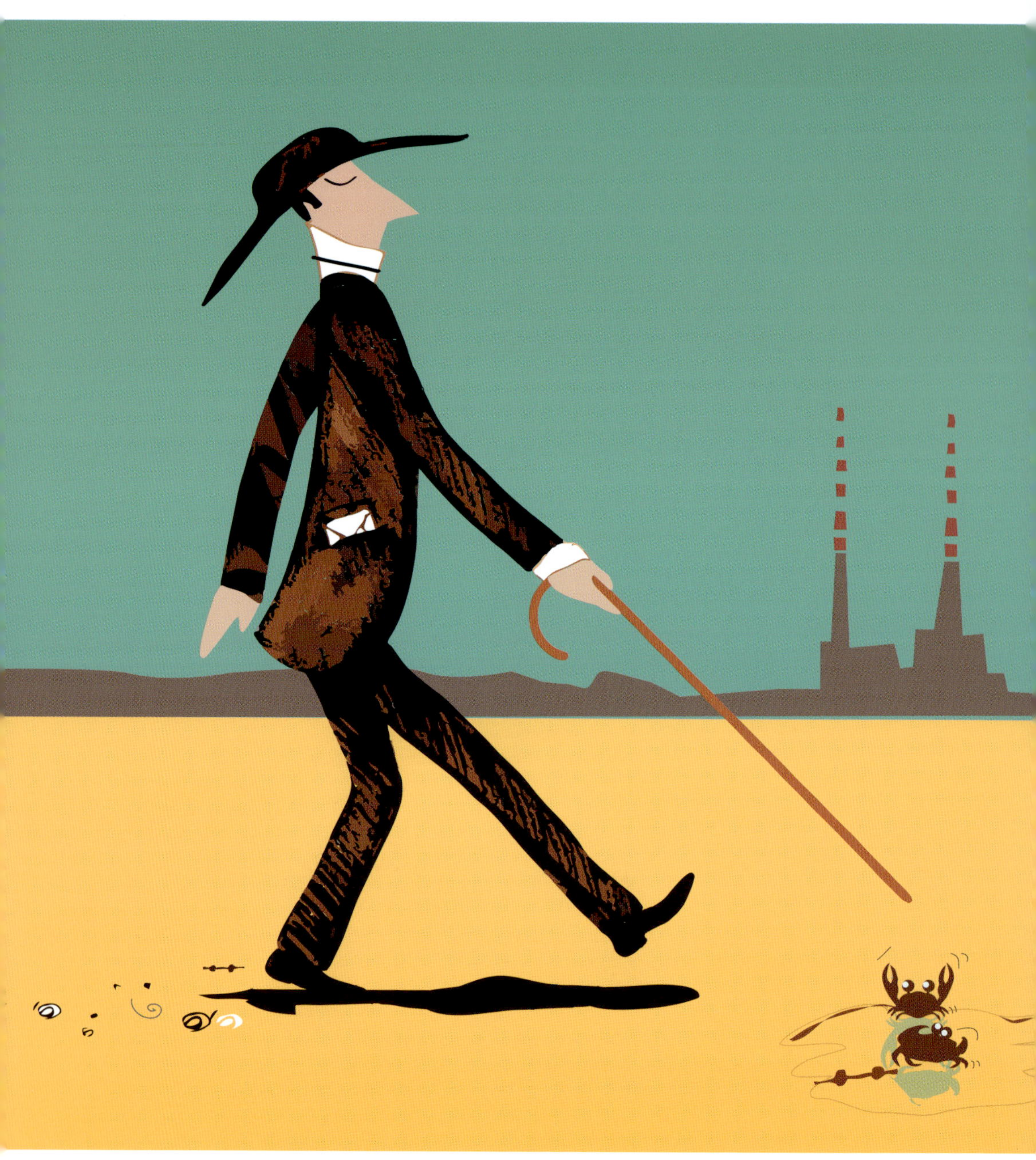

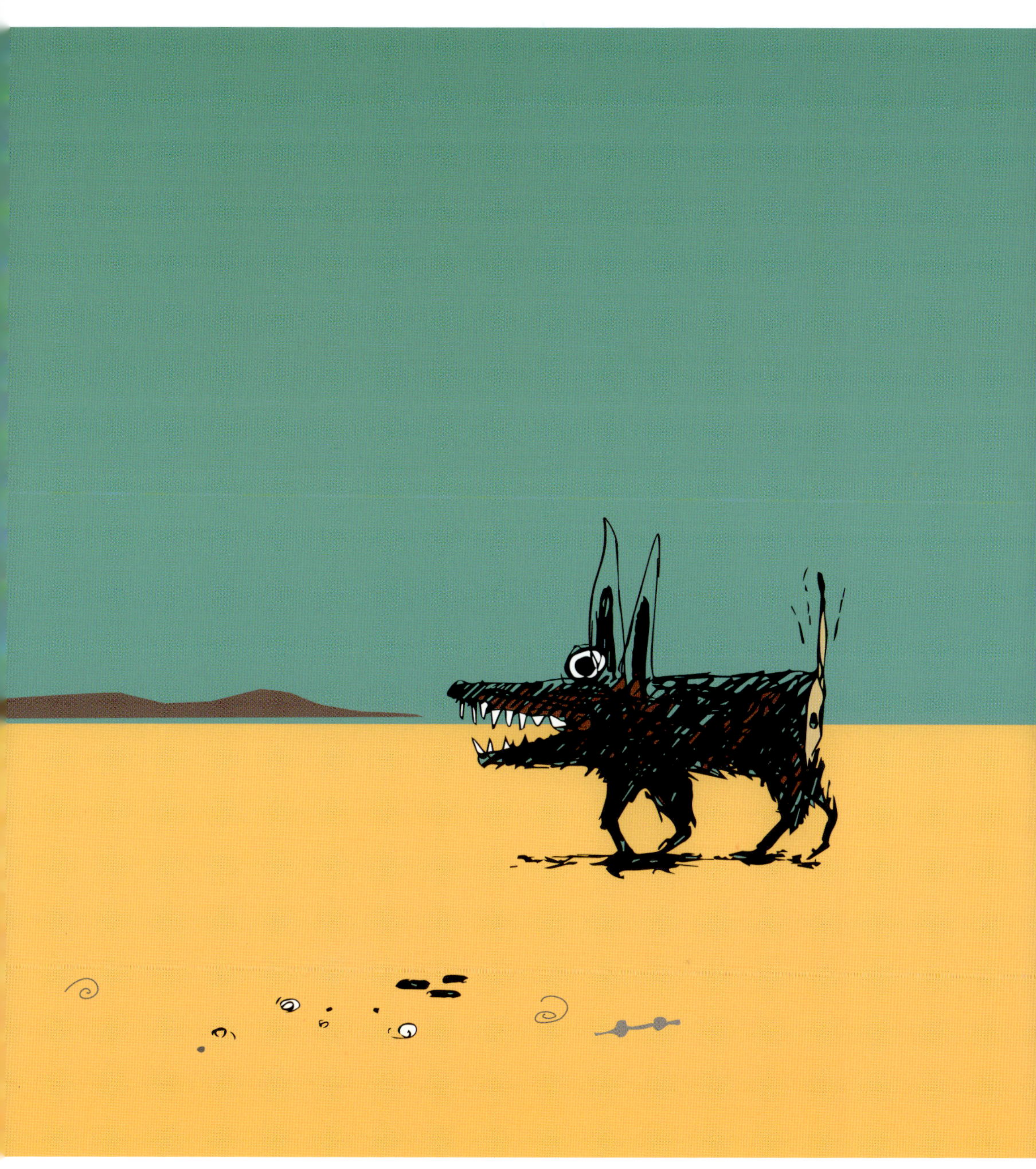

SANDYMOUNT STRAND, JAMES FRANCIS MOORE

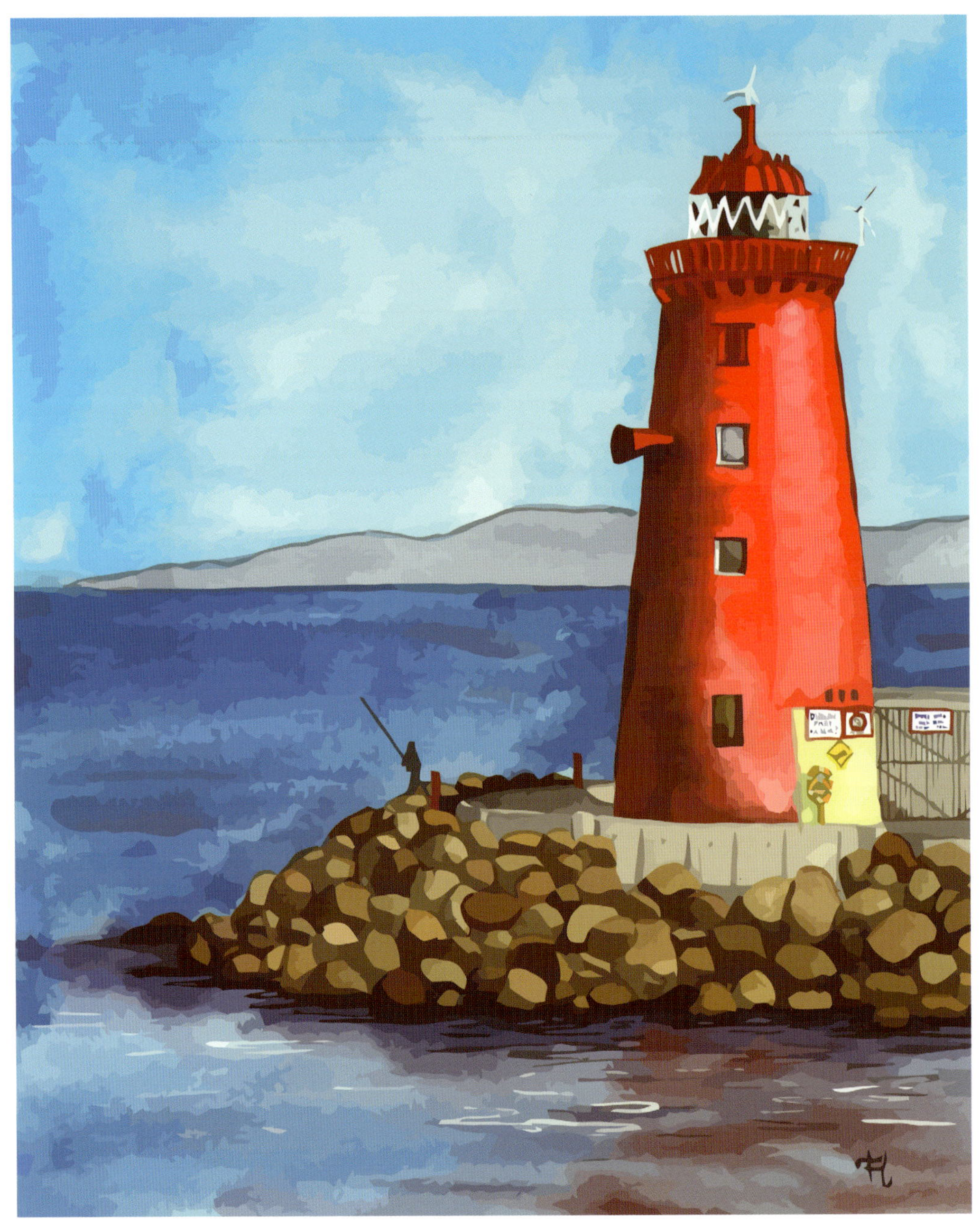

POOLBEG LIGHTHOUSE, TERRI KELLEHER

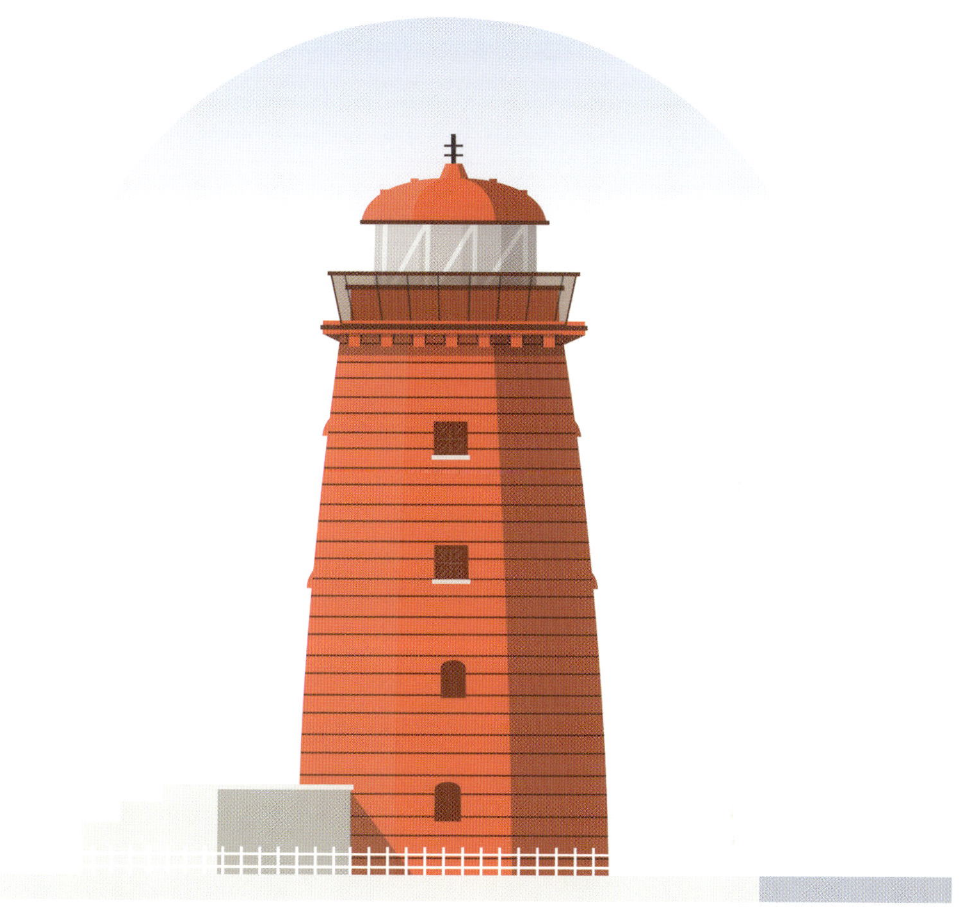

POOLBEG LIGHTHOUSE
- CO. DUBLIN, IRELAND -

Poolbeg Lighthouse, Al Power

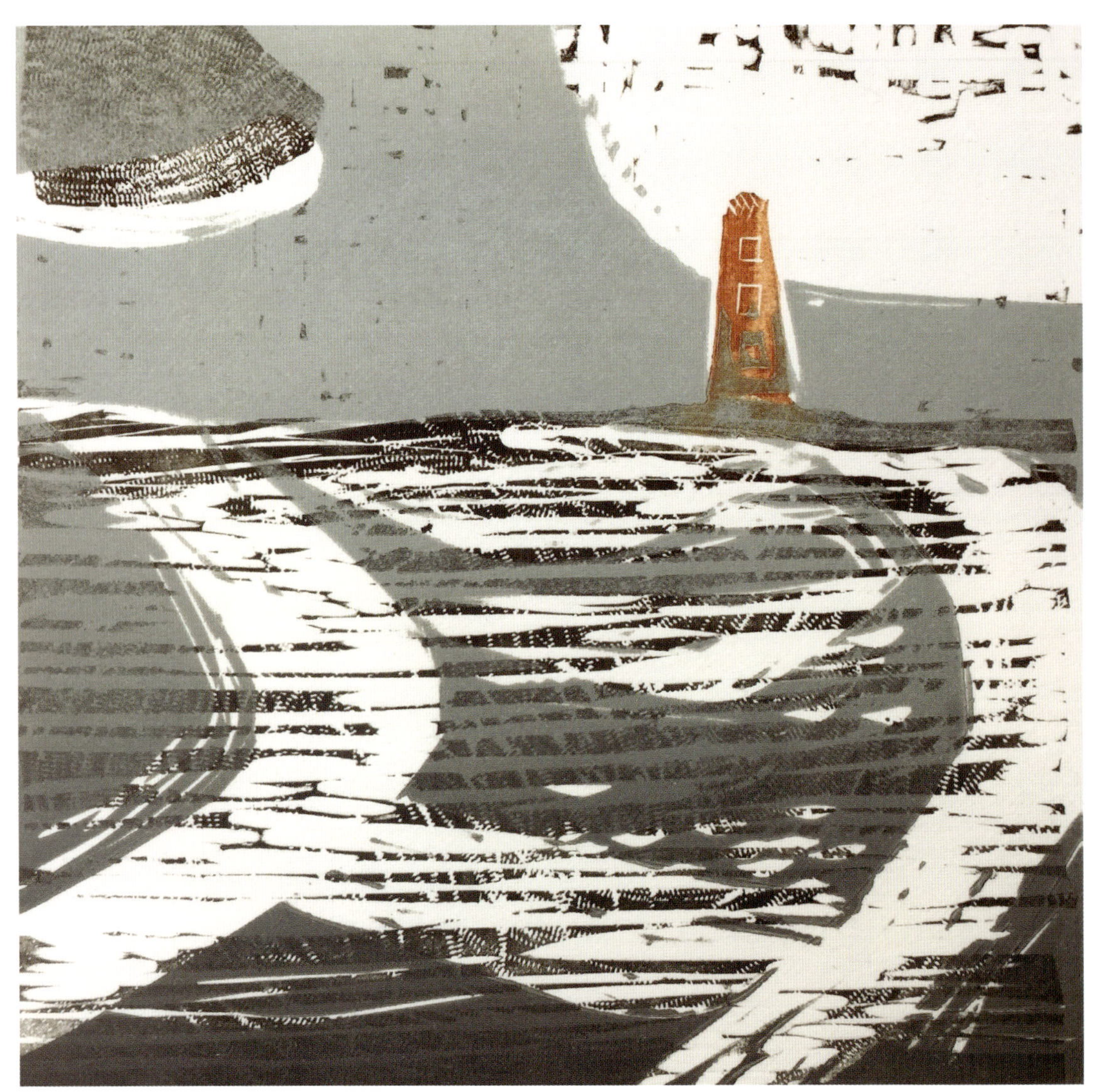

POOLBEG LIGHTHOUSE, MARTA WAKULA-MAC

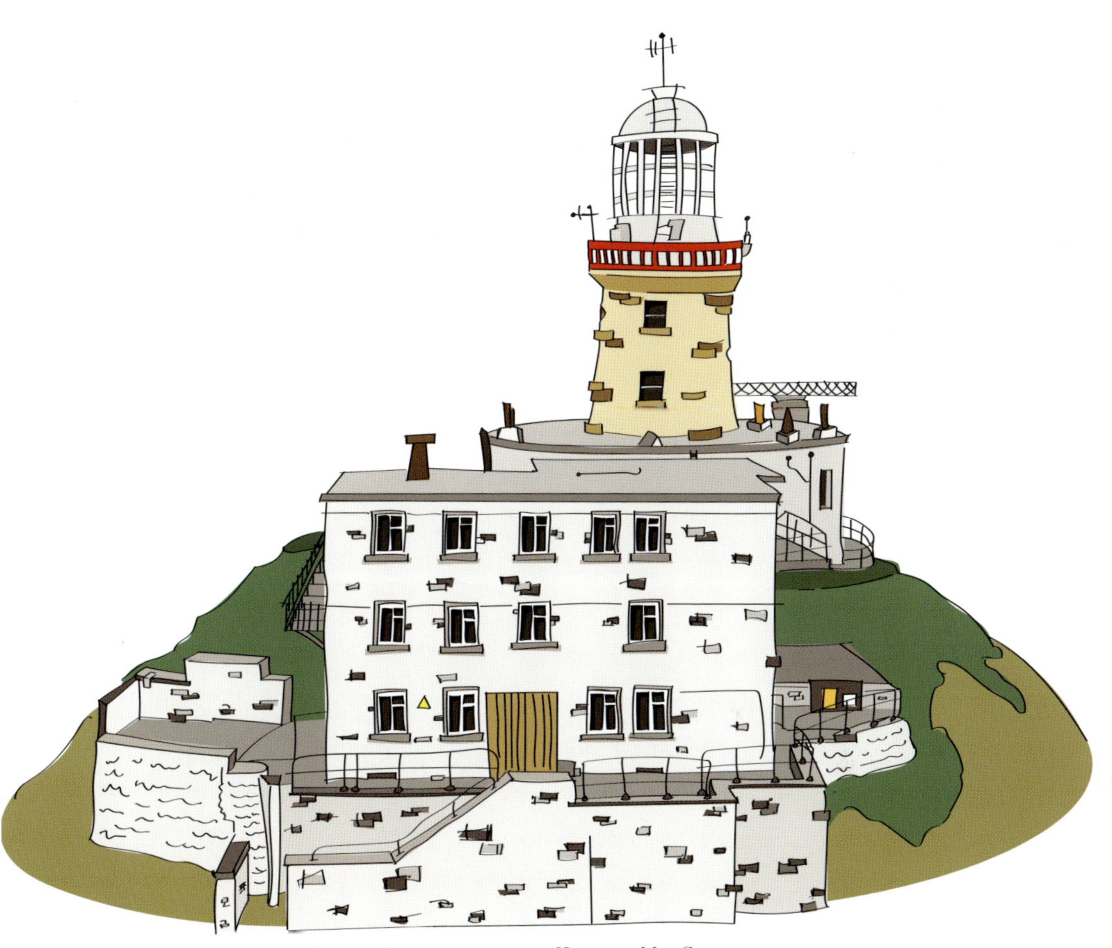

BAILY LIGHTHOUSE, KEVIN McGUINNESS

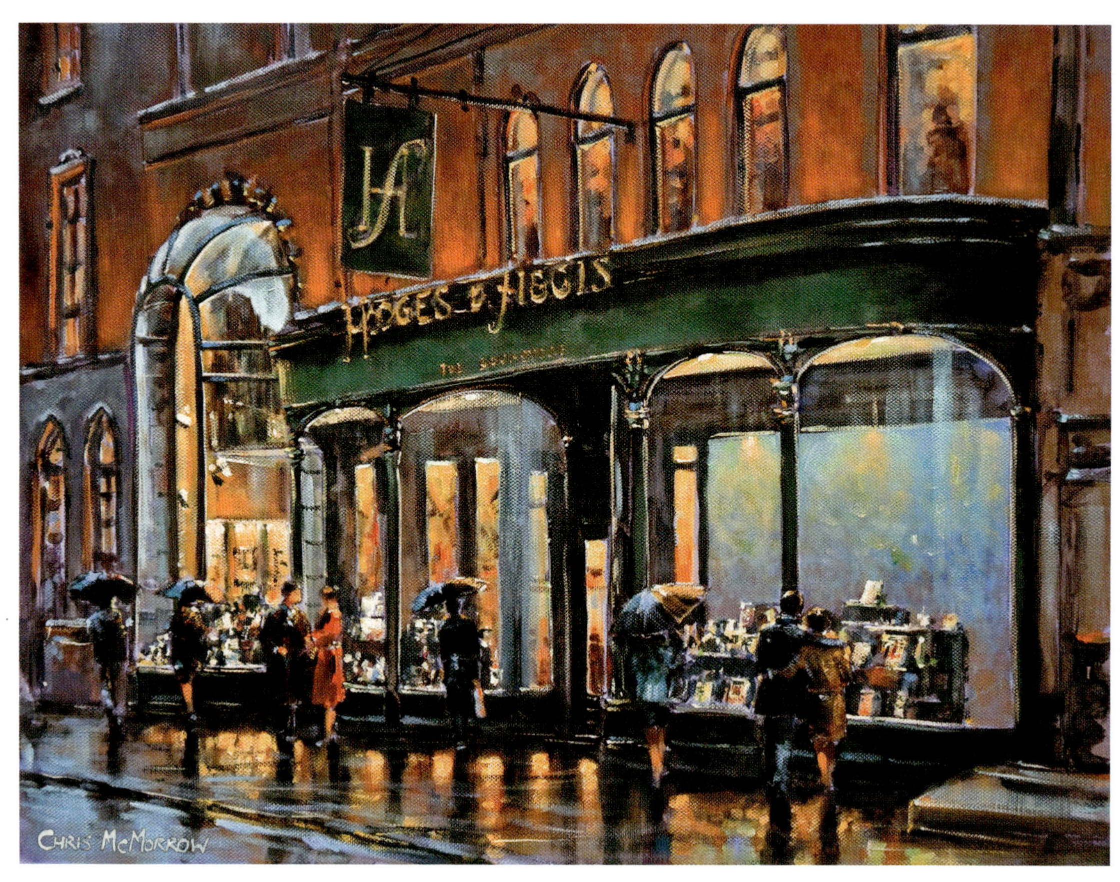

HODGES FIGGIS BOOKSTORE, CHRIS McMORROW

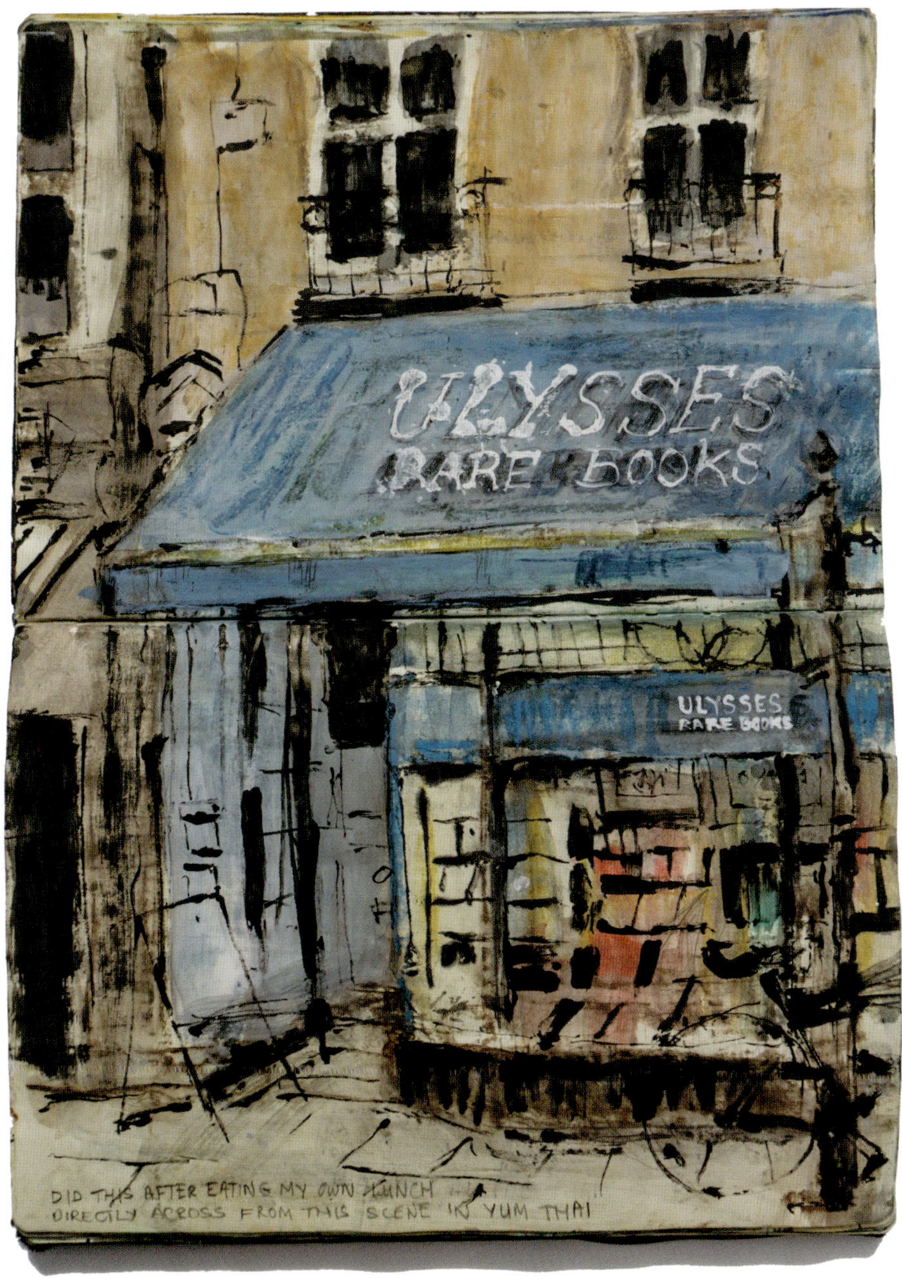

ULYSSES RARE BOOKS, DUKE STREET, JAMES FRANCIS MOORE

71

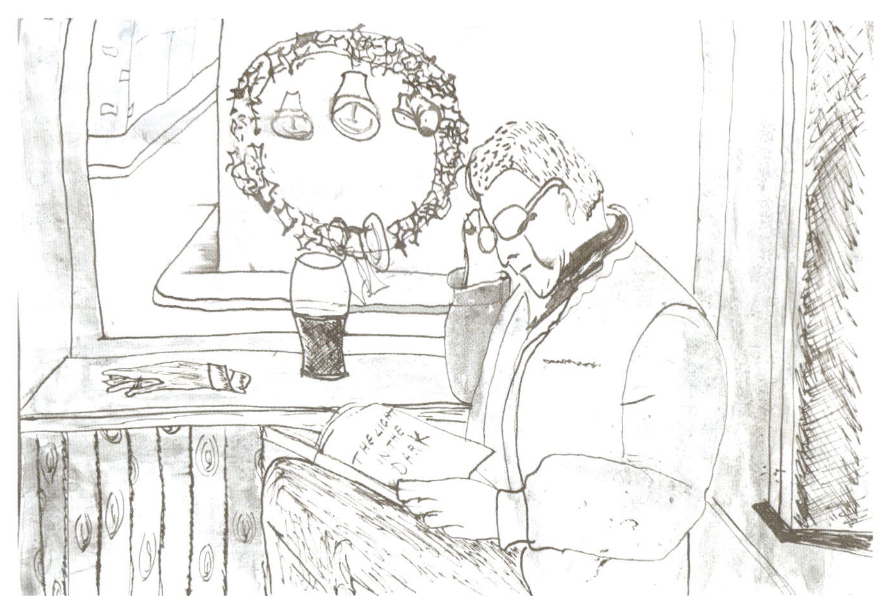

The Duke Pub, Kate Kavanagh

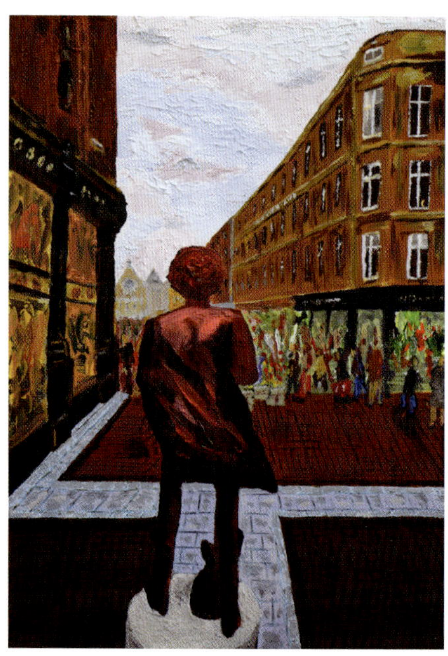

Facing toward South Anne Street, Leo Tierney

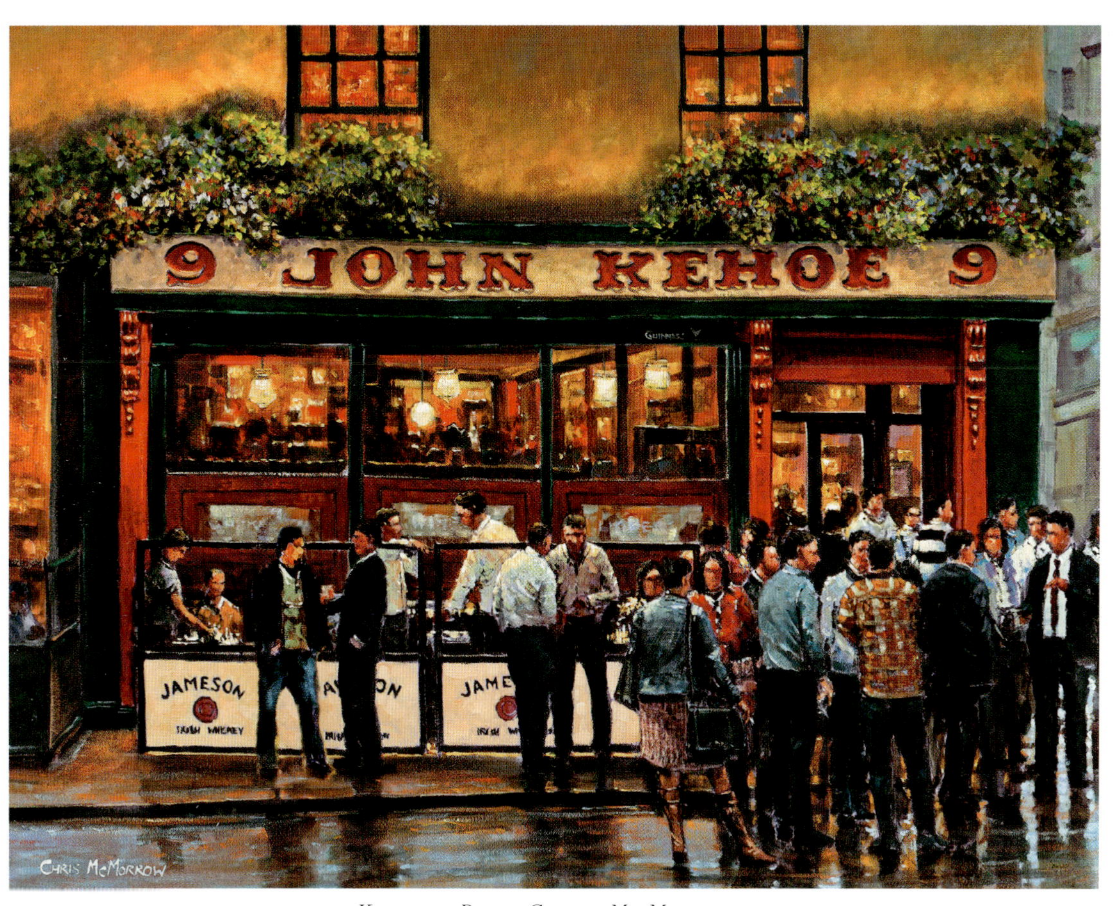

KEHOES PUB, CHRIS McMORROW

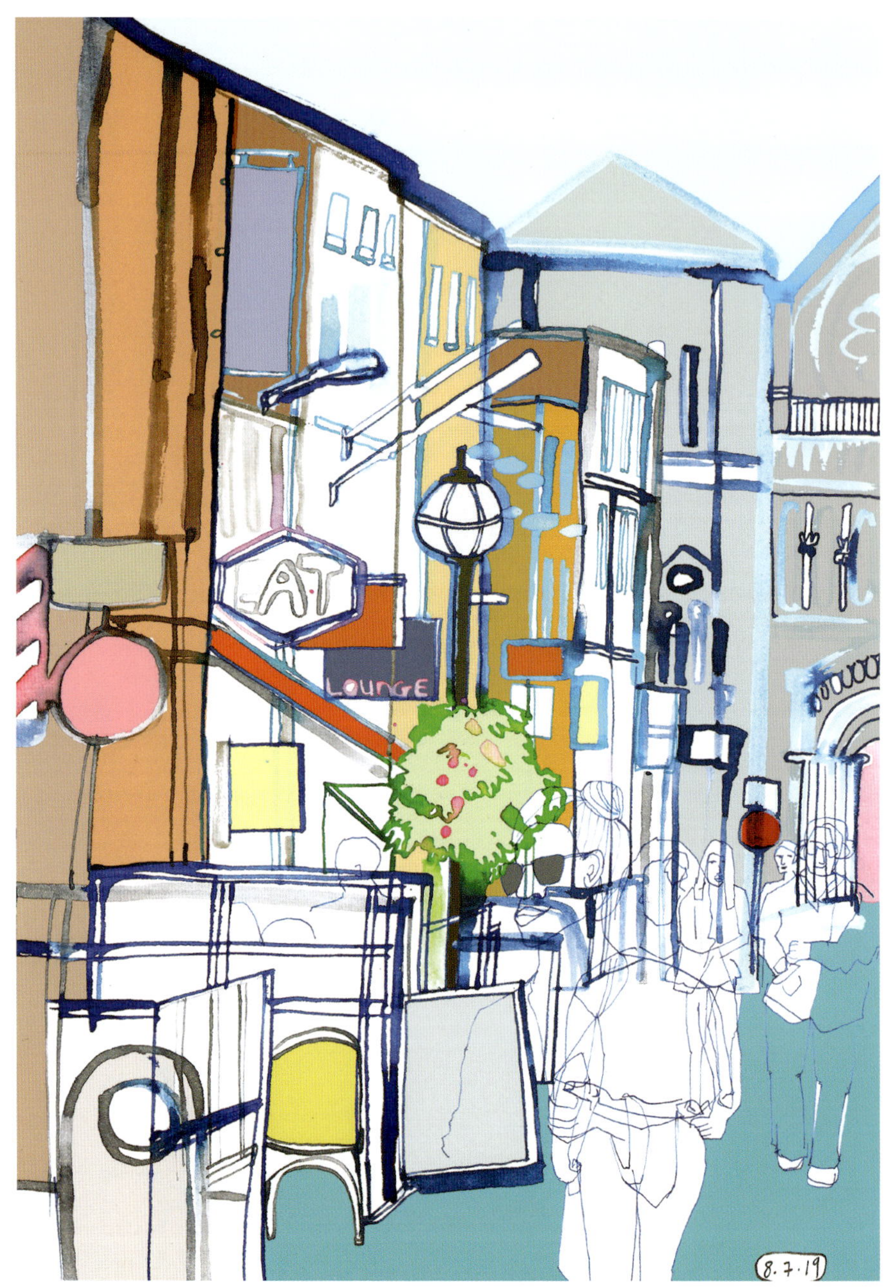

SOUTH ANNE STREET, EVA KELLY

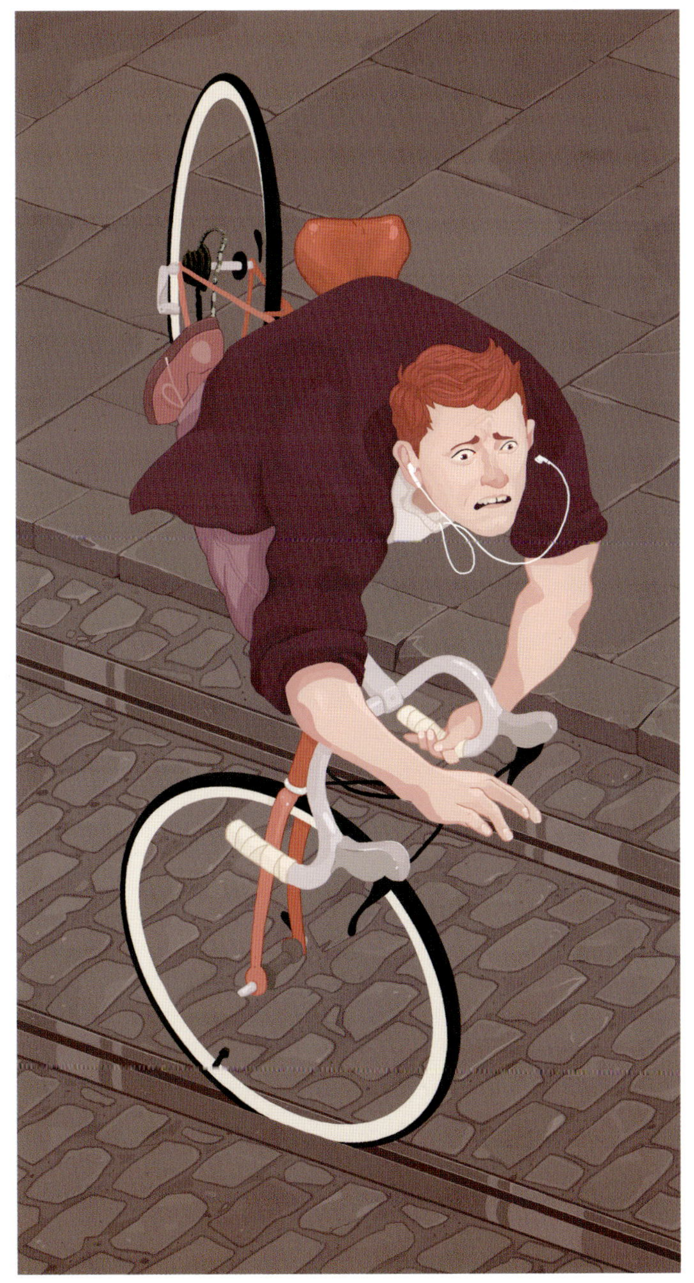

LUAS FLIP, ROB TORRANS

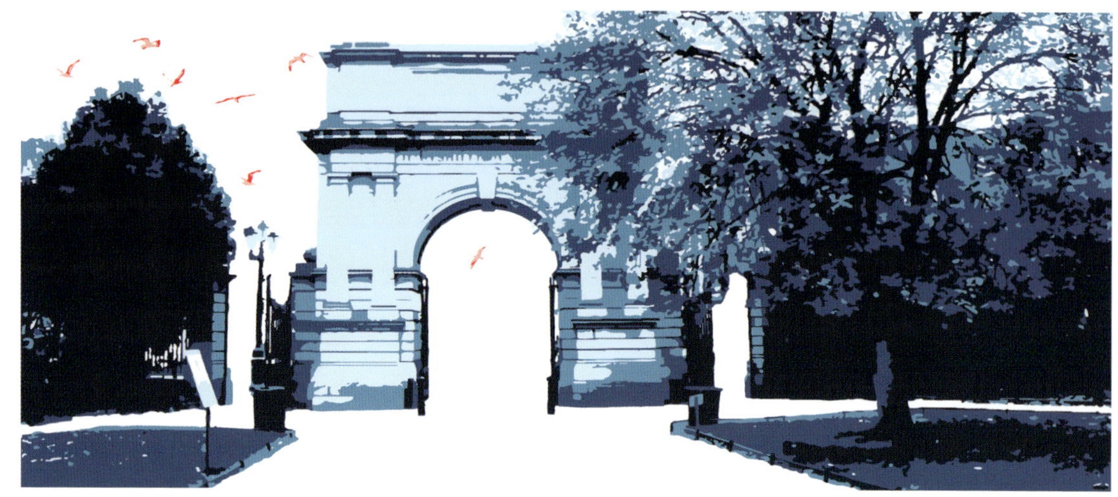

St Stephen's Green, Amy Hennesey

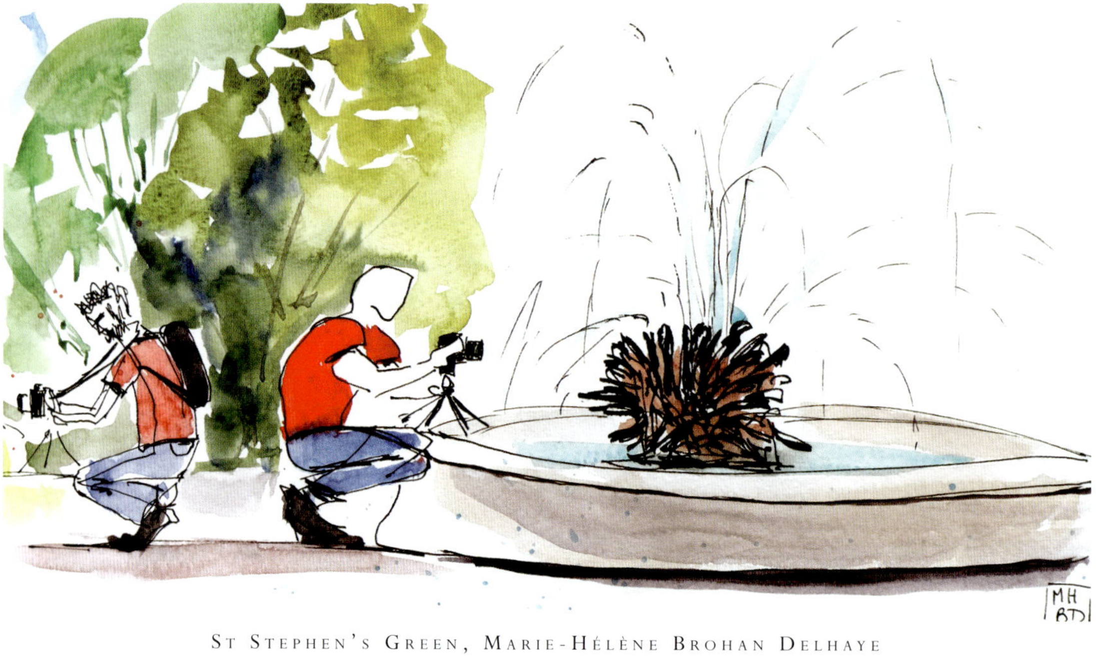

St Stephen's Green, Marie-Hélène Brohan Delhaye

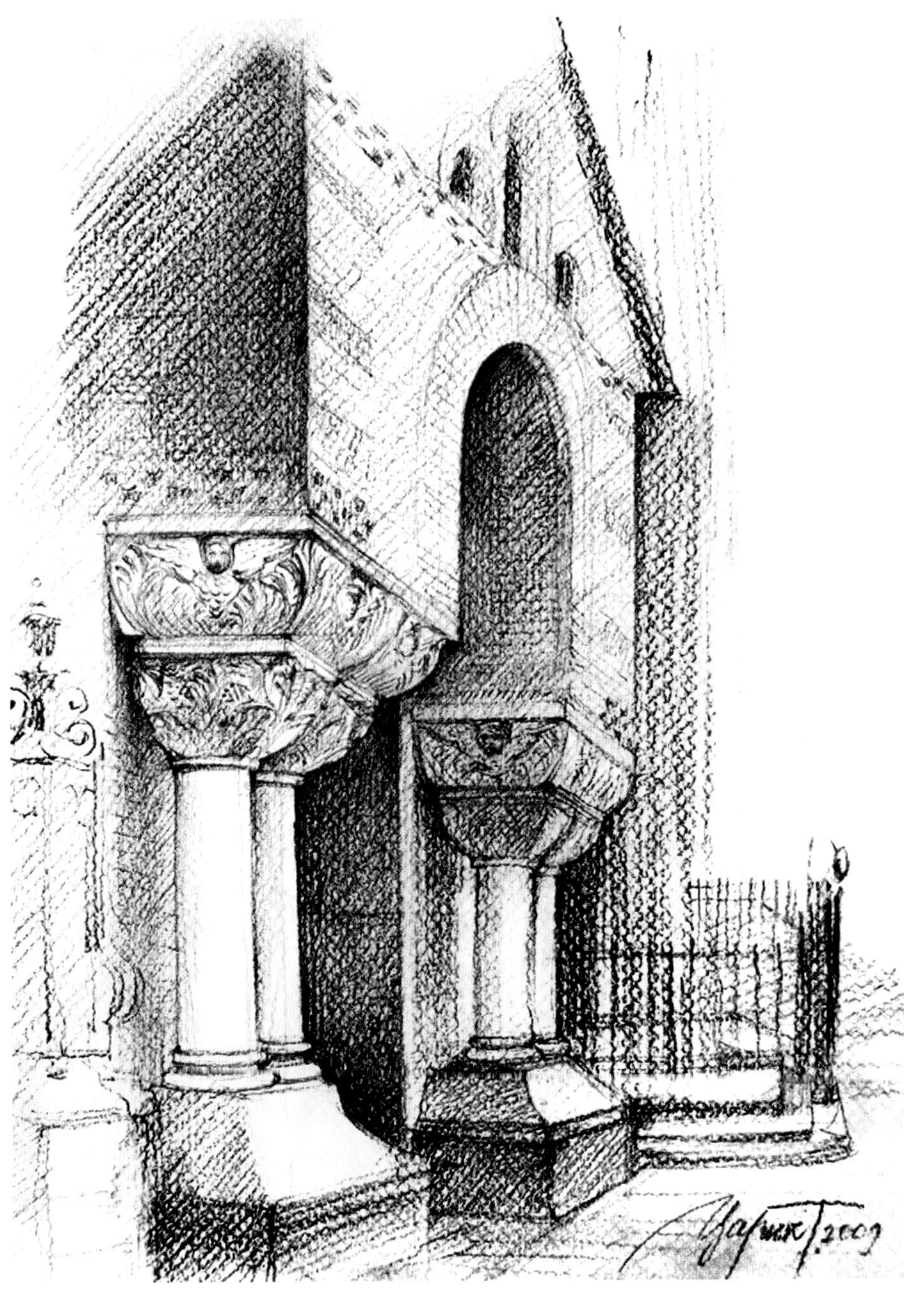

St Stephen's green, Tetyana Tsaryk

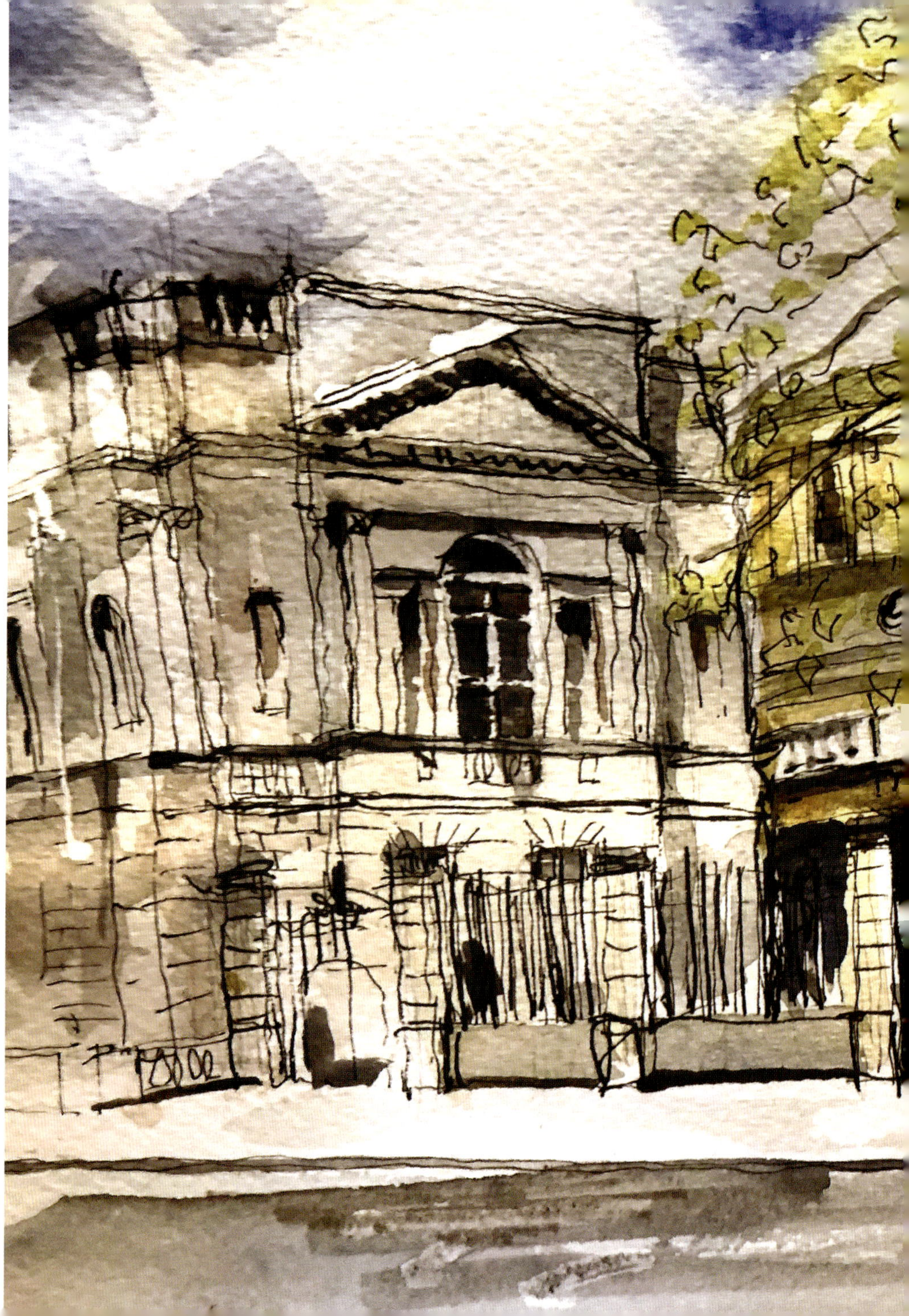

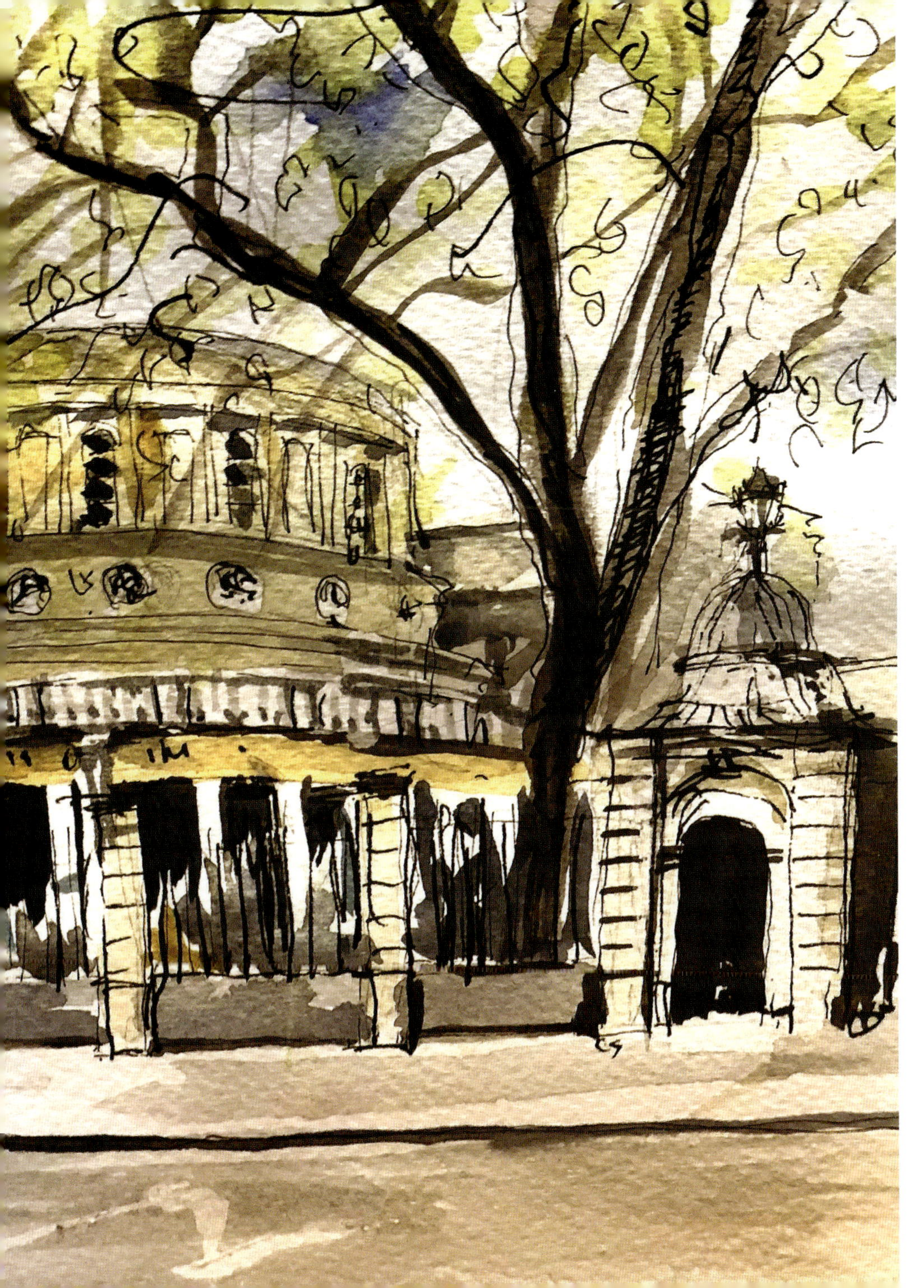

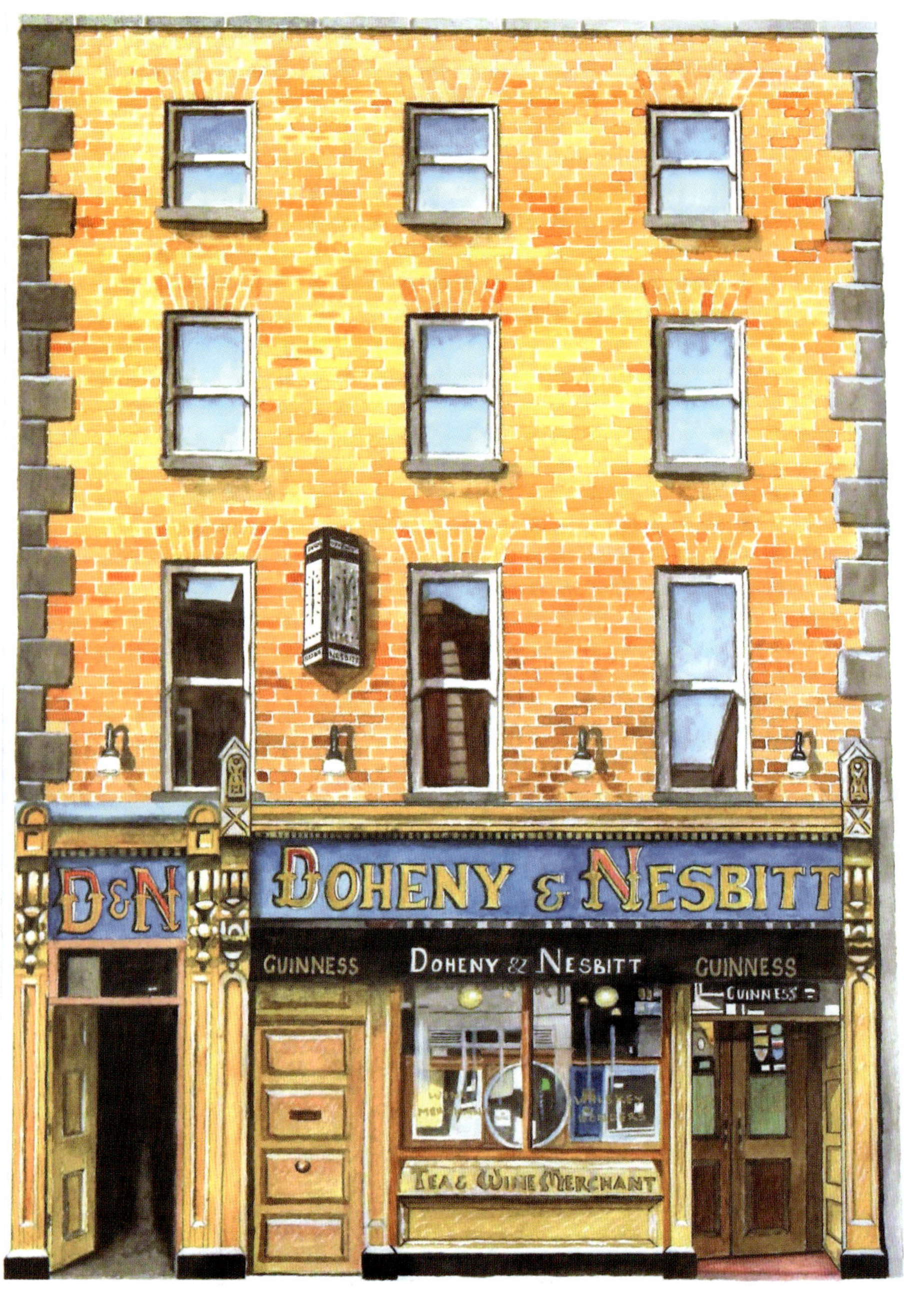

DOHENY AND NESBITT, BRIAN O'NEILL
PREVIOUS TWO PAGES: NATIONAL LIBRARY, CAITRIONA SHAFFREY

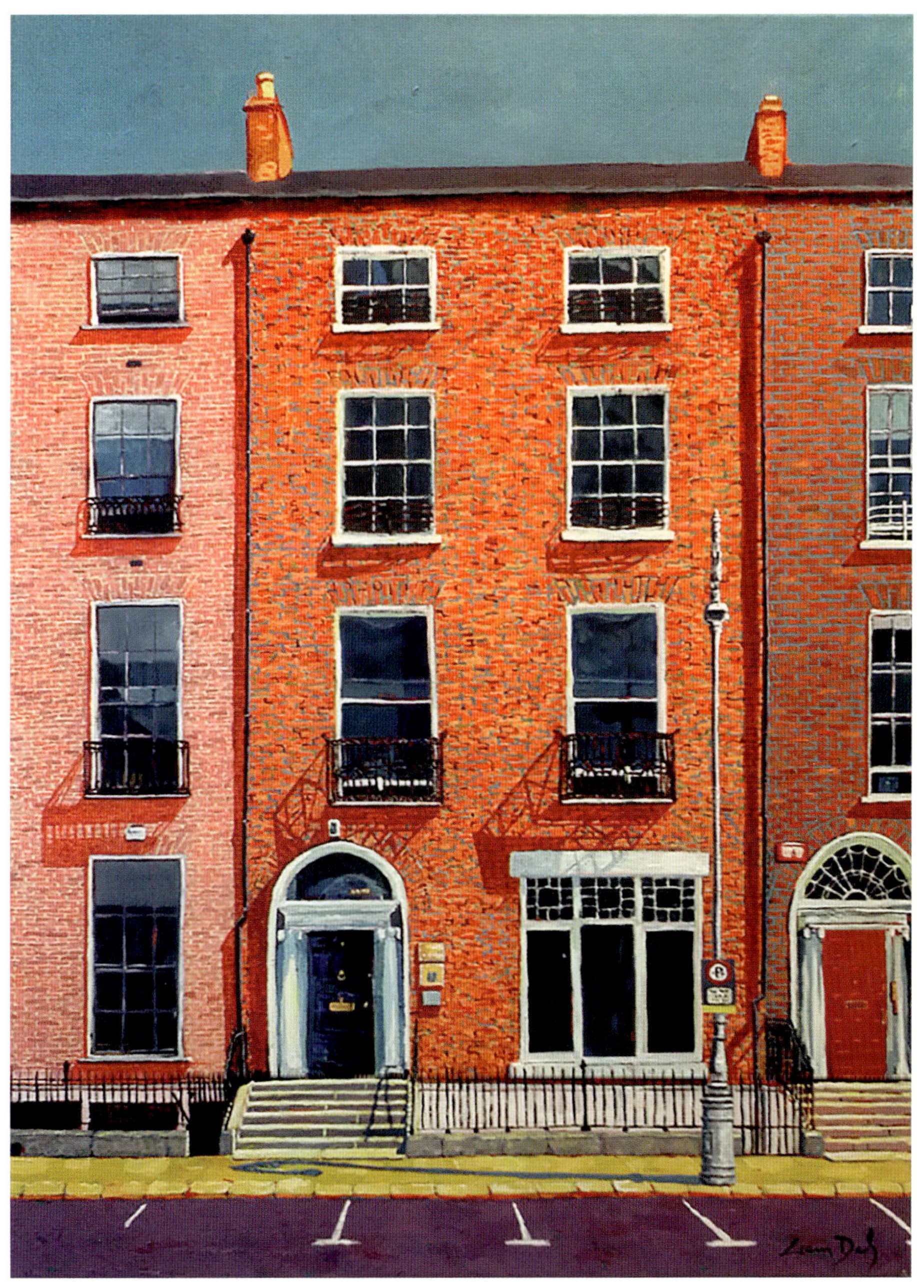

FITZWILLIAM SQUARE, LIAM DALY

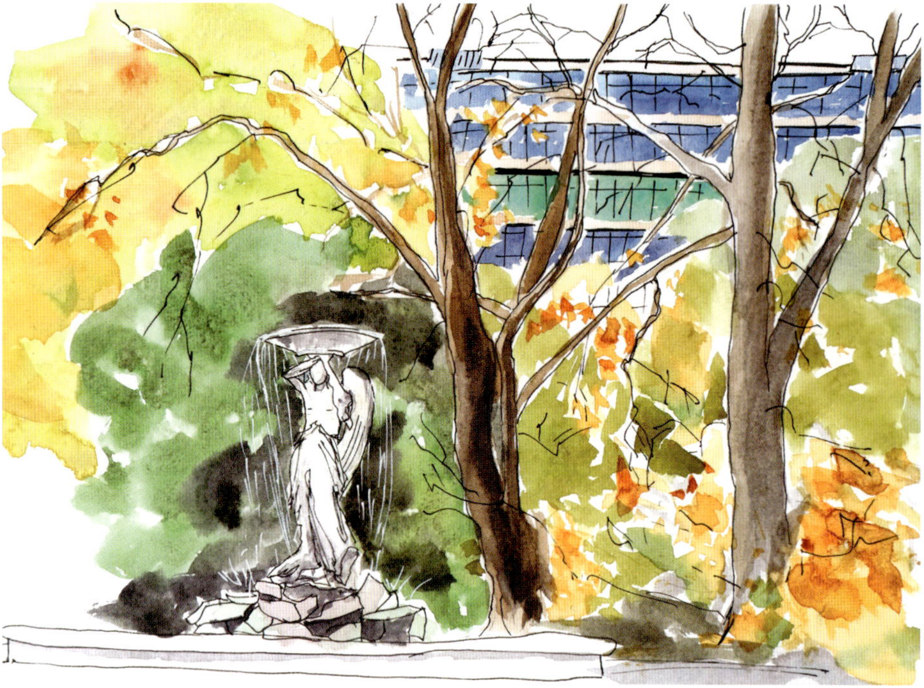

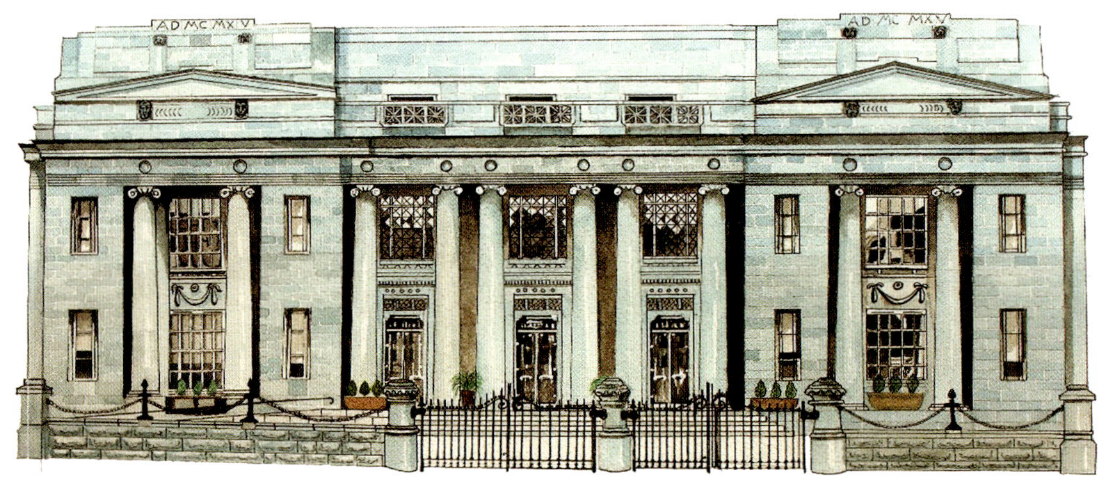

IVEAGH GARDENS, MARIE-HÉLÈNE BROHAN DELHAYE

NATIONAL CONCERT HALL, BRIAN O'NEILL

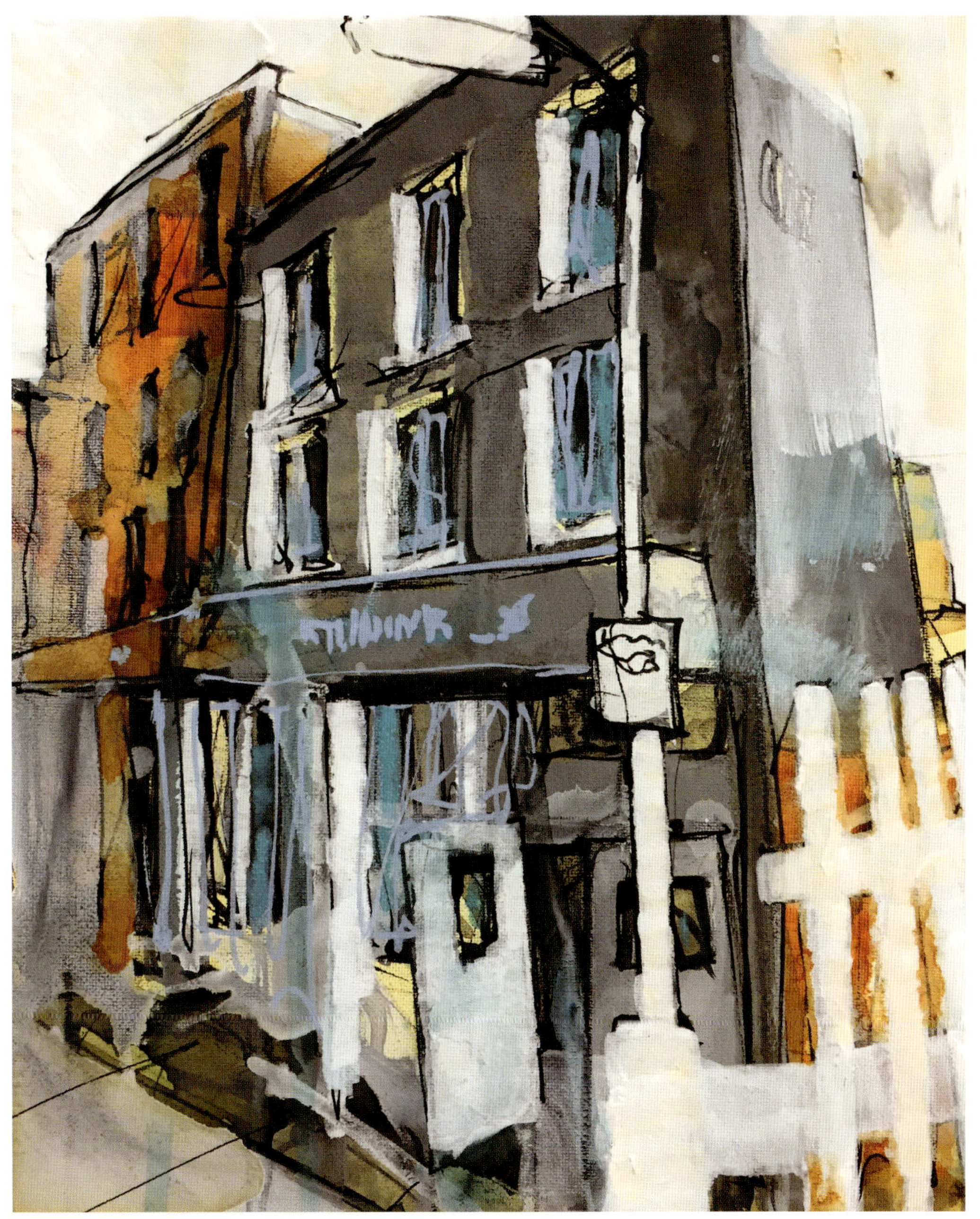

THE LUCKY DUCK, PETE MONAGHAN

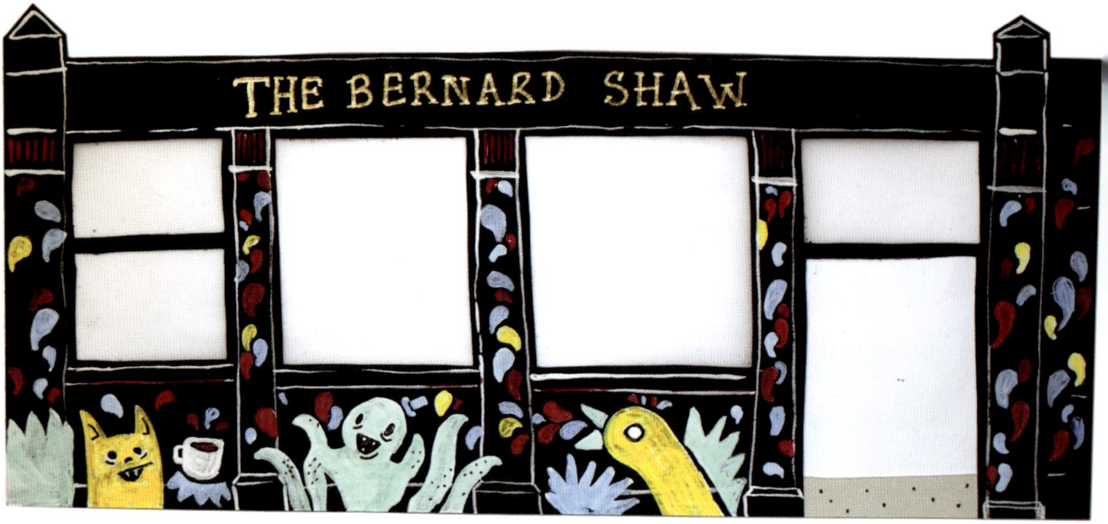

THE BERNARD SHAW, JESSICA ROONEY DEANE

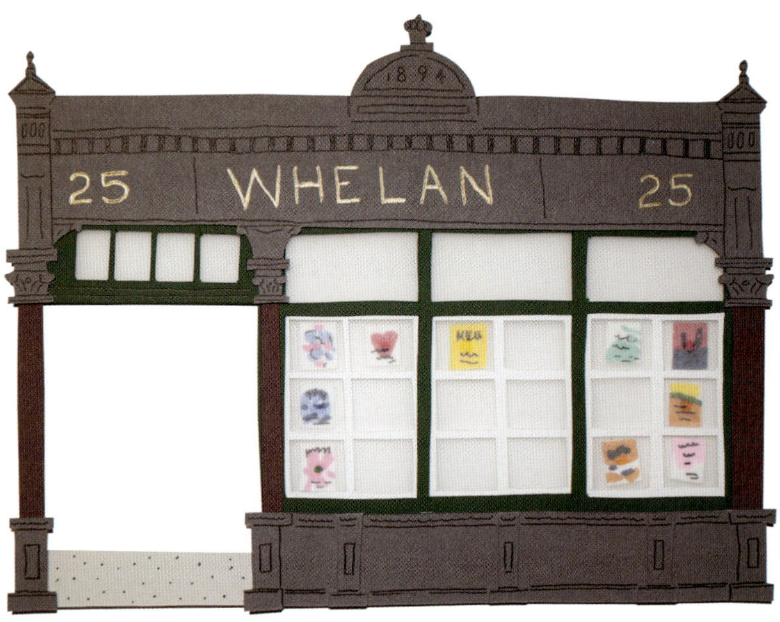

WHELAN'S, JESSICA ROONEY DEANE

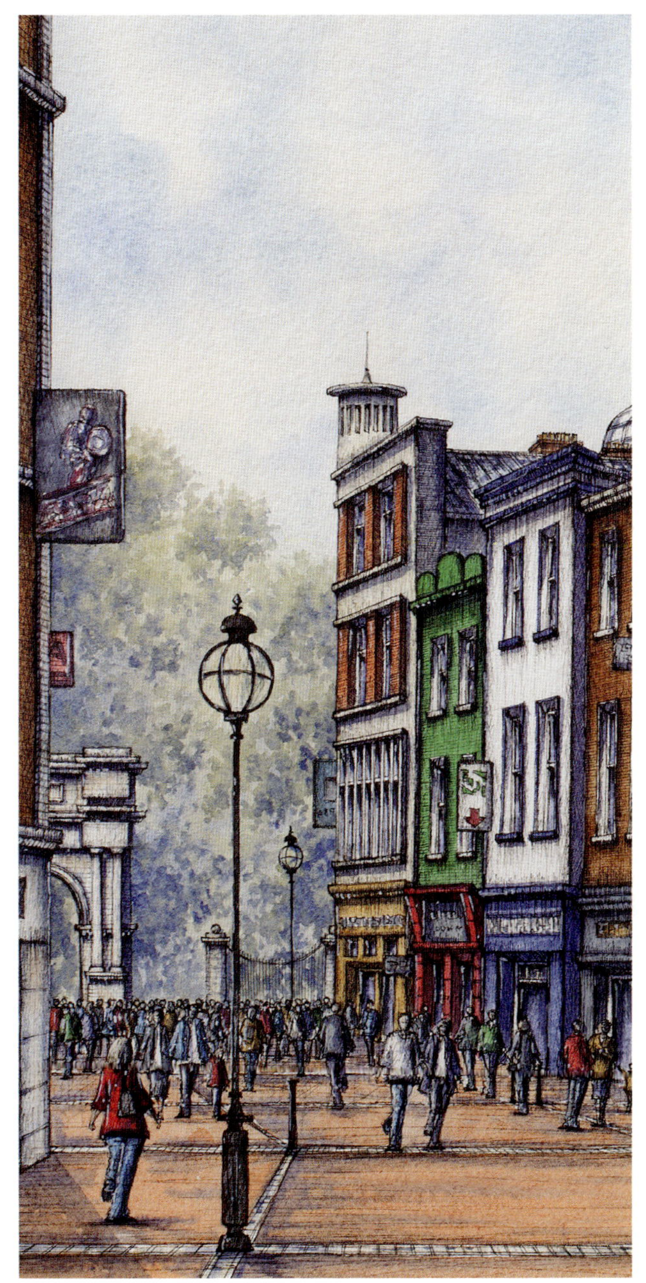

GRAFTON STREET, JIM SCULLY

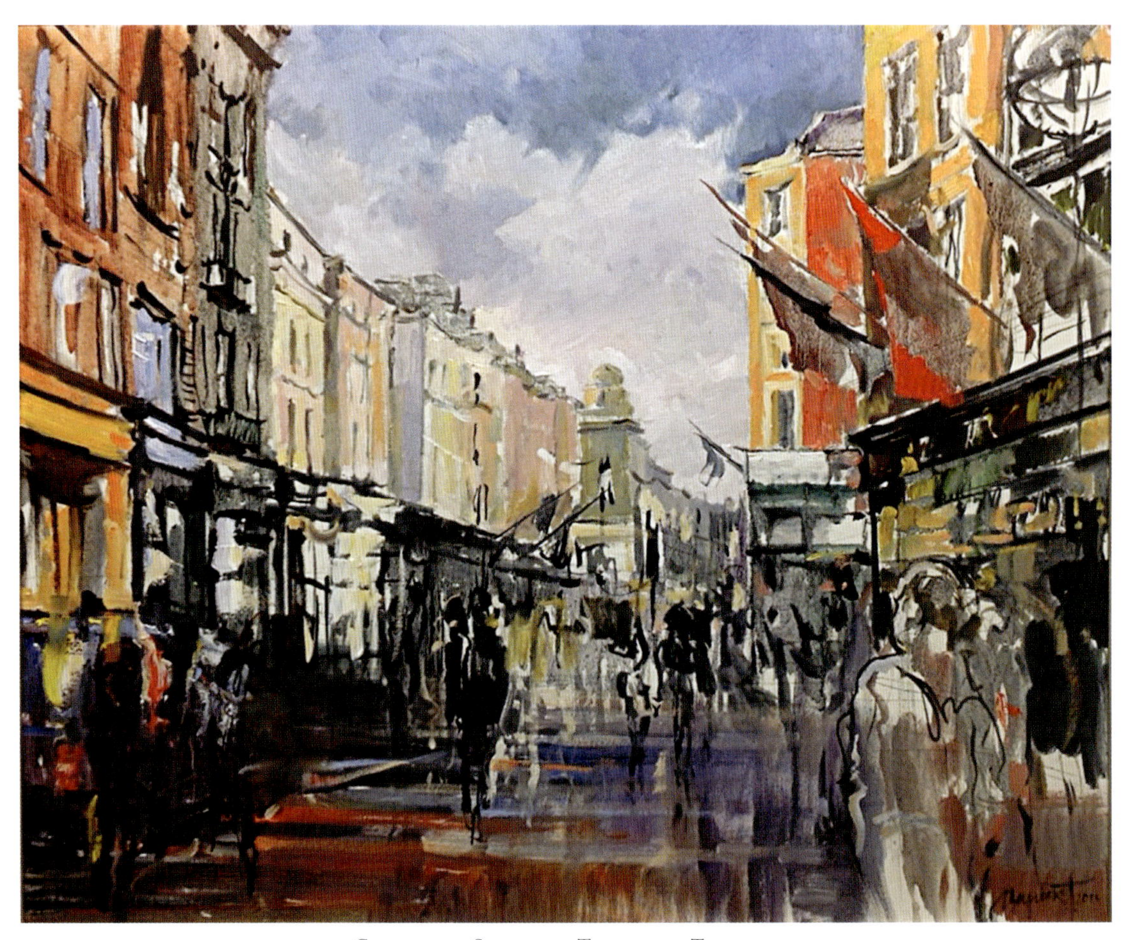

GRAFTON STREET, TETYANA TSARYK

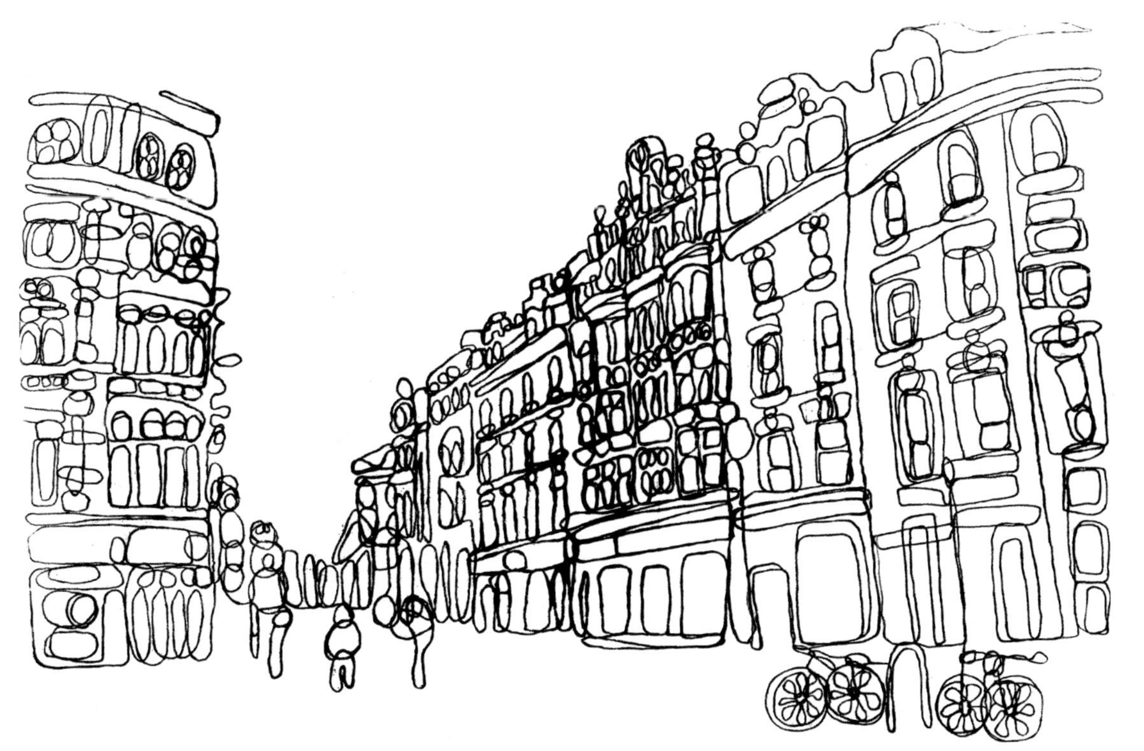

GRAFTON STREET, TRACEY FLYNN

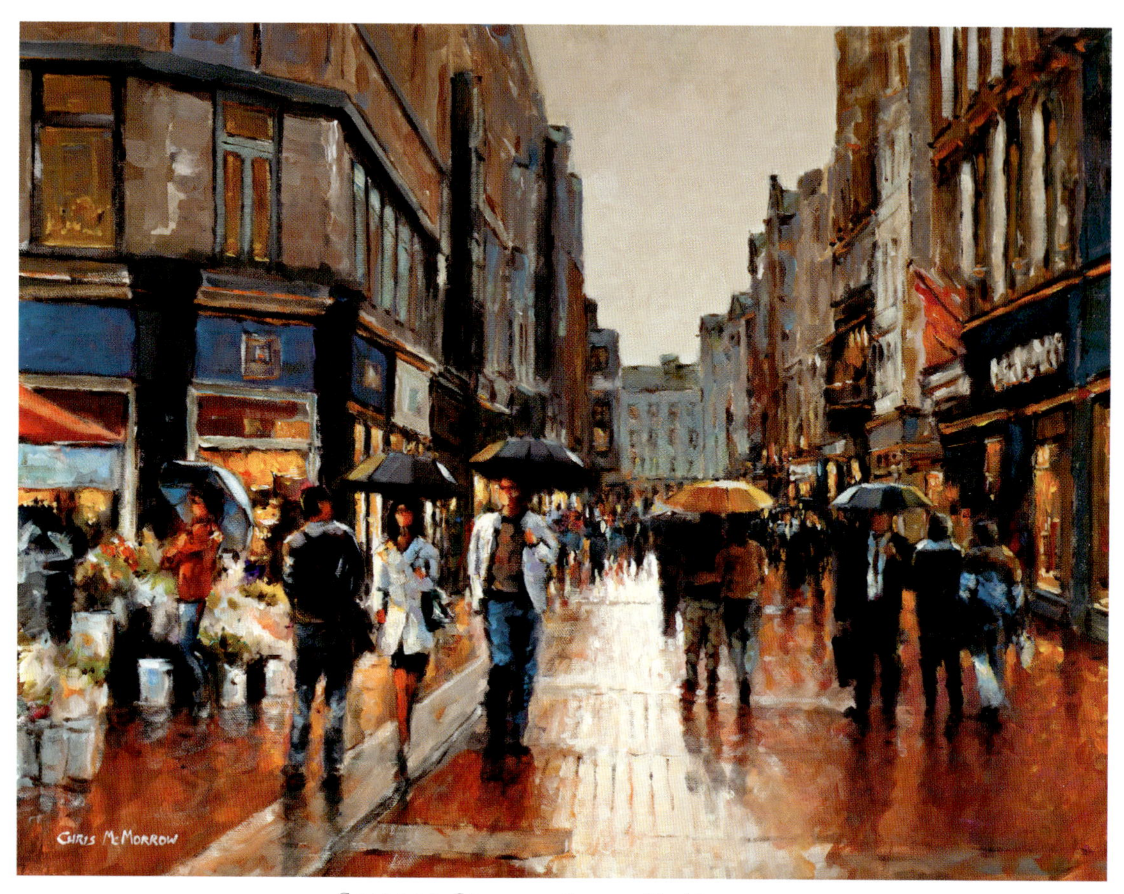

GRAFTON STREET, CHRIS MCMORROW

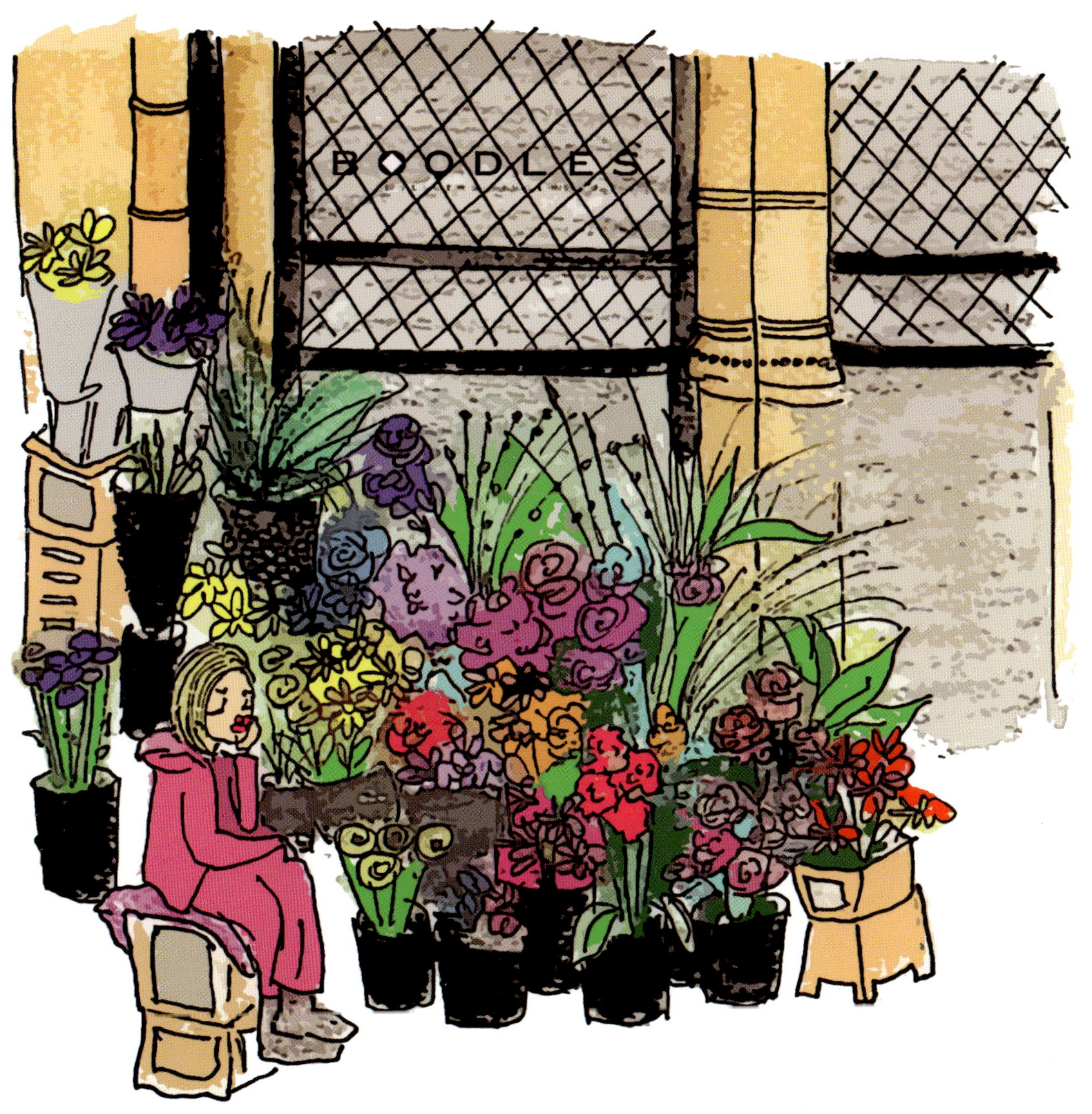

GRAFTON STREET, SHAUNA HARRISON

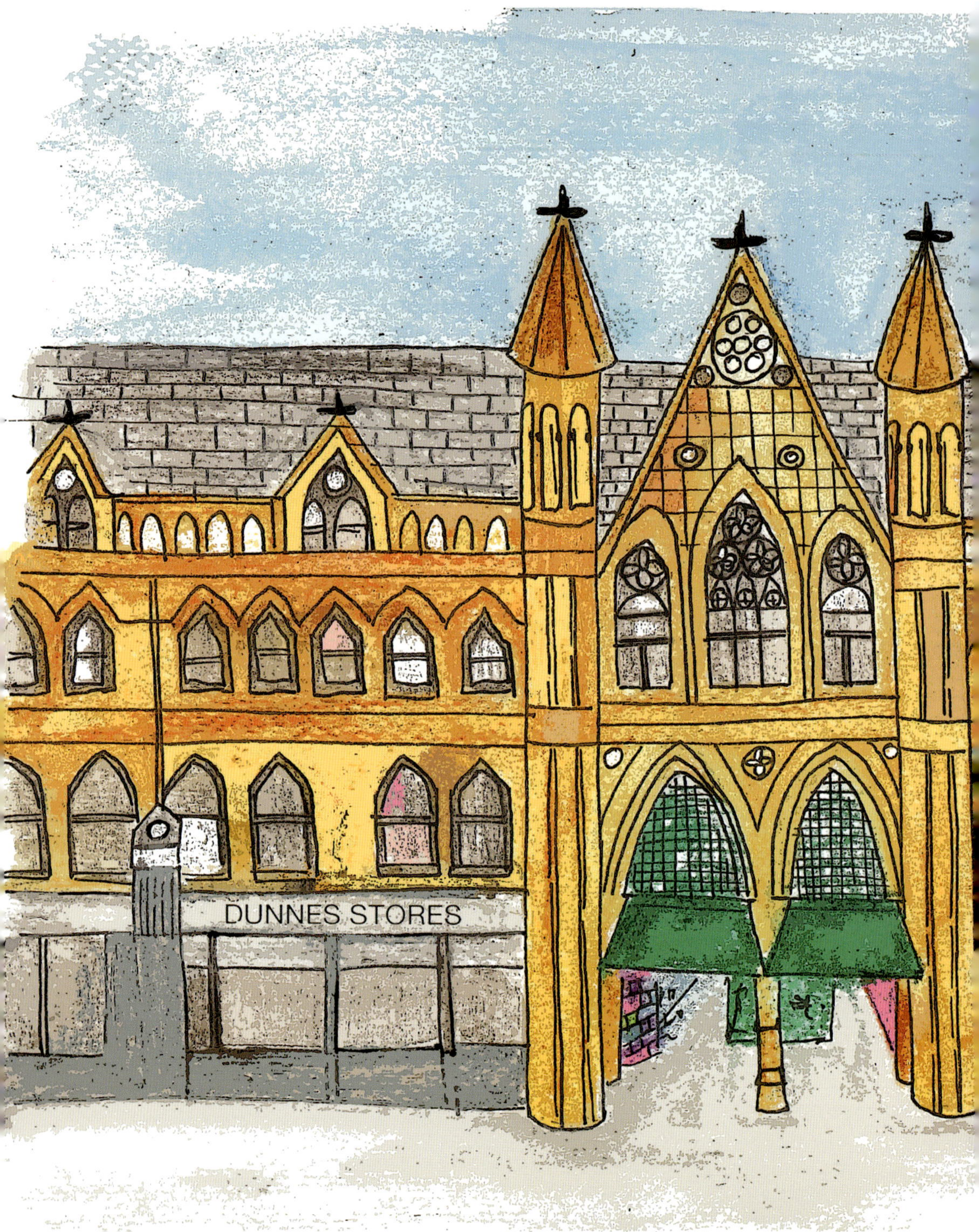
DUNNES STORES

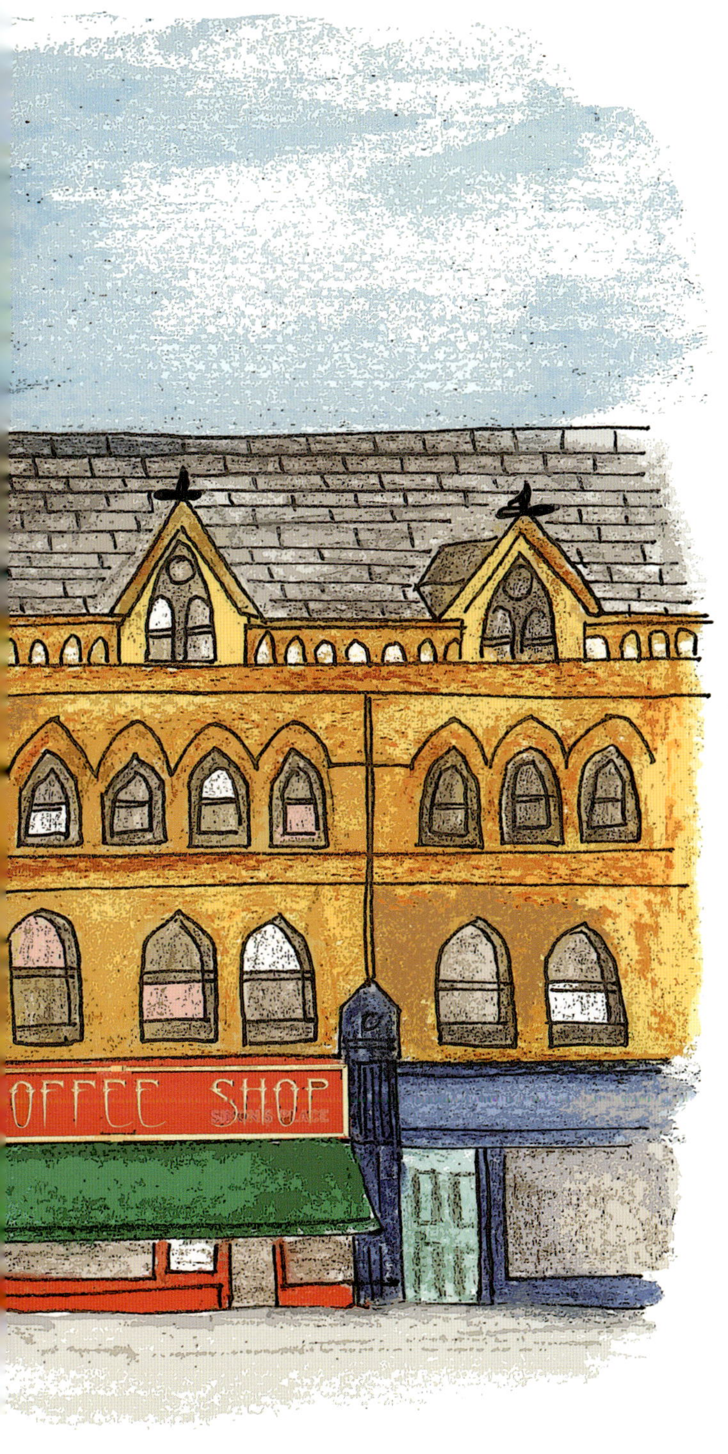

GEORGE'S STREET,
SHAUNA HARRISON

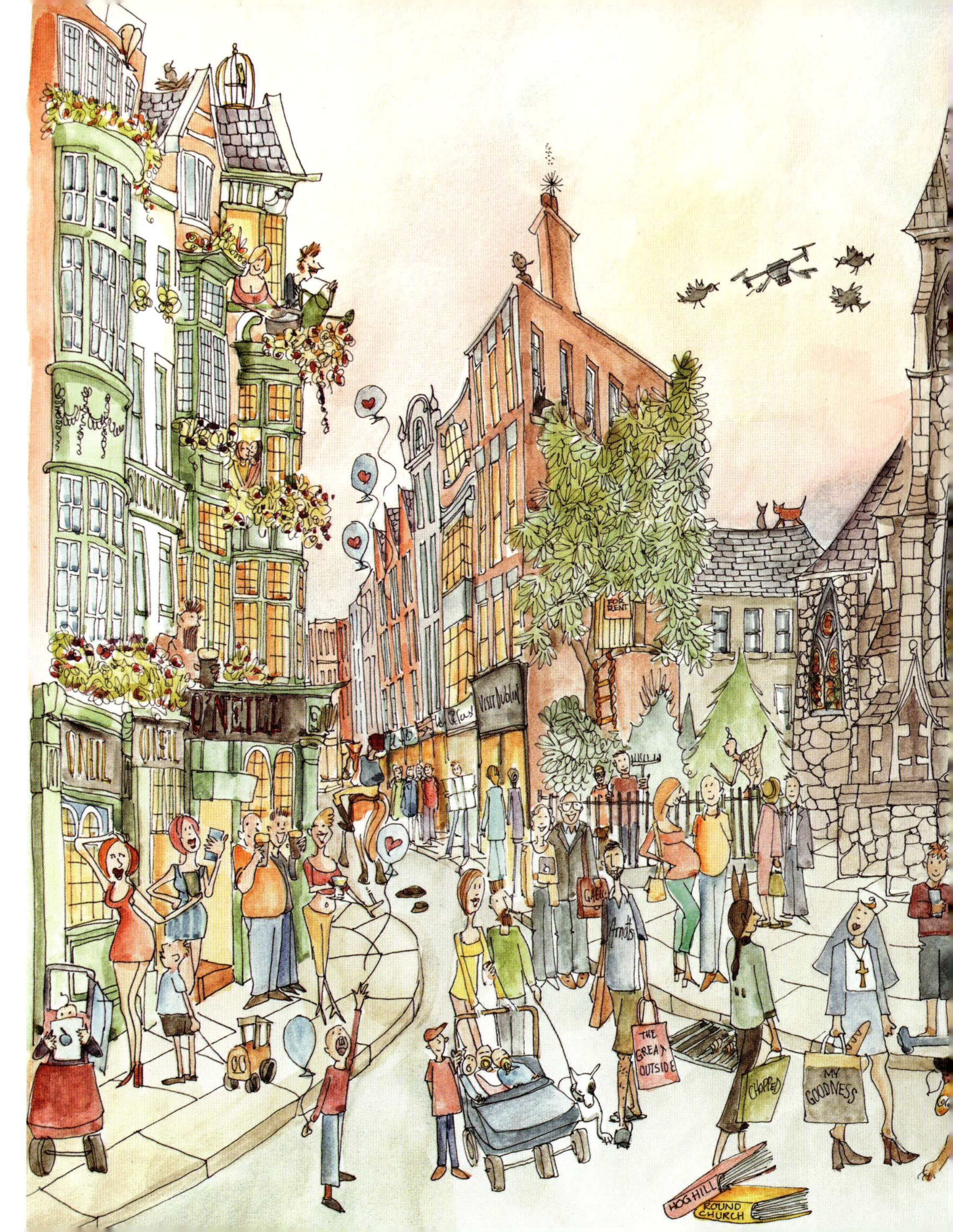
O'NEILL
O'NEILL
O'NEILL
VISIT DUBLIN
FOR RENT
THE GREAT OUTSIDE
CHOPPED
MY GOODNESS
HOG HILL
ROUND CHURCH
Arnolds

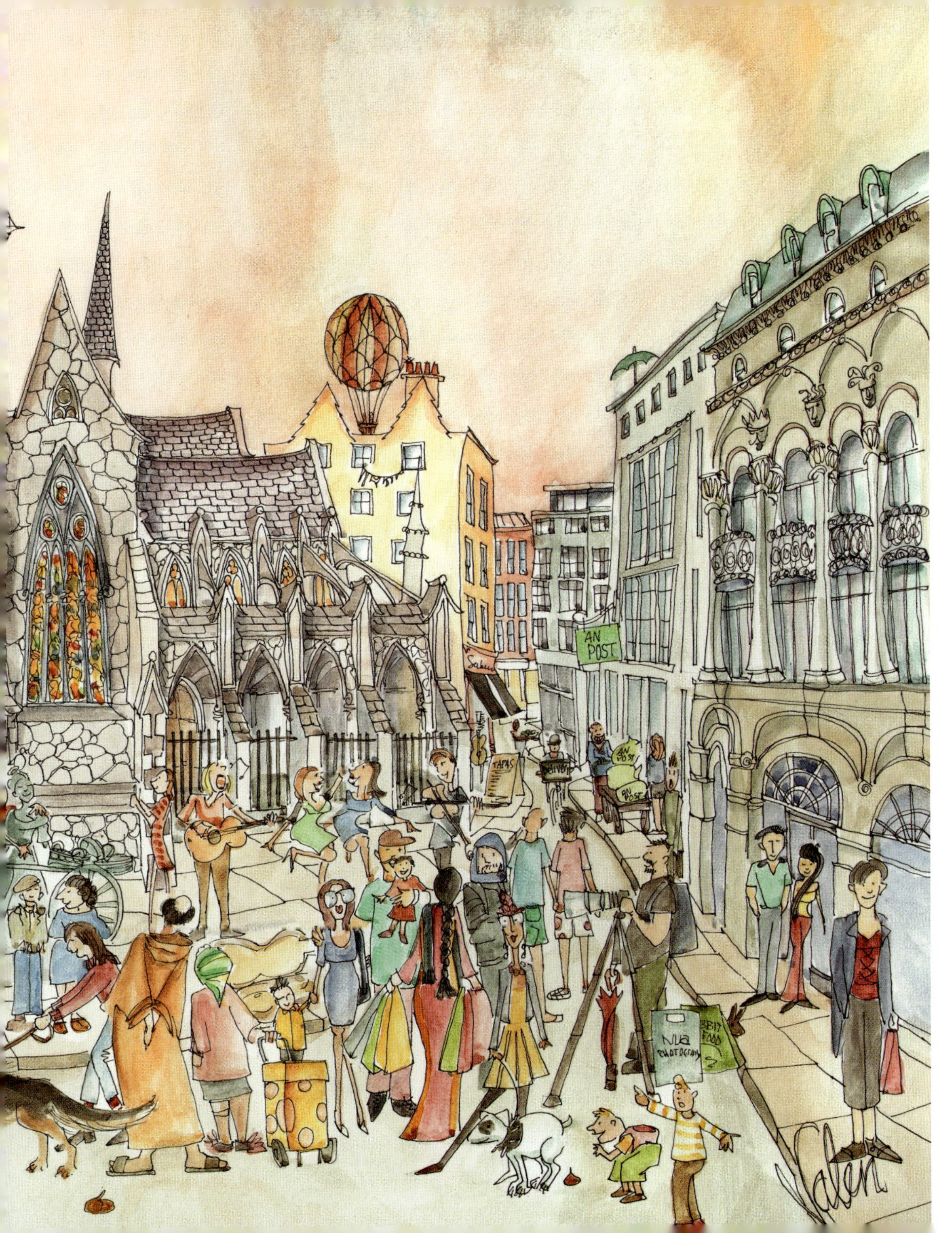

AN POST
AN POST
AN POST
Deliver
TAPAS
Saba
NUA PHOTOGRAPHY
BIT FOOD
Valeri

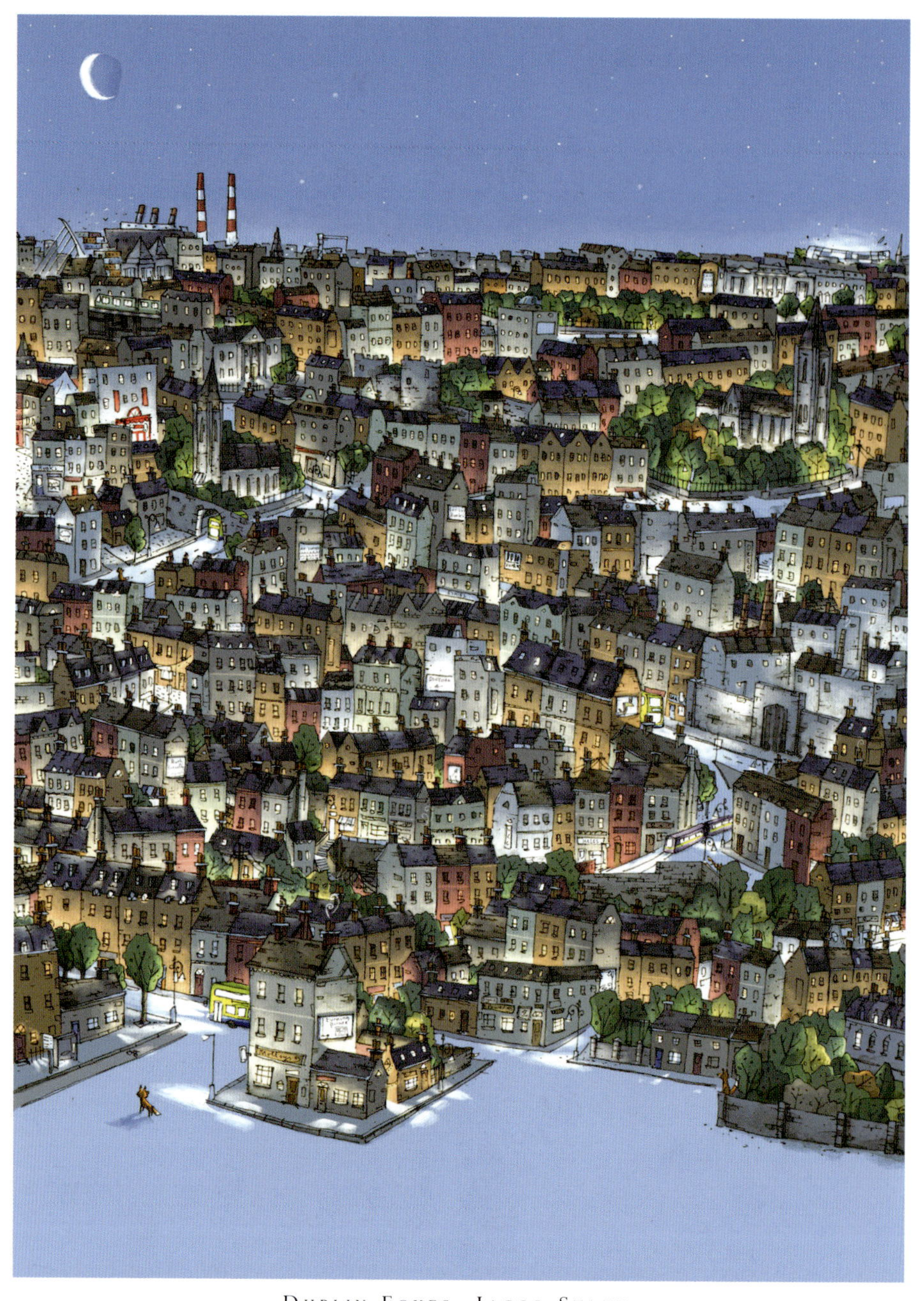

DUBLIN FOXES, JACOB STACK
PREVIOUS TWO PAGES: ST ANDREW'S STREET, VALERI BYRNE

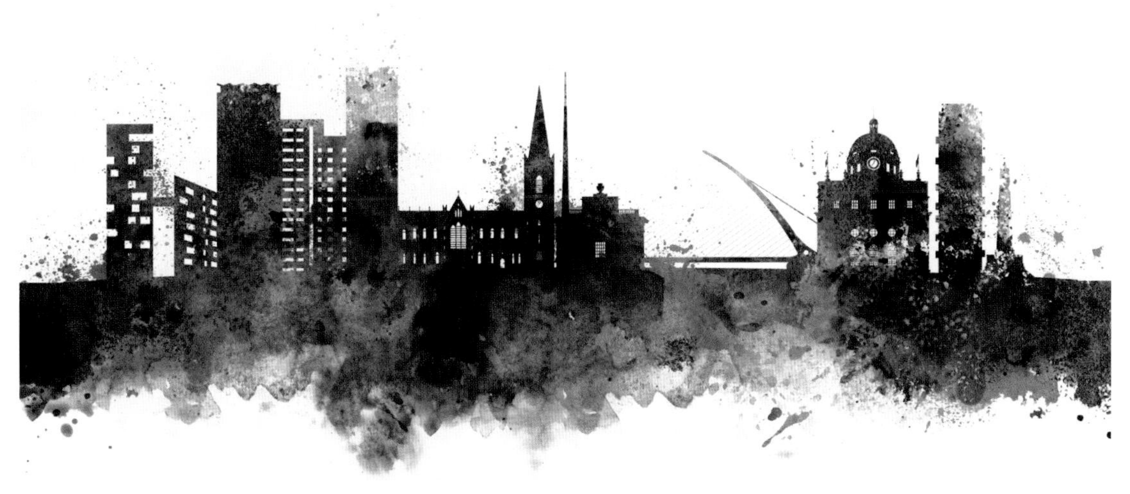

DUBLIN CITY SKYLINE, PICO MAC

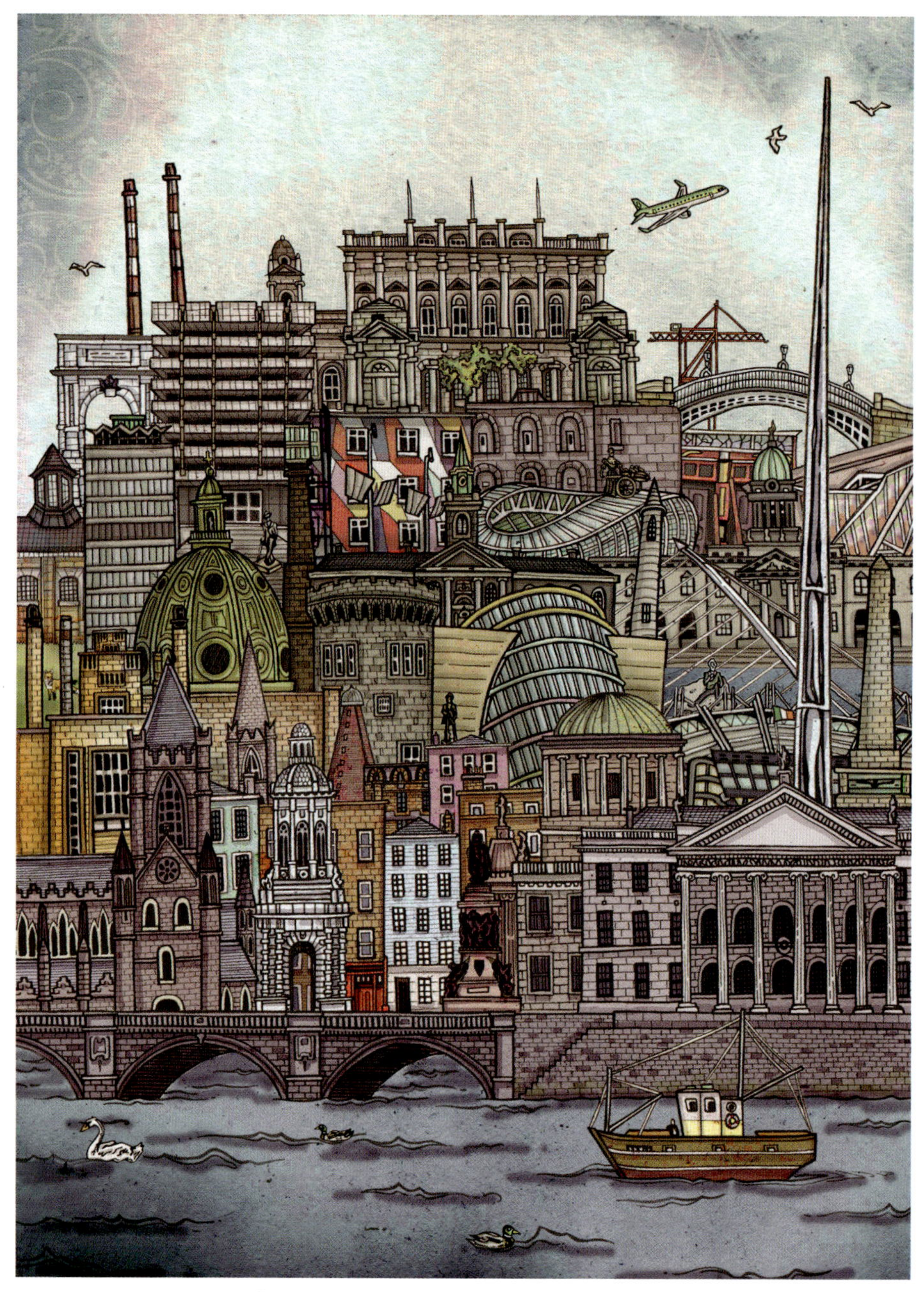

DUBLIN CITYSCAPE, JOHN ROONEY

SAINT PATRICK'S CATHEDRAL

DUBLIN

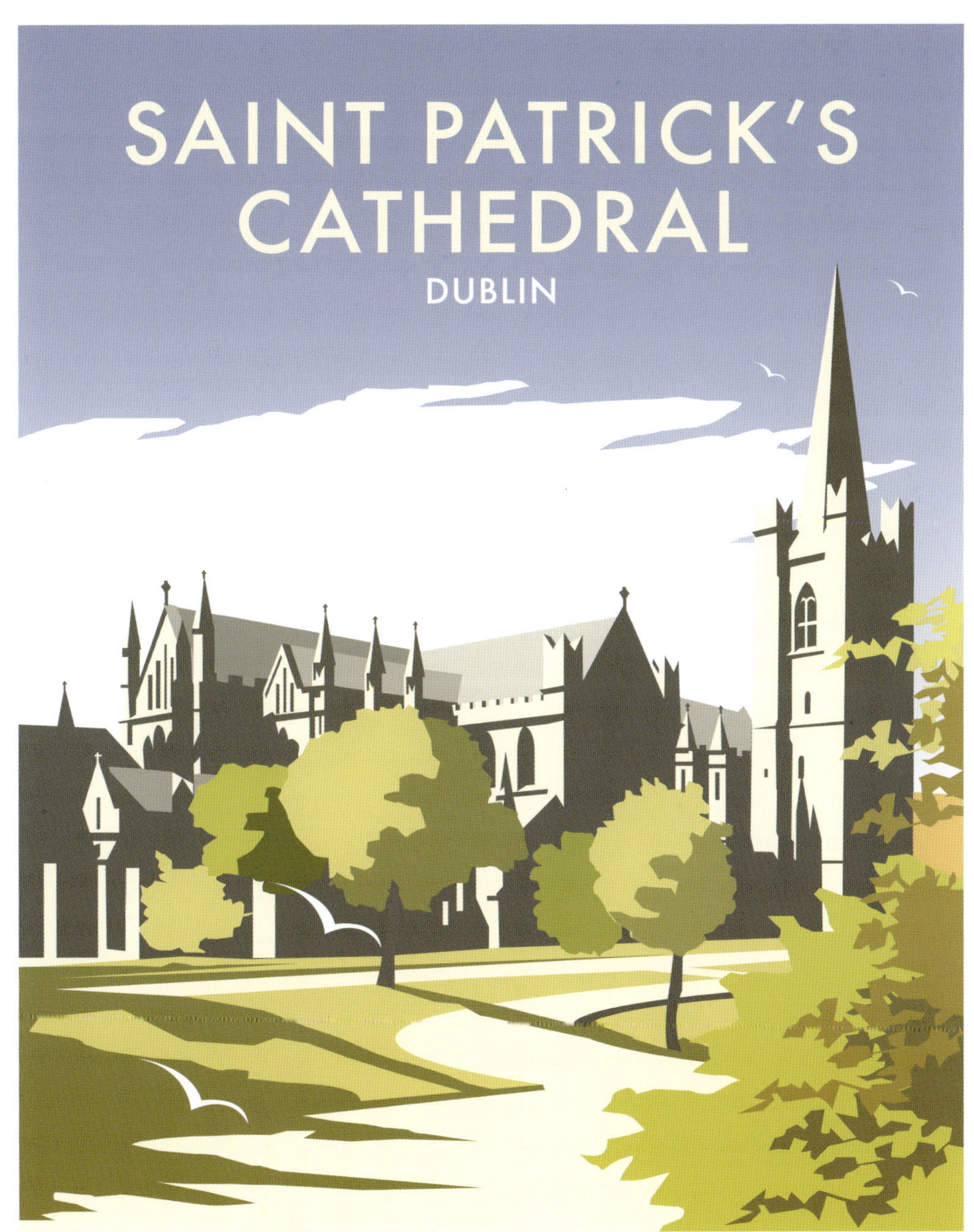

St Patrick's Cathedral, Dave Thompson

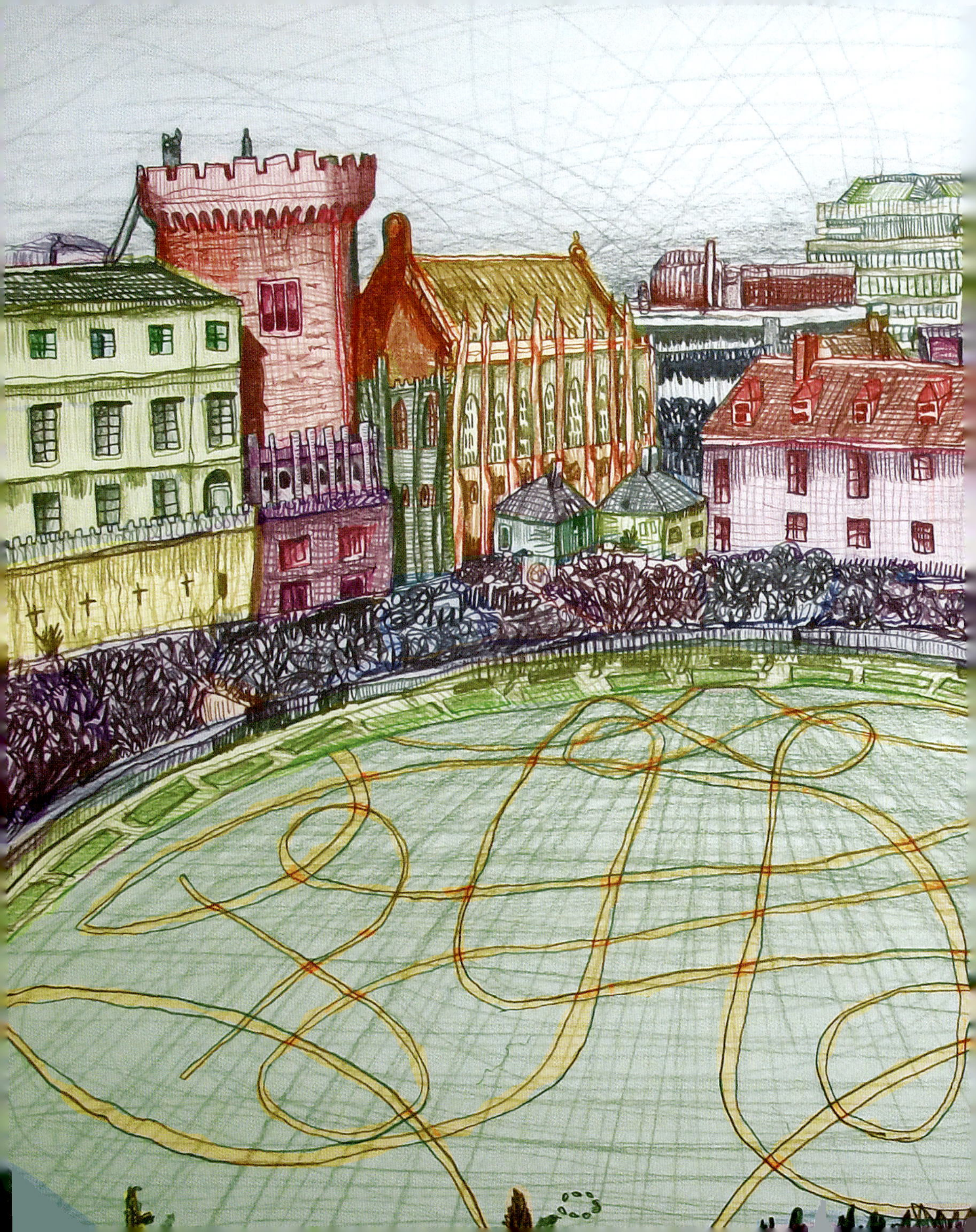

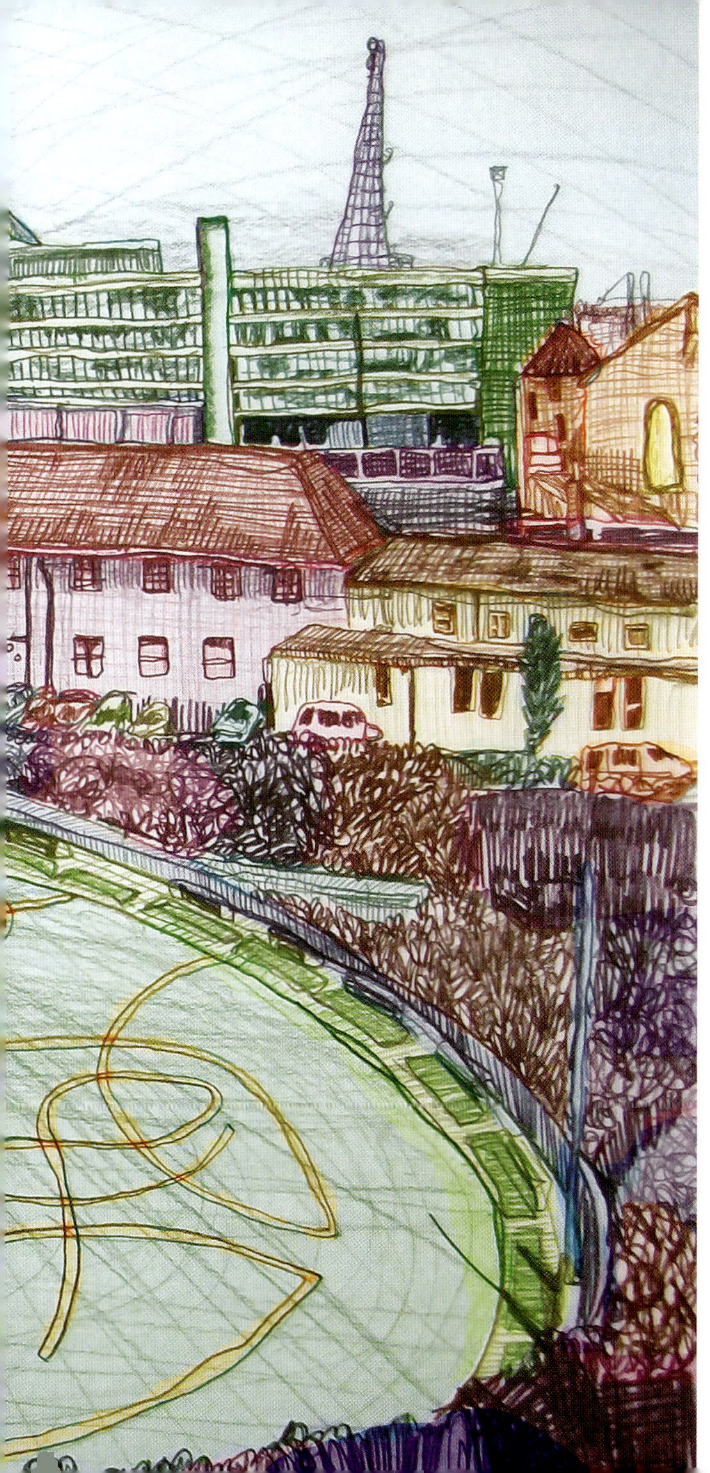

Dubh Linn Garden,
Anna Gwenllian

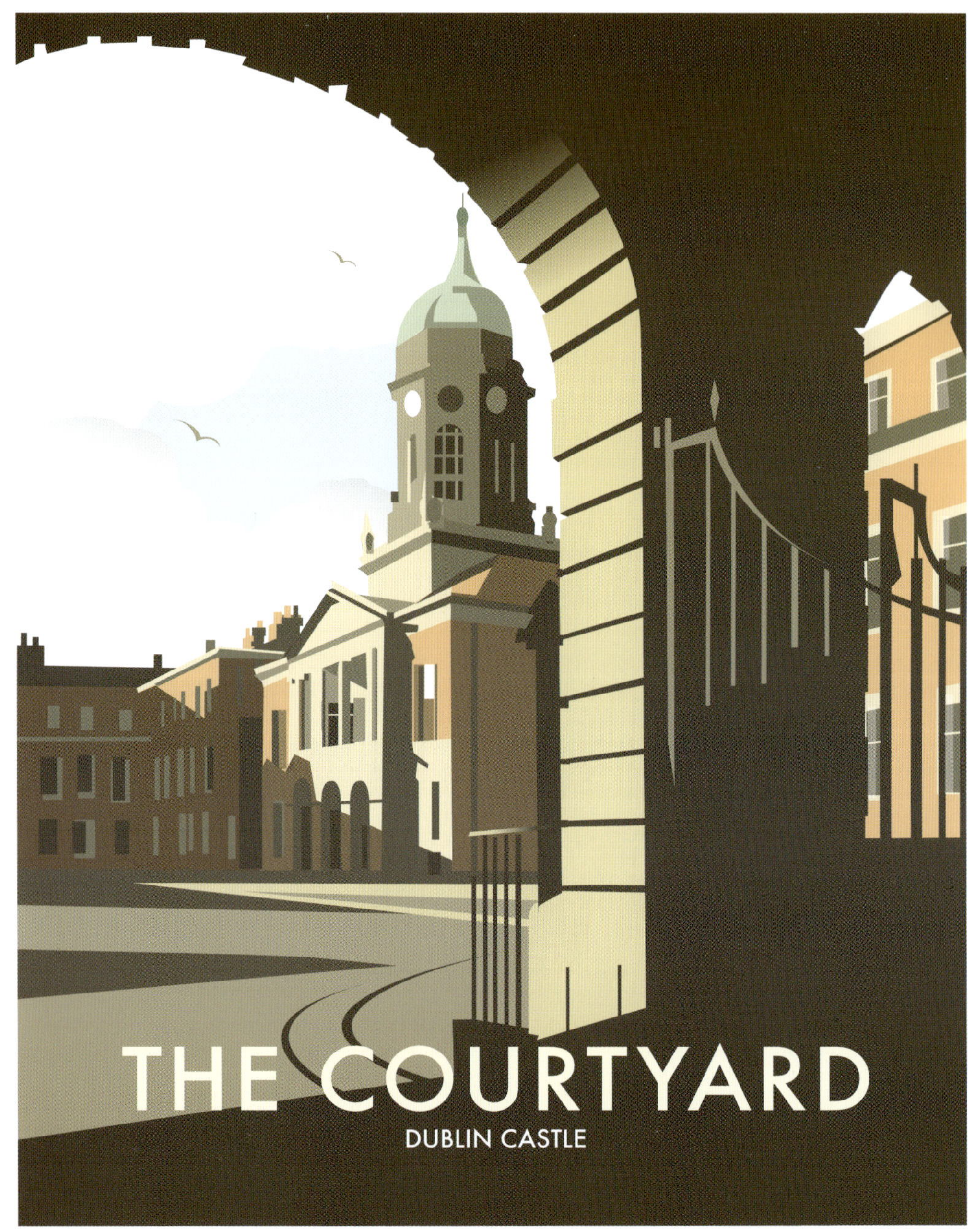

DUBLIN CASTLE, DAVE THOMPSON

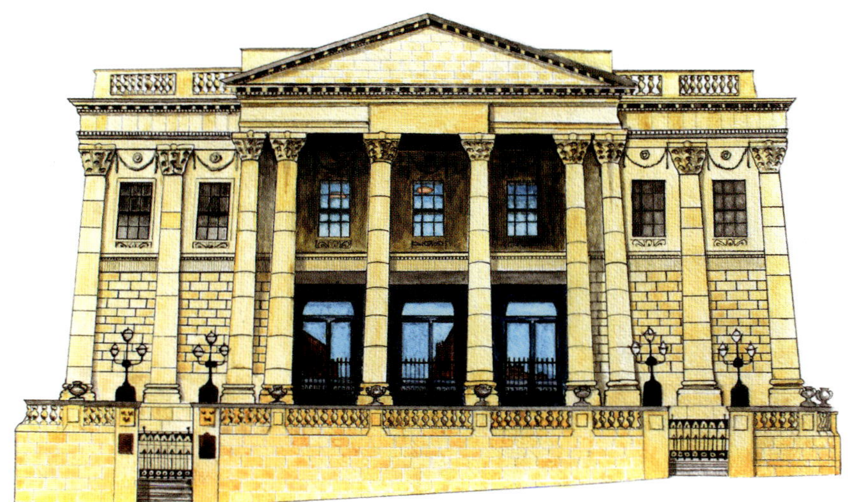

City Hall, Brian O'Neill

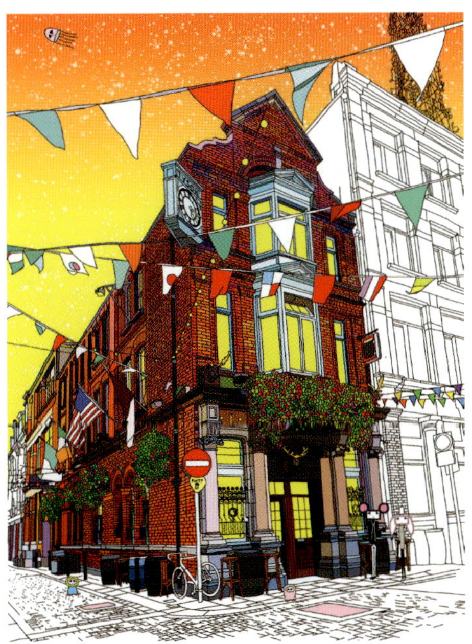

The Stag's Head, Sketchy

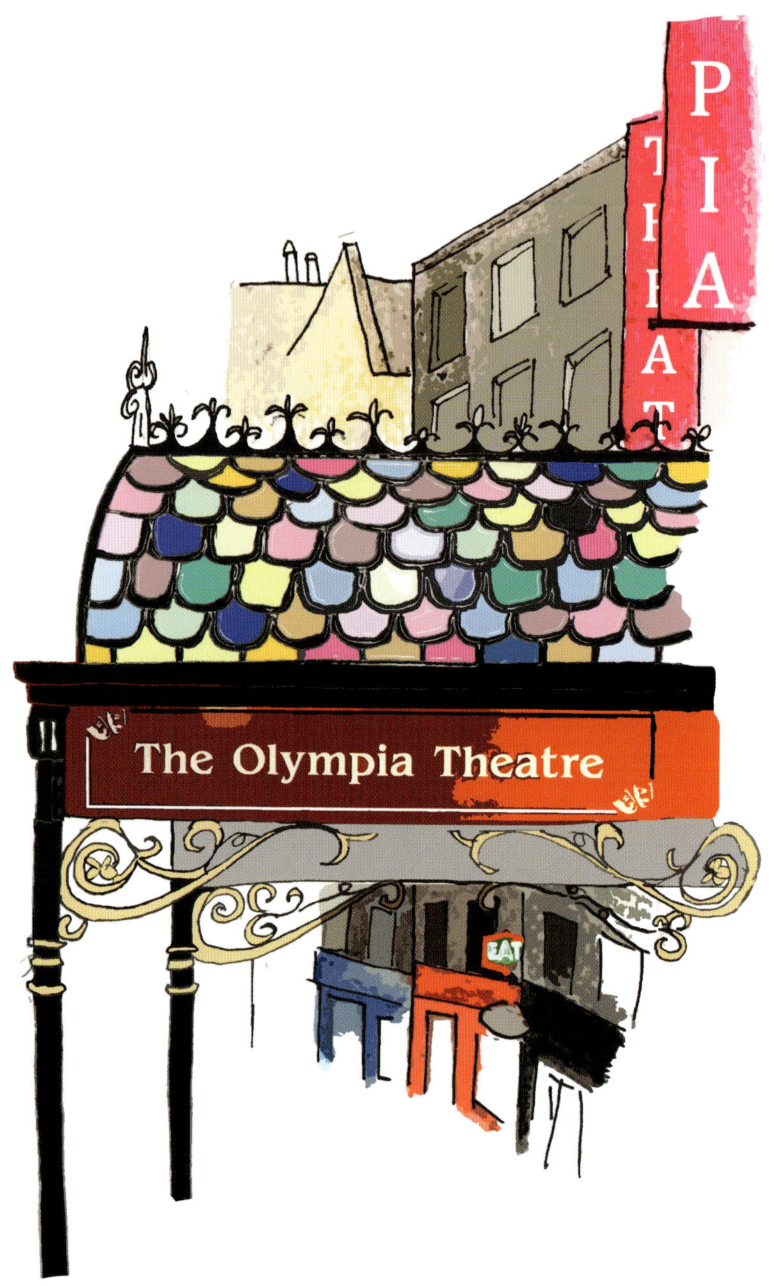

OLYMPIA THEATRE, SHAUNA HARRISON

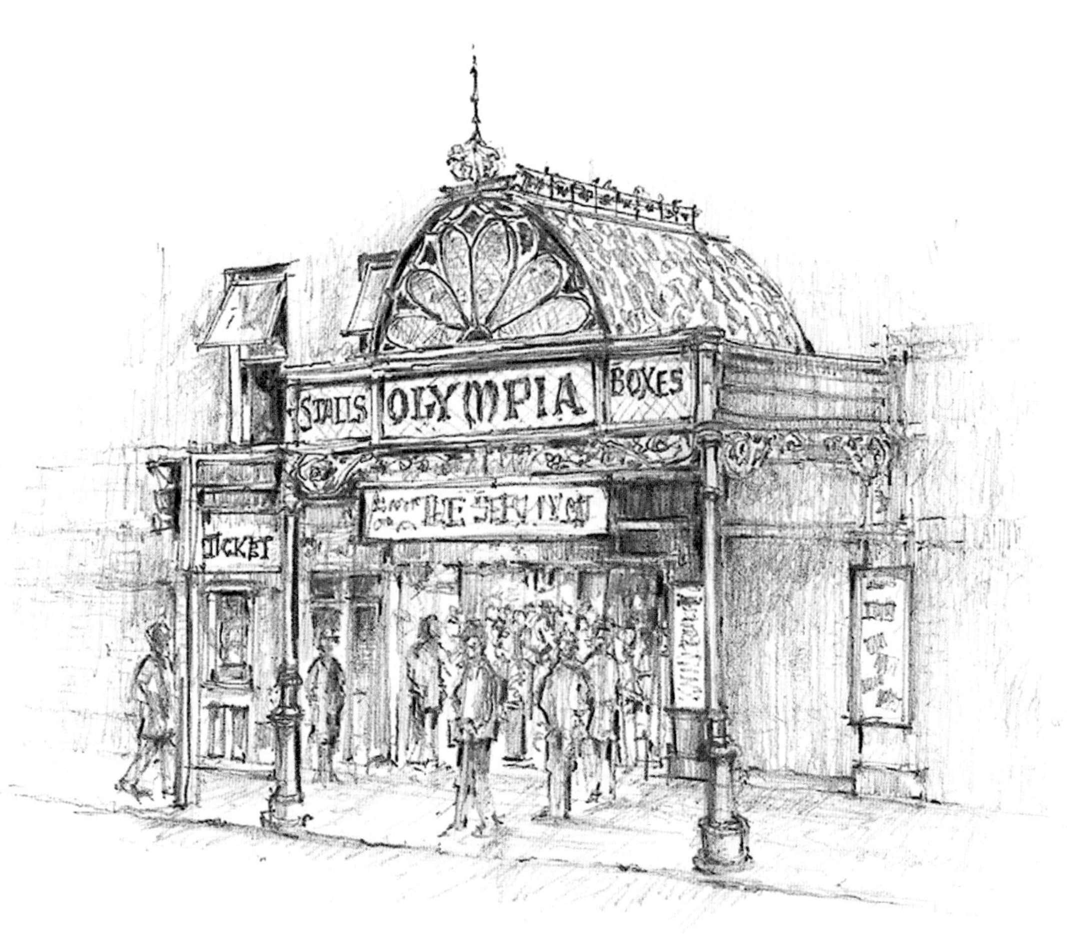

OLYMPIA THEATRE, DESMOND McCARTHY

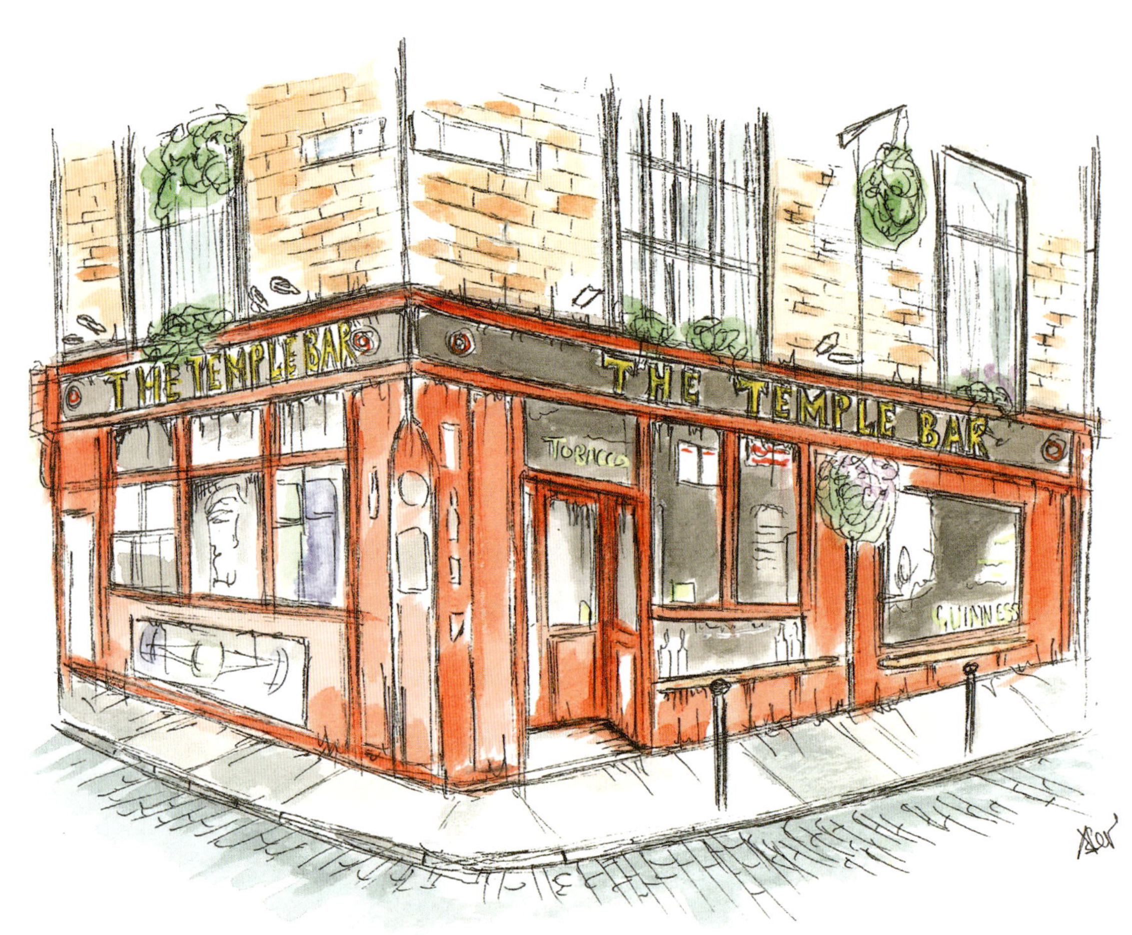

THE TEMPLE BAR, VICTORIA WOOD

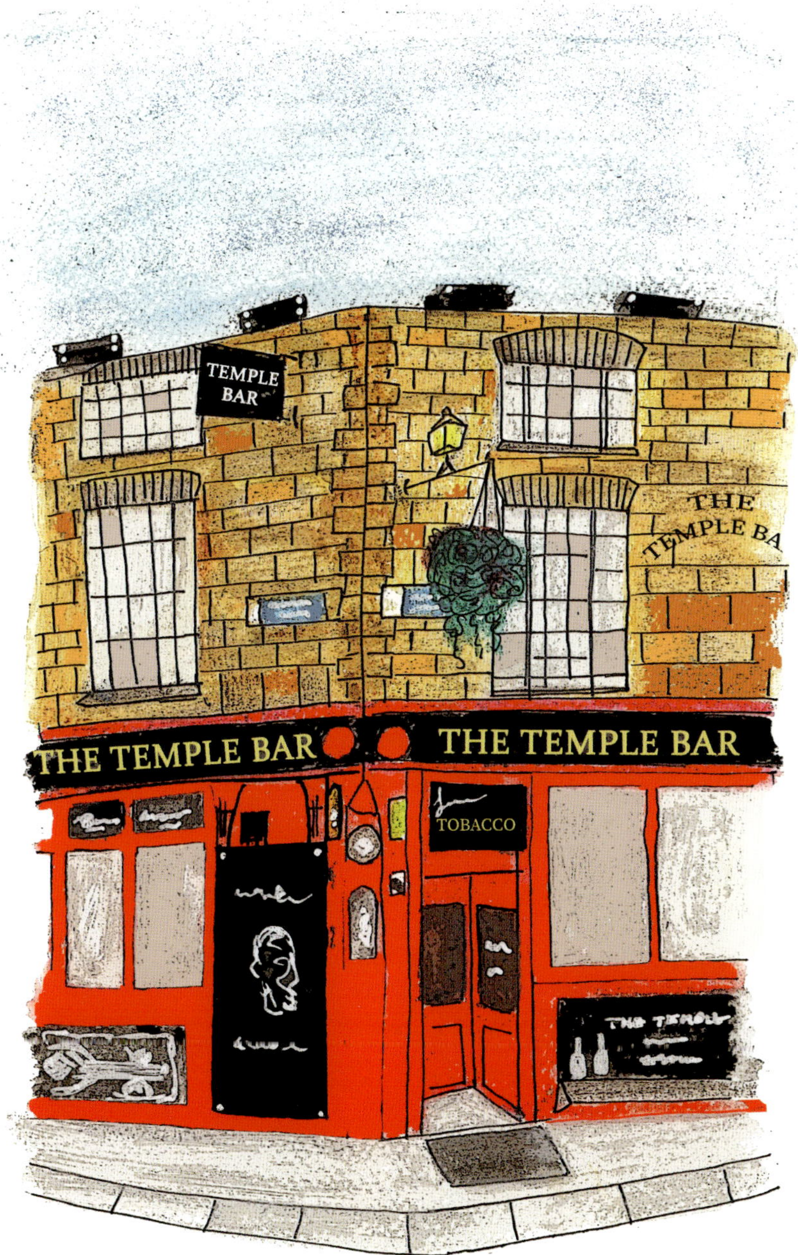

The Temple Bar, Shauna Harrison

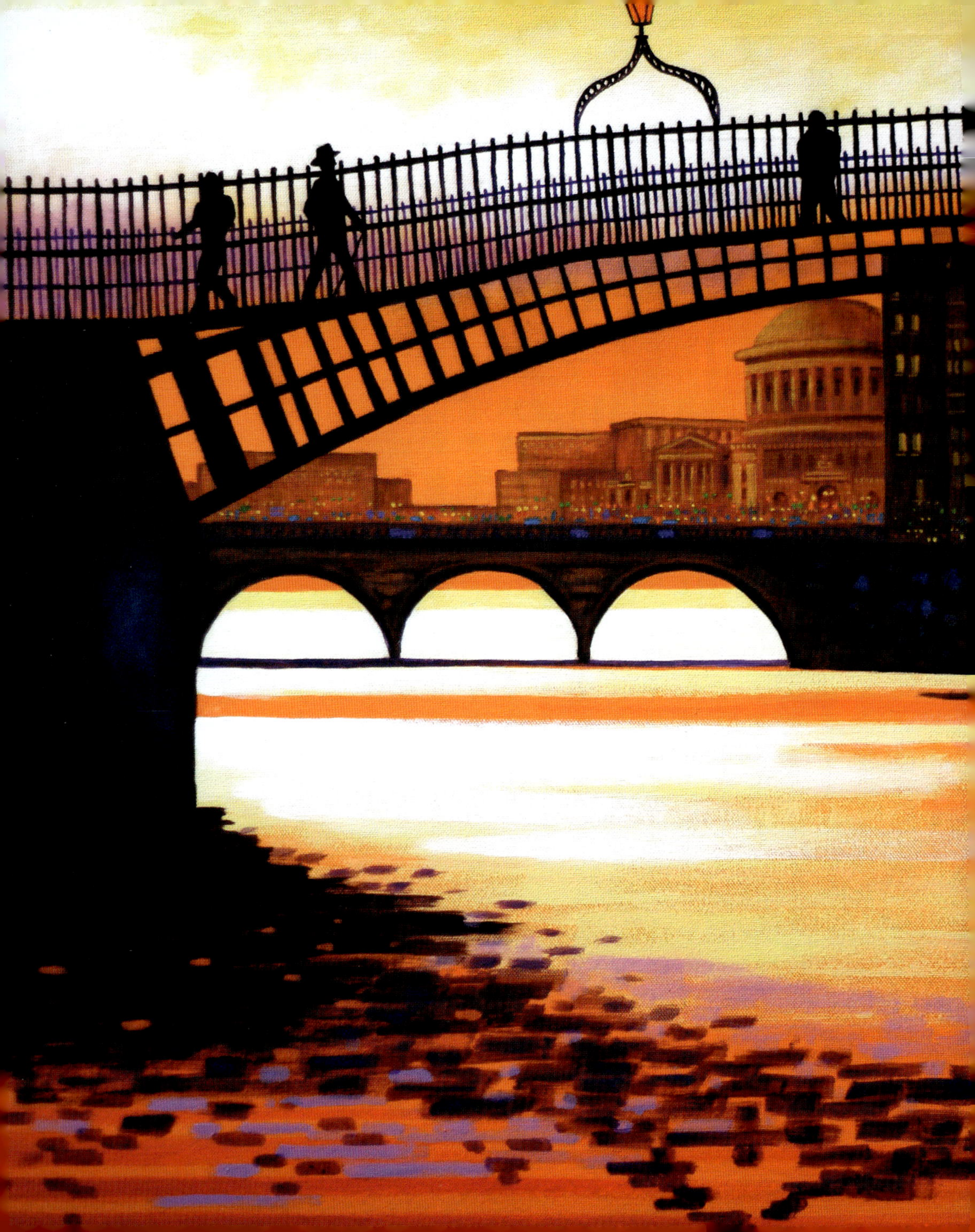

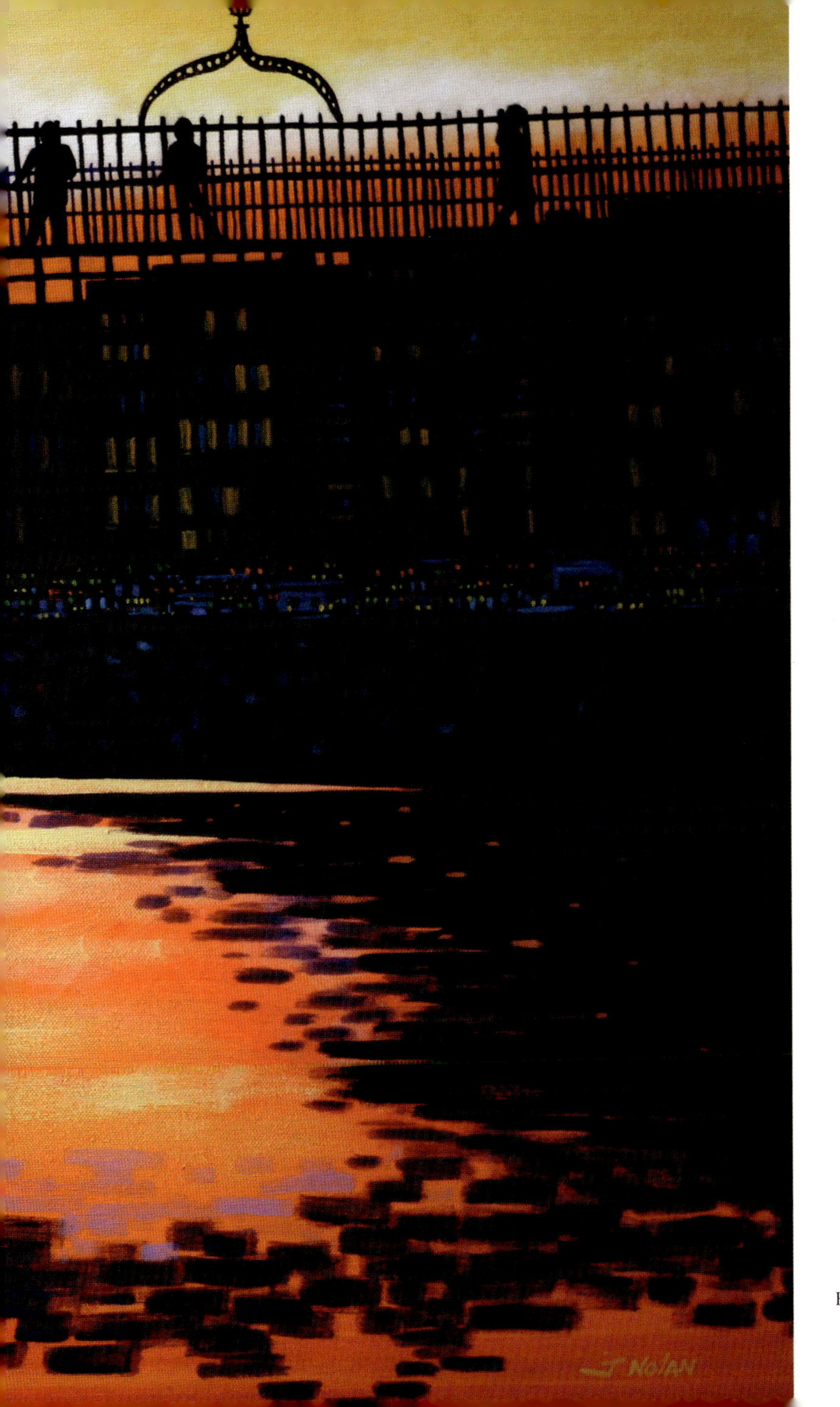

CROSSING THE
HA'PENNY BRIDGE,
JOHN NOLAN

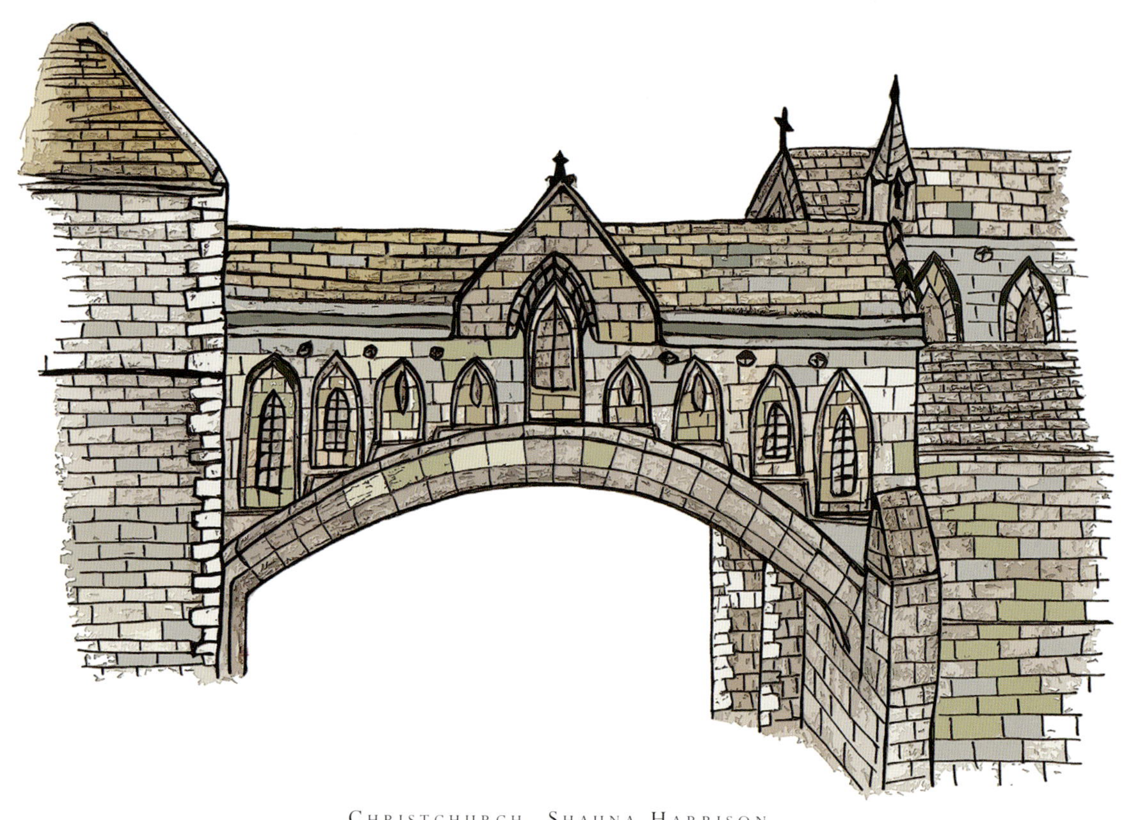

Christchurch, Shauna Harrison

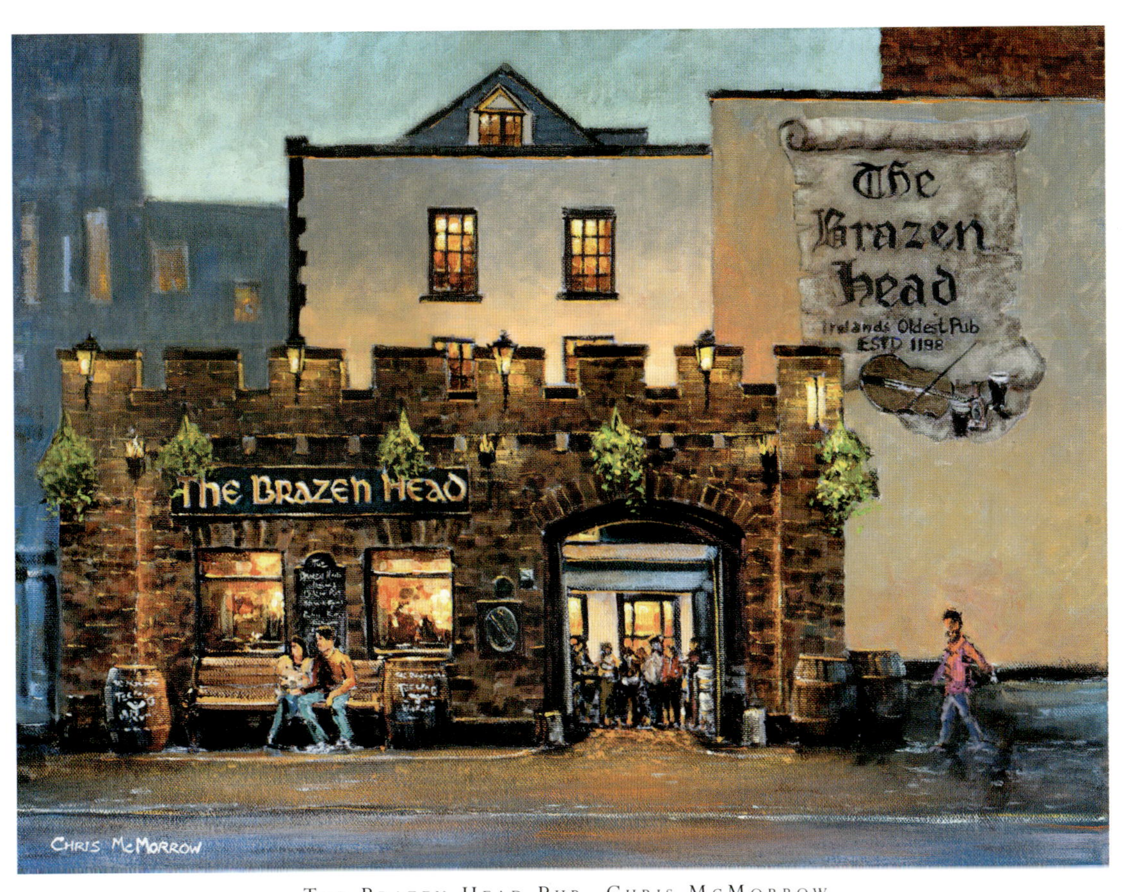

THE BRAZEN HEAD PUB, CHRIS MCMORROW

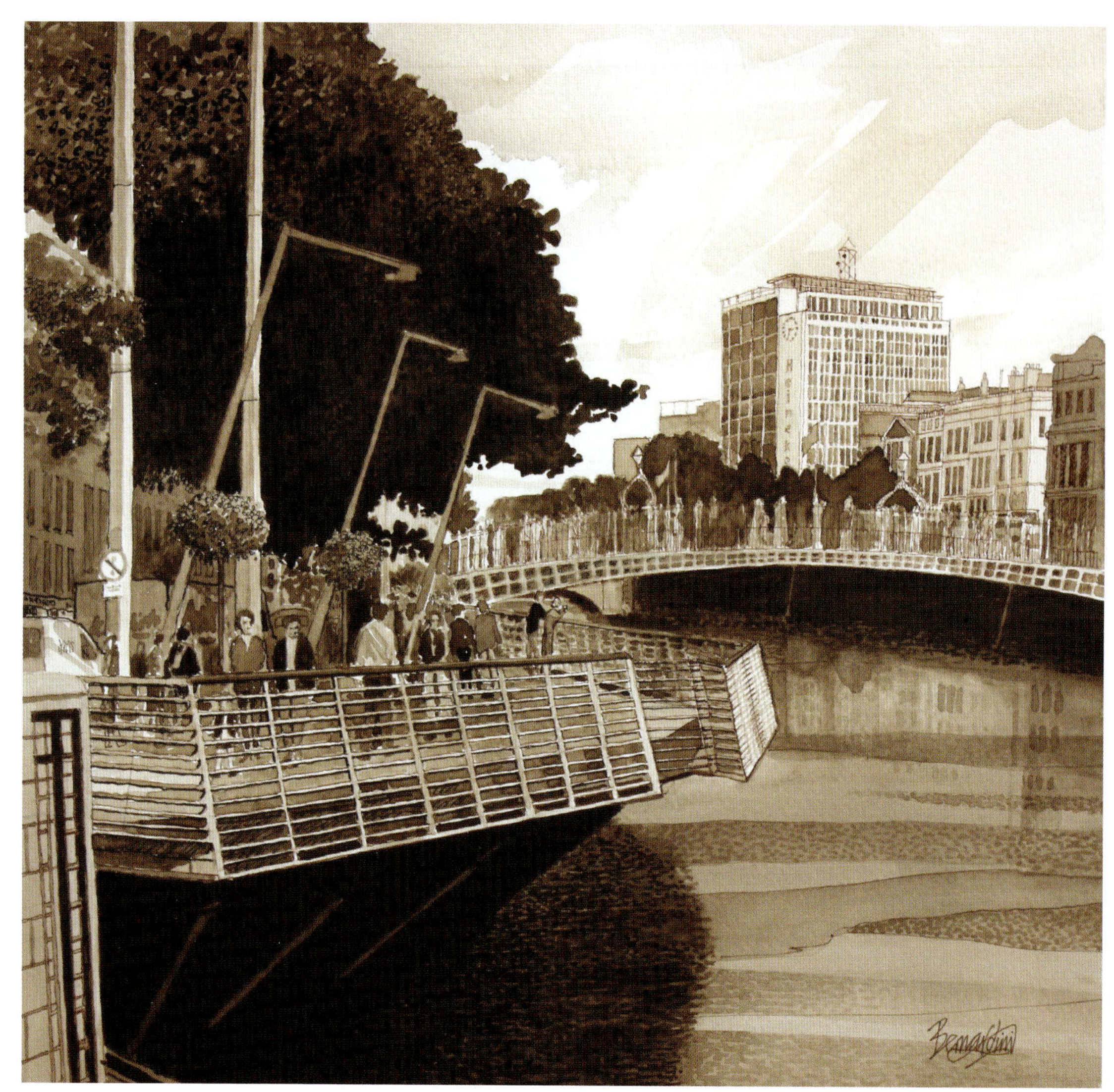

B O A R D W A L K , W A L T E R B E R N A R D I N I

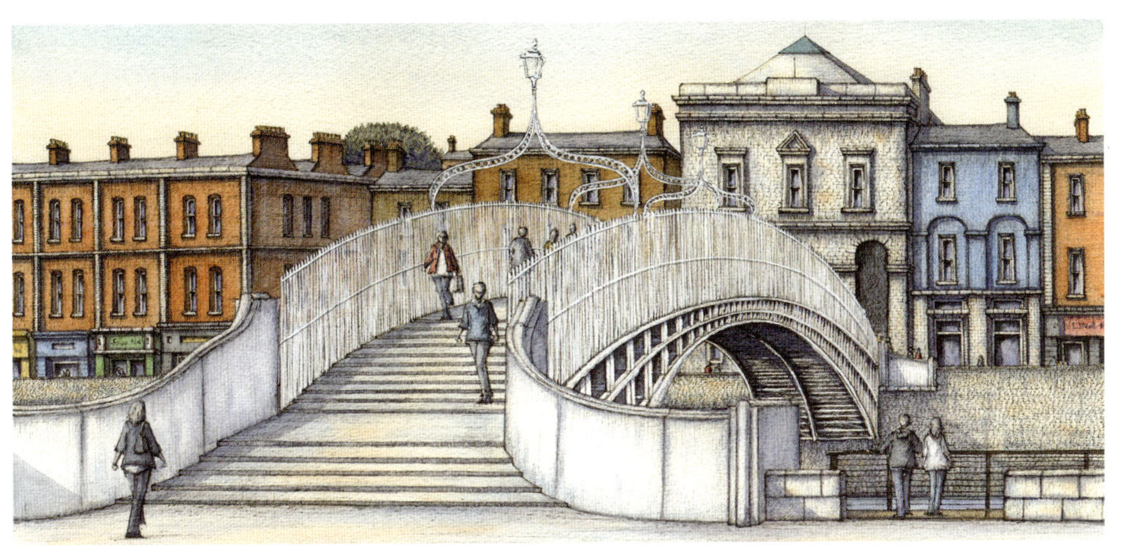

HA'PENNY BRIDGE, JIM SCULLY

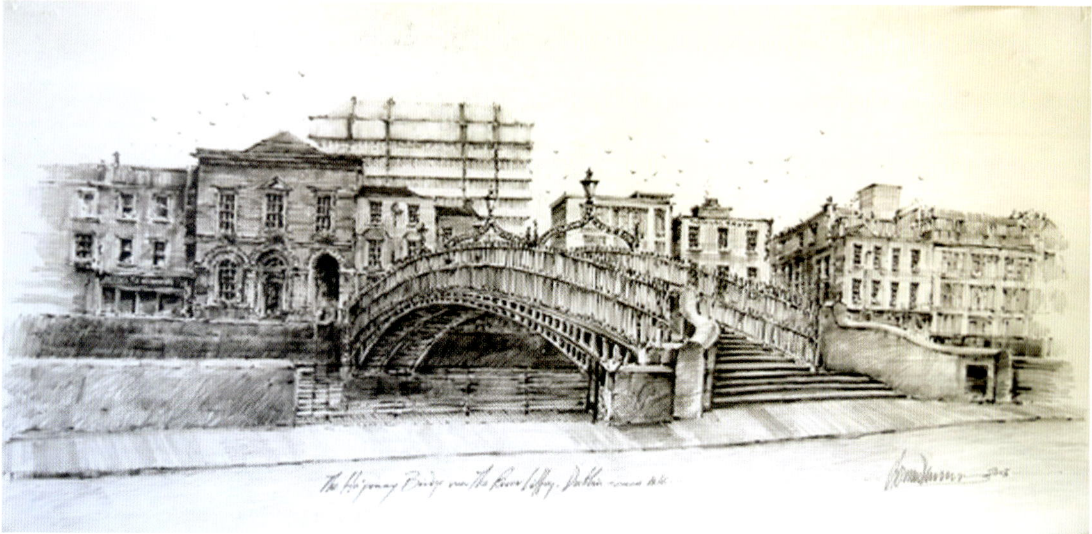

HA'PENNY BRIDGE, DESMOND MCCARTHY

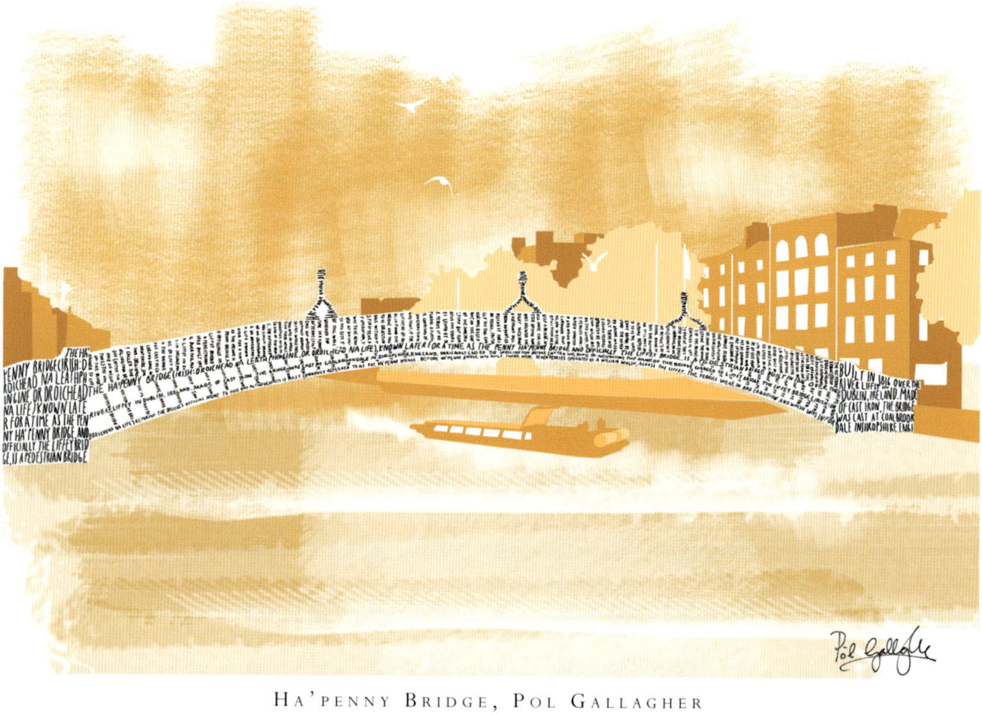

HA'PENNY BRIDGE, POL GALLAGHER

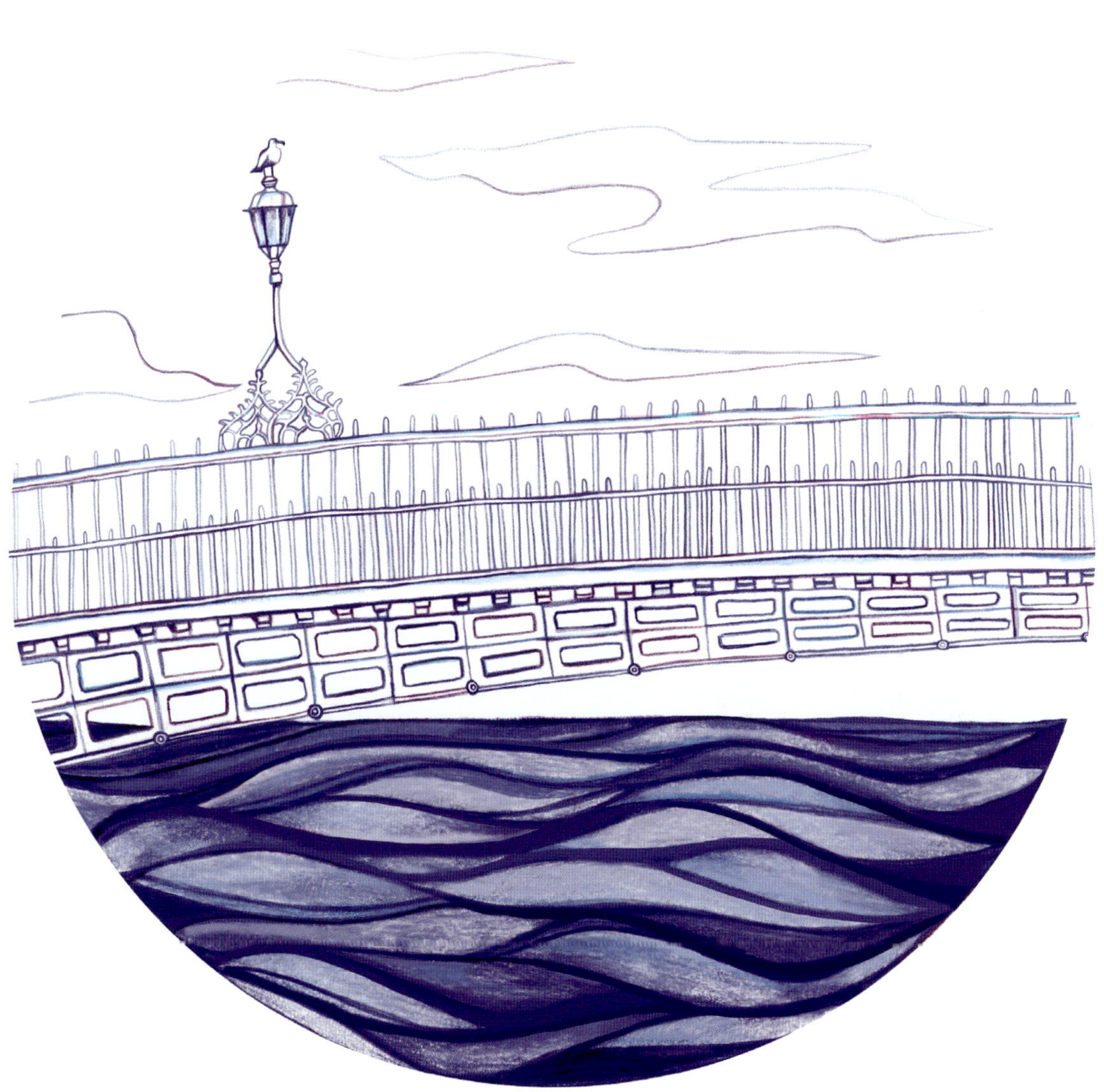

Ha'penny Bridge, Claudine O'Sullivan

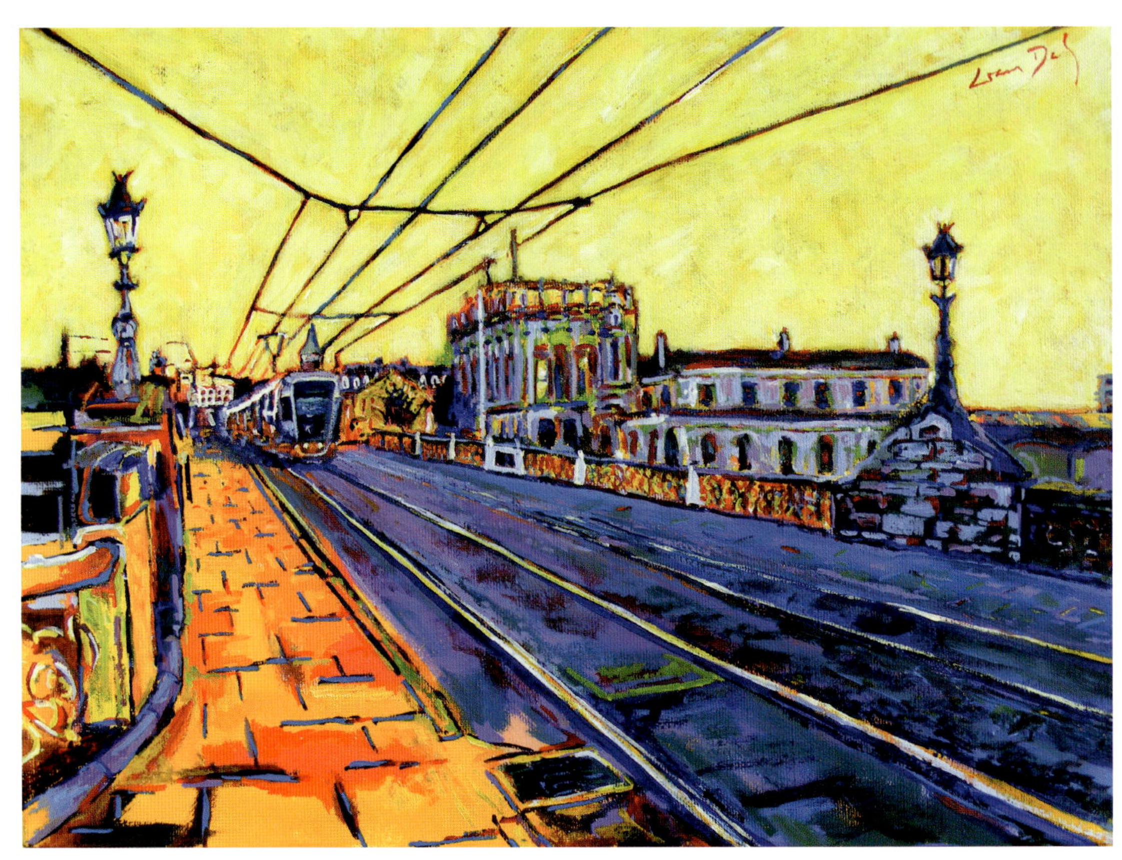

HEUSTON, LIAM DALY

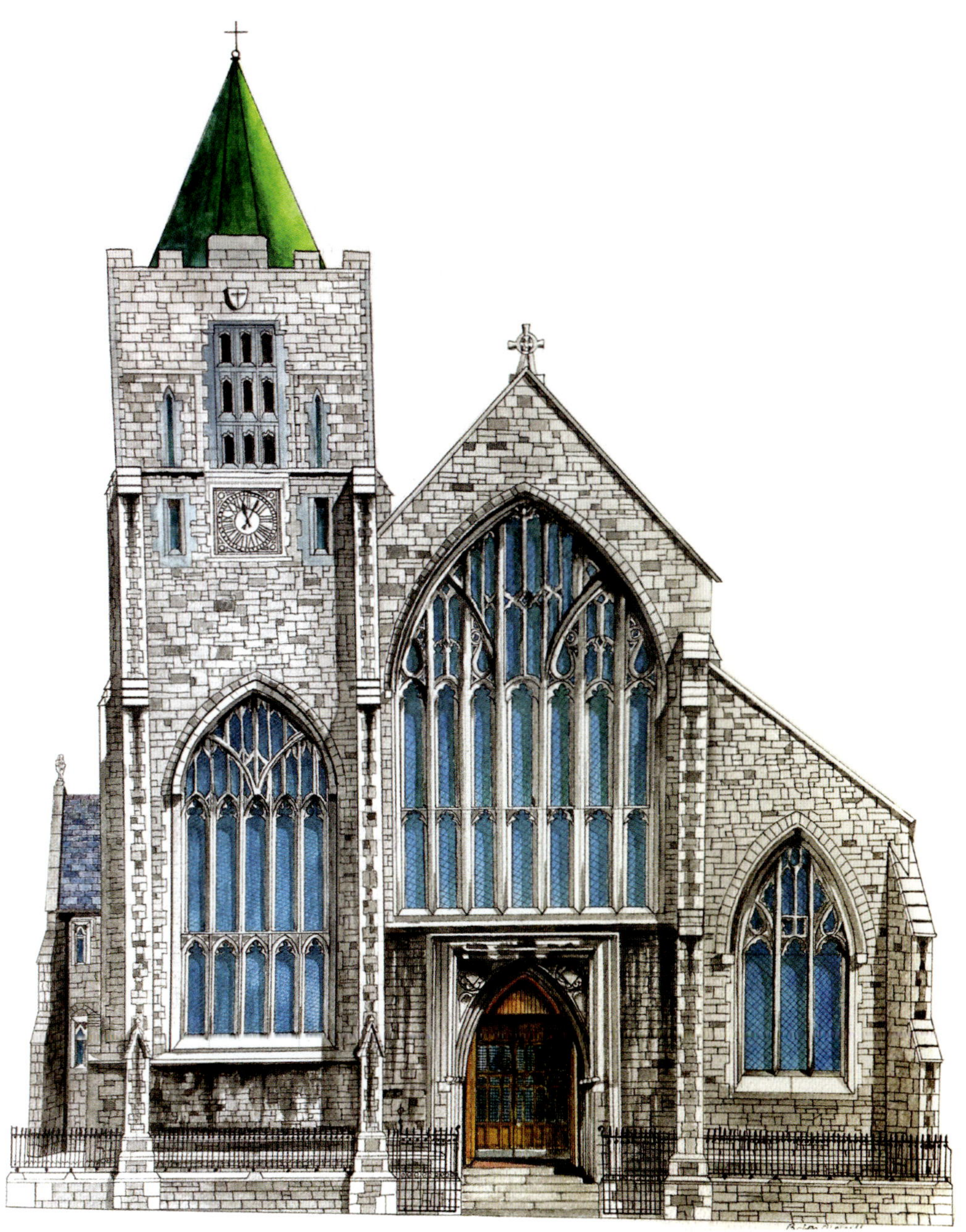

St Catherine's Church, Brian O'Neill

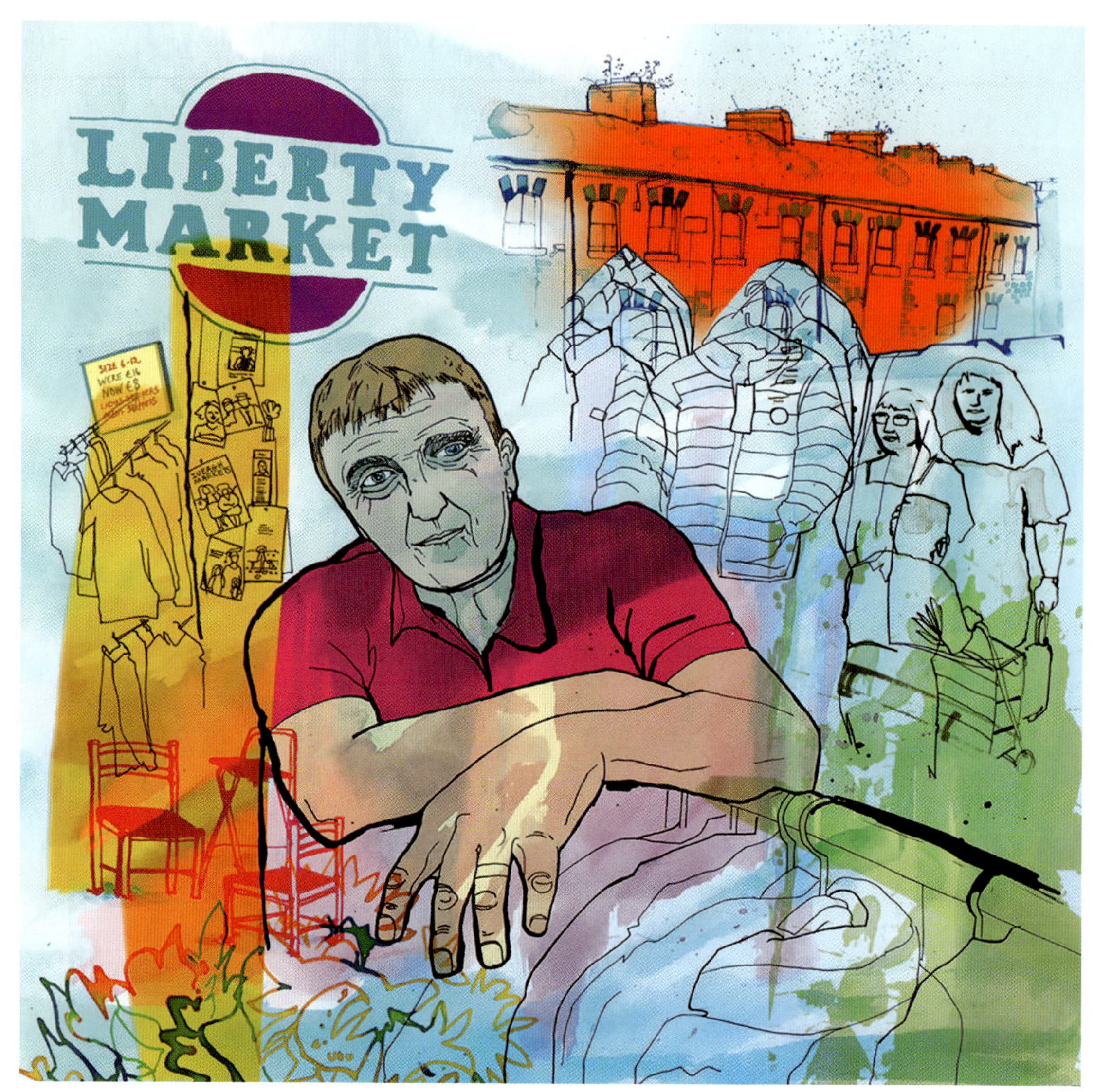

LIBERTY STREET MARKET, EVA KELLY

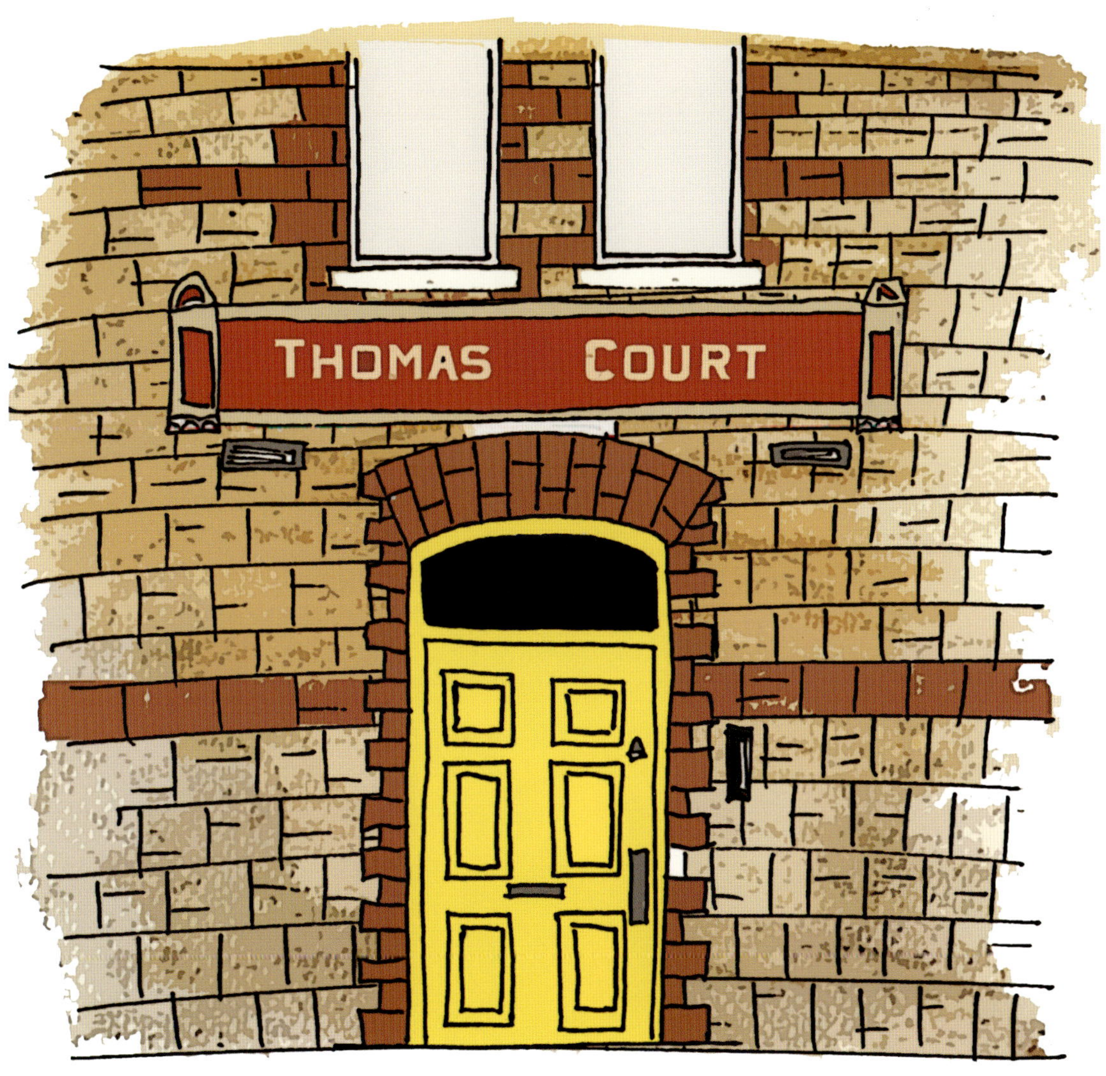

THE LIBERTIES, SHAUNA HARRISON

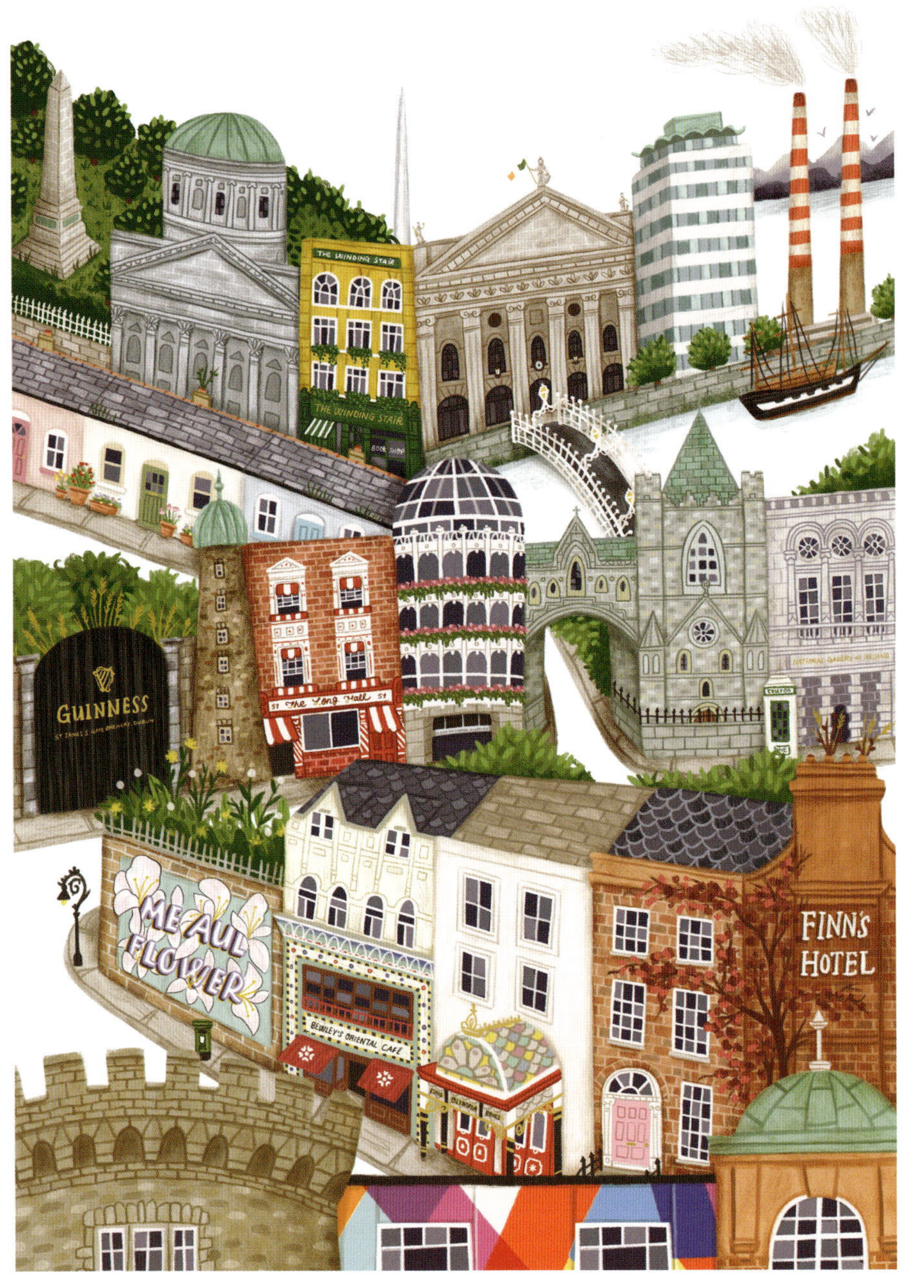

MY FAIR CITY, RACHEL CORCORAN

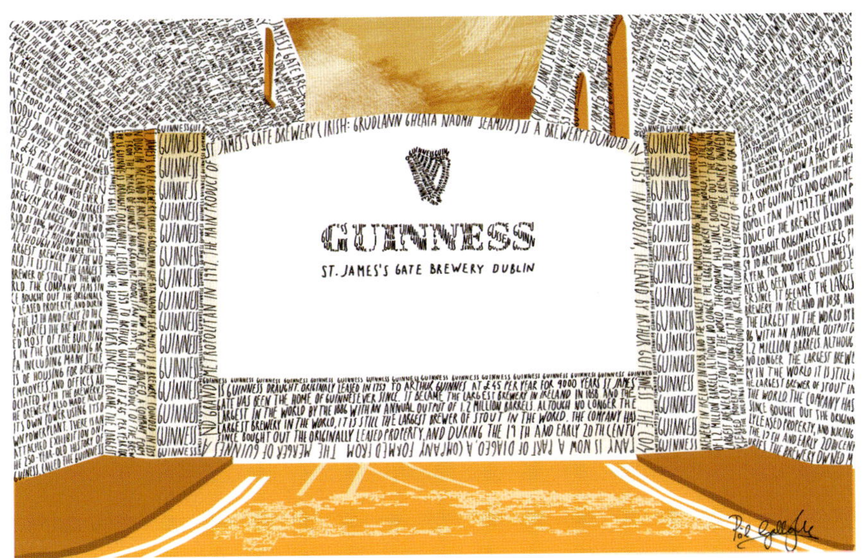

St James's Gate, Pol Gallagher

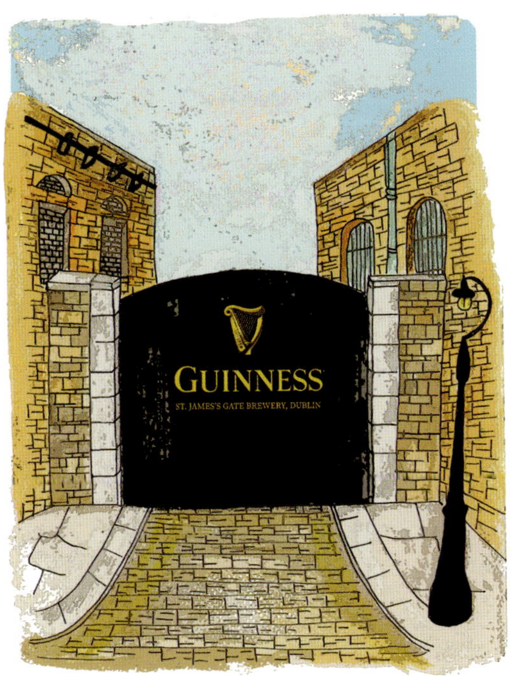

St James's Gate, Shauna Harrison

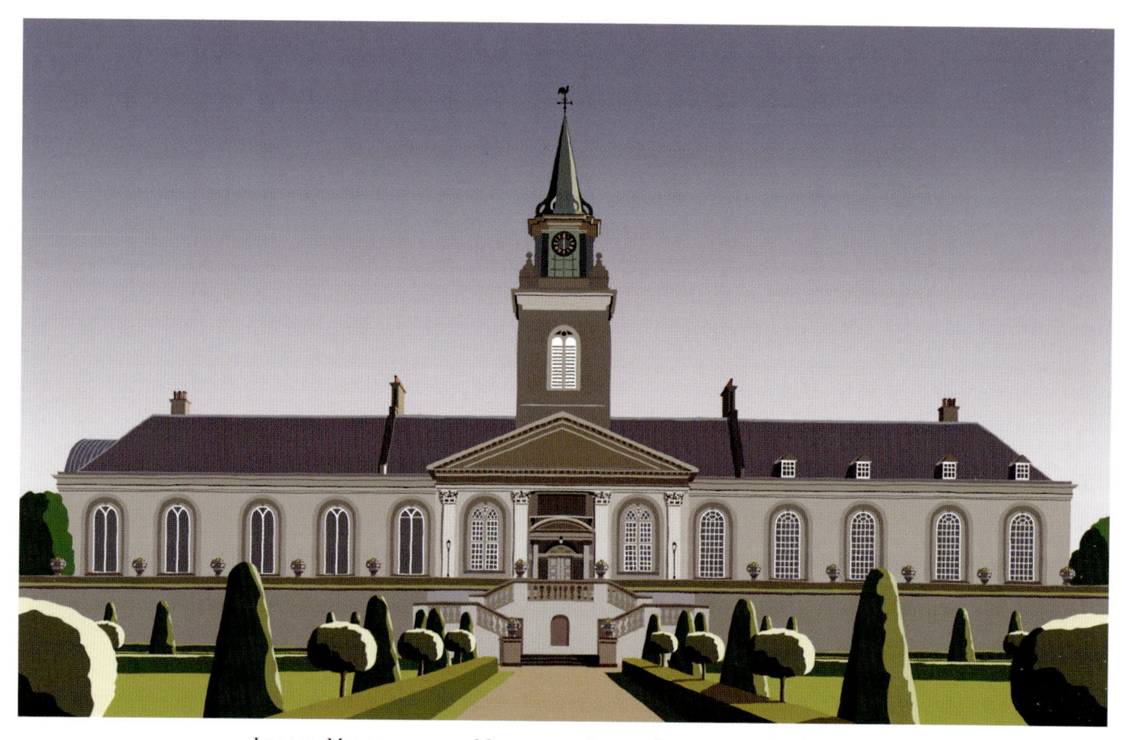

IRISH MUSEUM OF MODERN ART, RICHARD O'NEILL

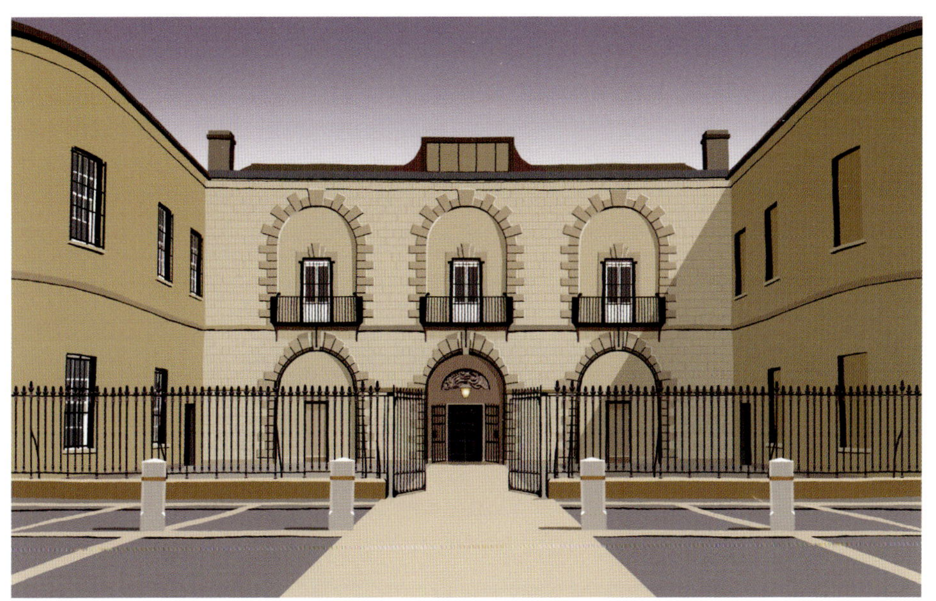

KILMAINHAM GAOL, RICHARD O'NEILL

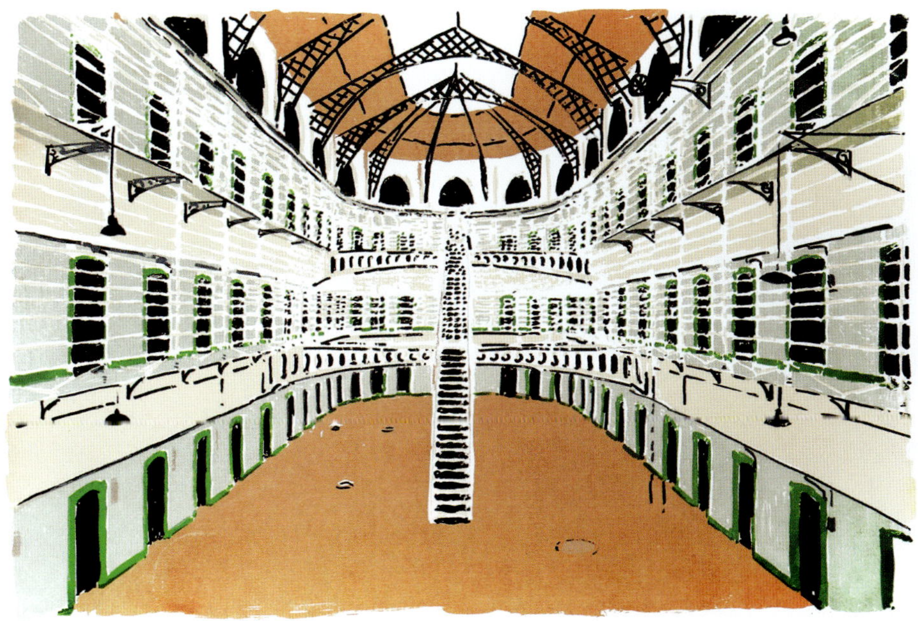

KILMAINHAM GAOL, JONATHAN BRENNAN

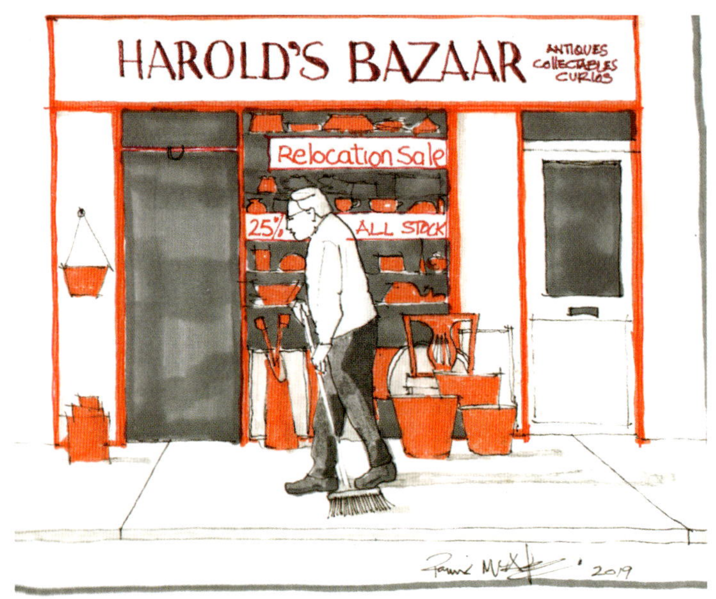

HAROLD'S CROSS, PATRICK MCAFEE

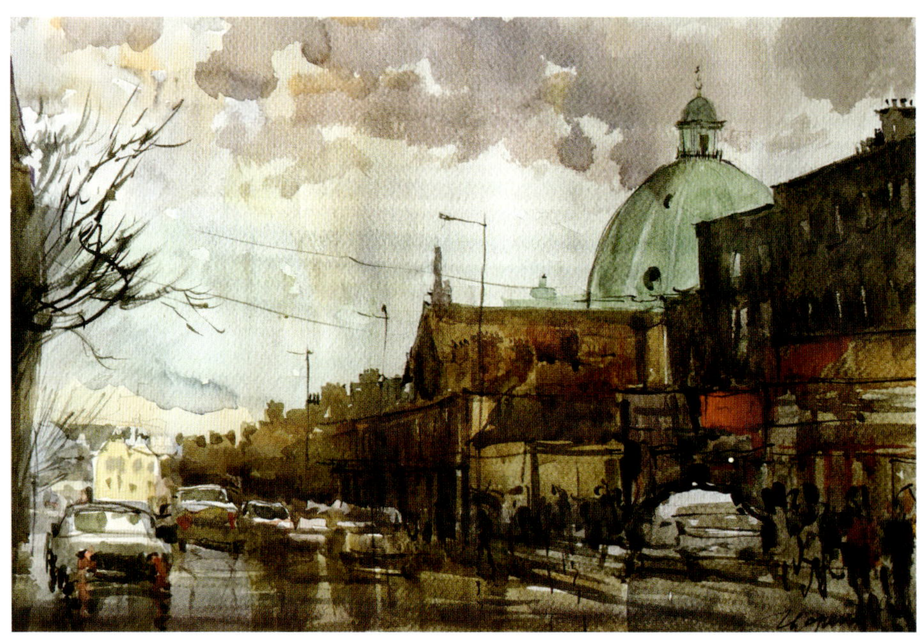

RATHMINES, TETYANA TSARYK

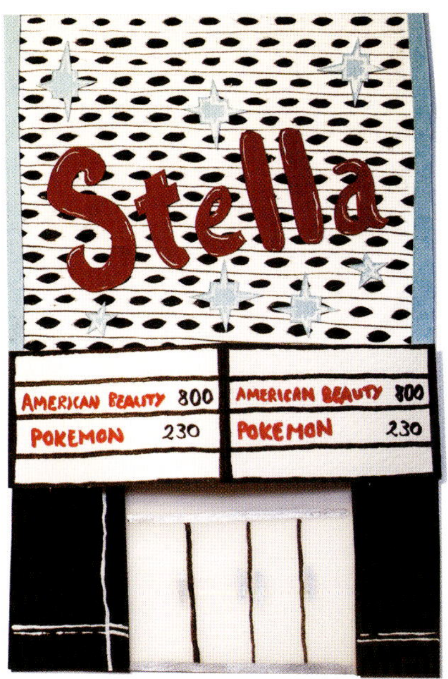

Stella
AMERICAN BEAUTY 800
POKEMON 230
AMERICAN BEAUTY 800
POKEMON 230

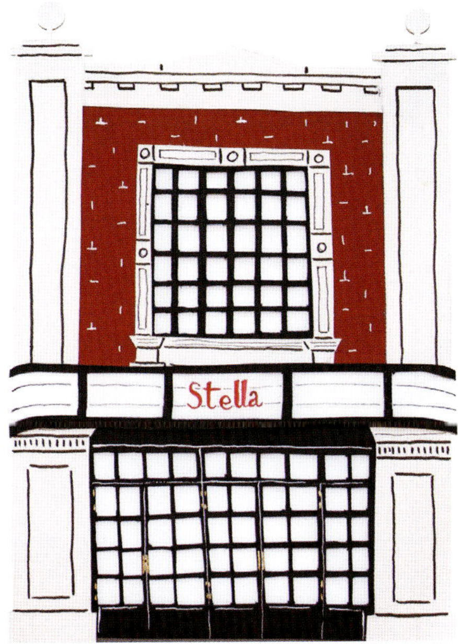

Stella

STELLA, JESSICA ROONEY DEANE

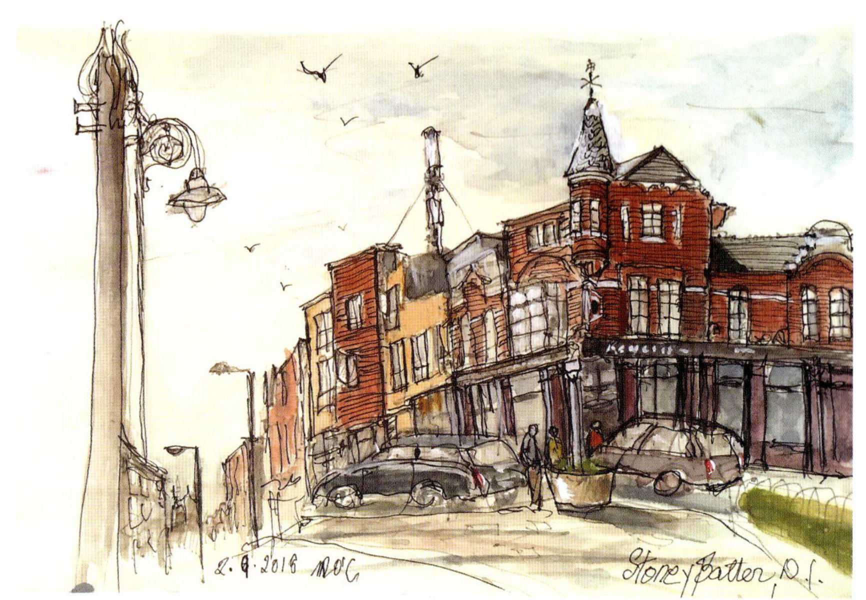

STONEYBATTER, MARY O'CARROLL

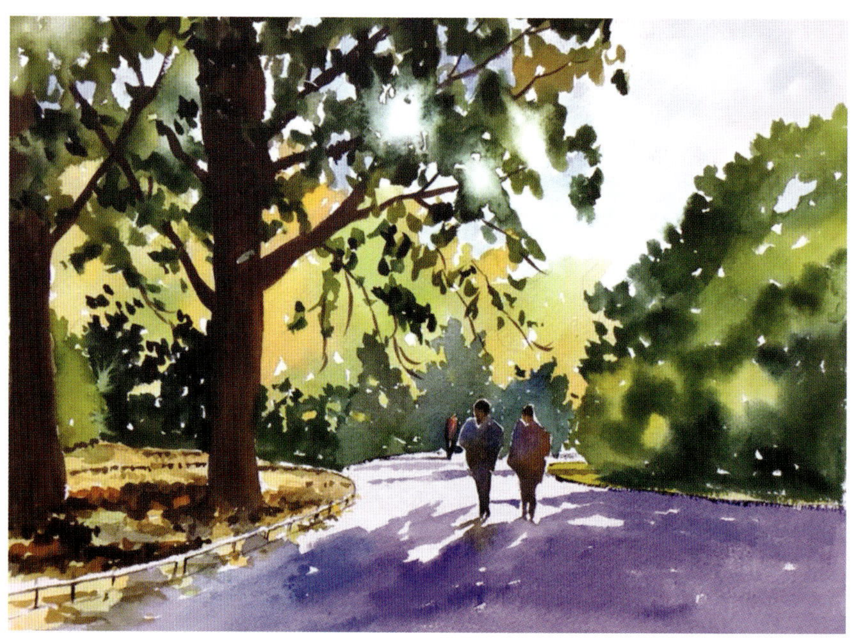

PHOENIX PARK, DERMOT BRENNAN

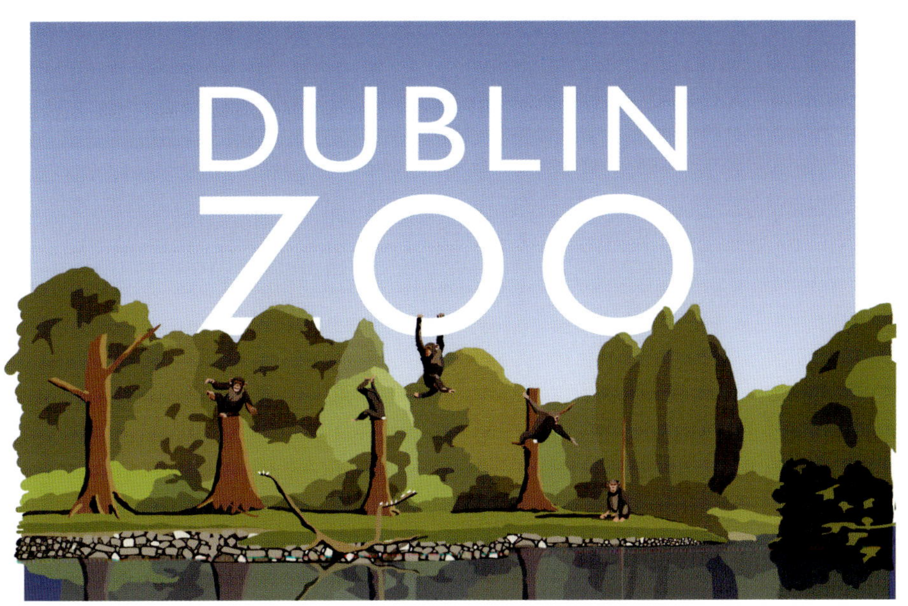

Dublin Zoo, Richard O'Neill

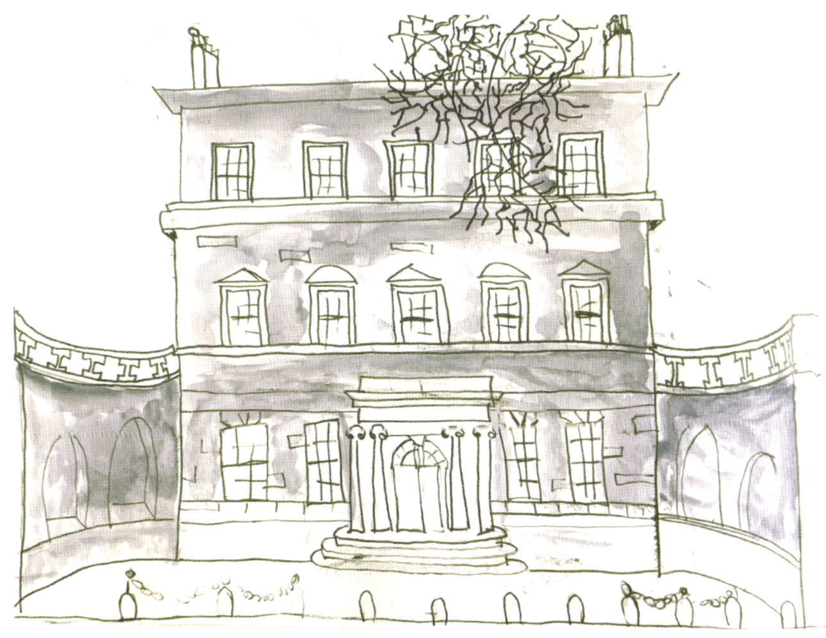

Dublin City Gallery, Kate Kavanagh

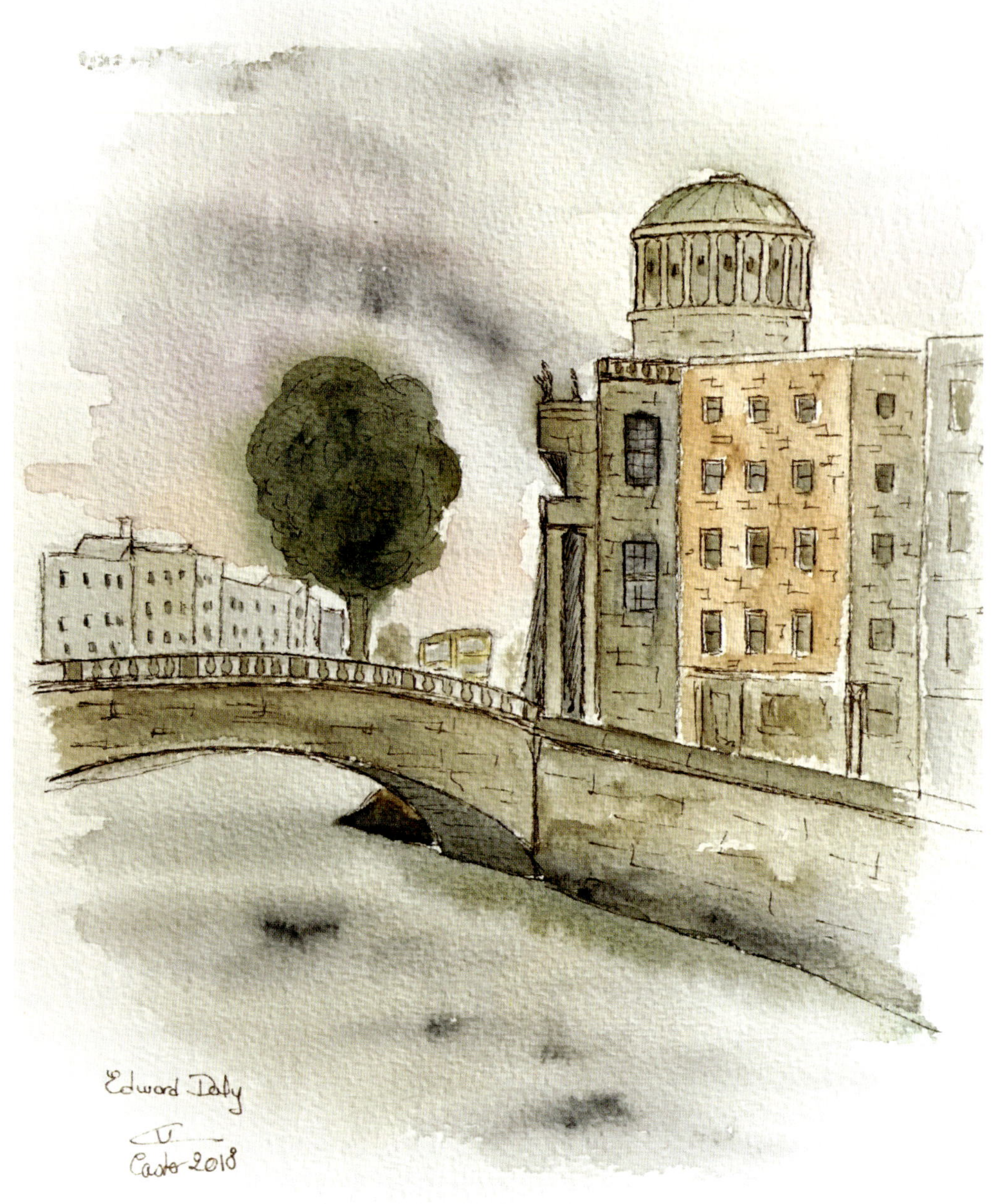

THE FOUR COURTS AND O'DONOVAN ROSSA BRIDGE, VÉRONIQUE CROMBÉ

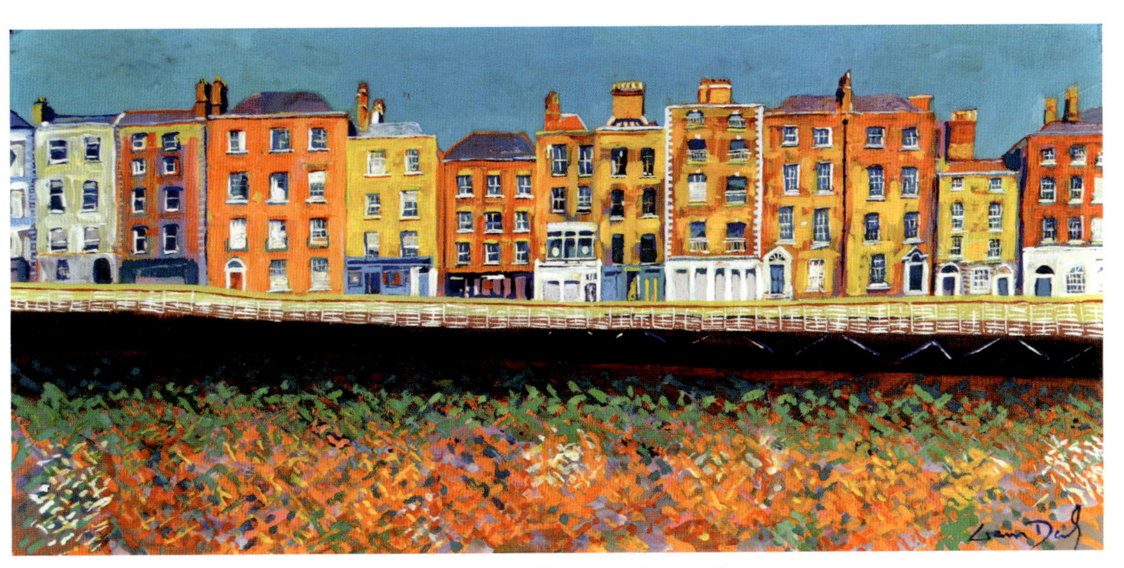

Ormond Quay Lower, Liam Daly

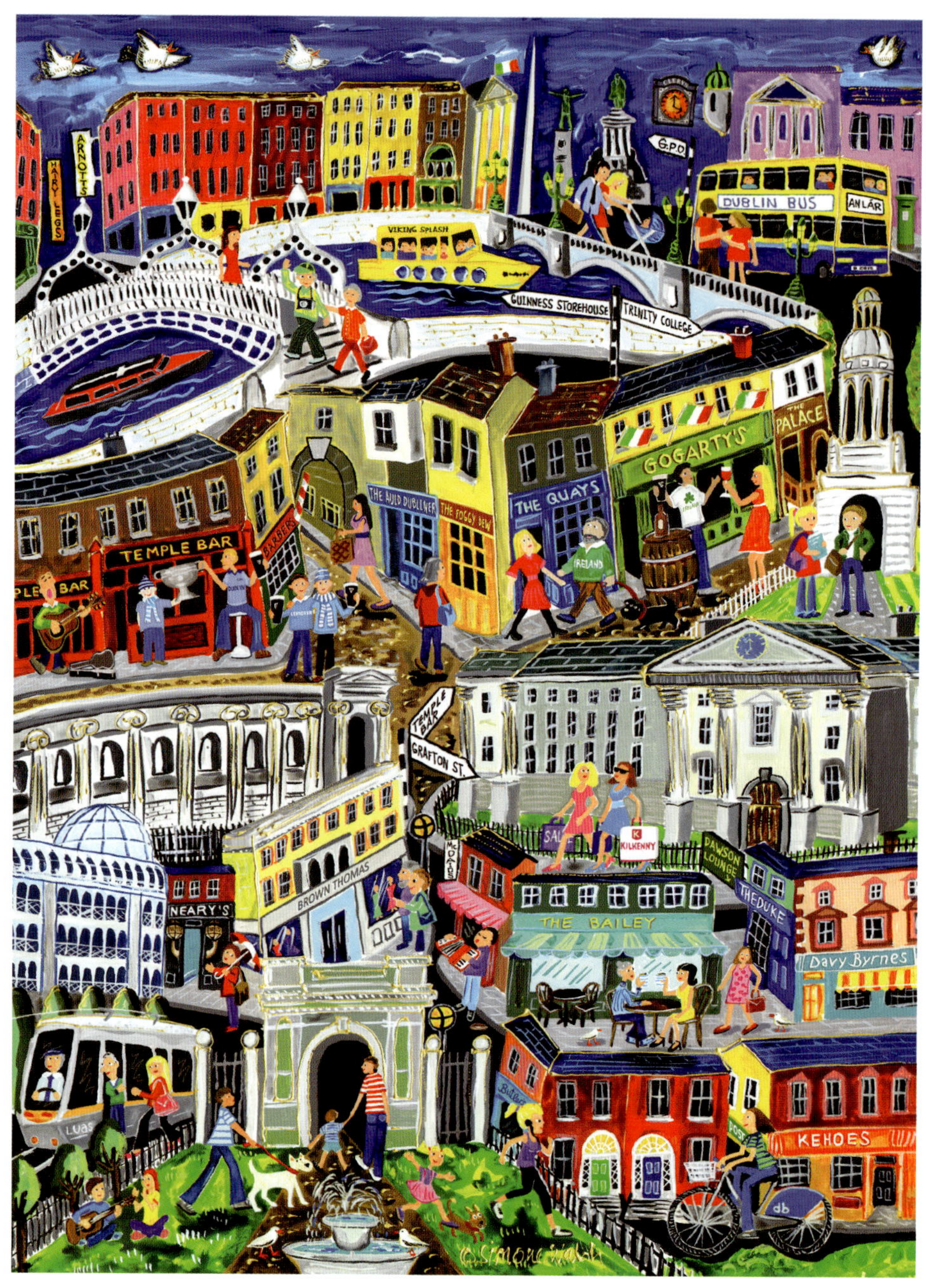

DUBLIN CITY, SIMONE WALSH

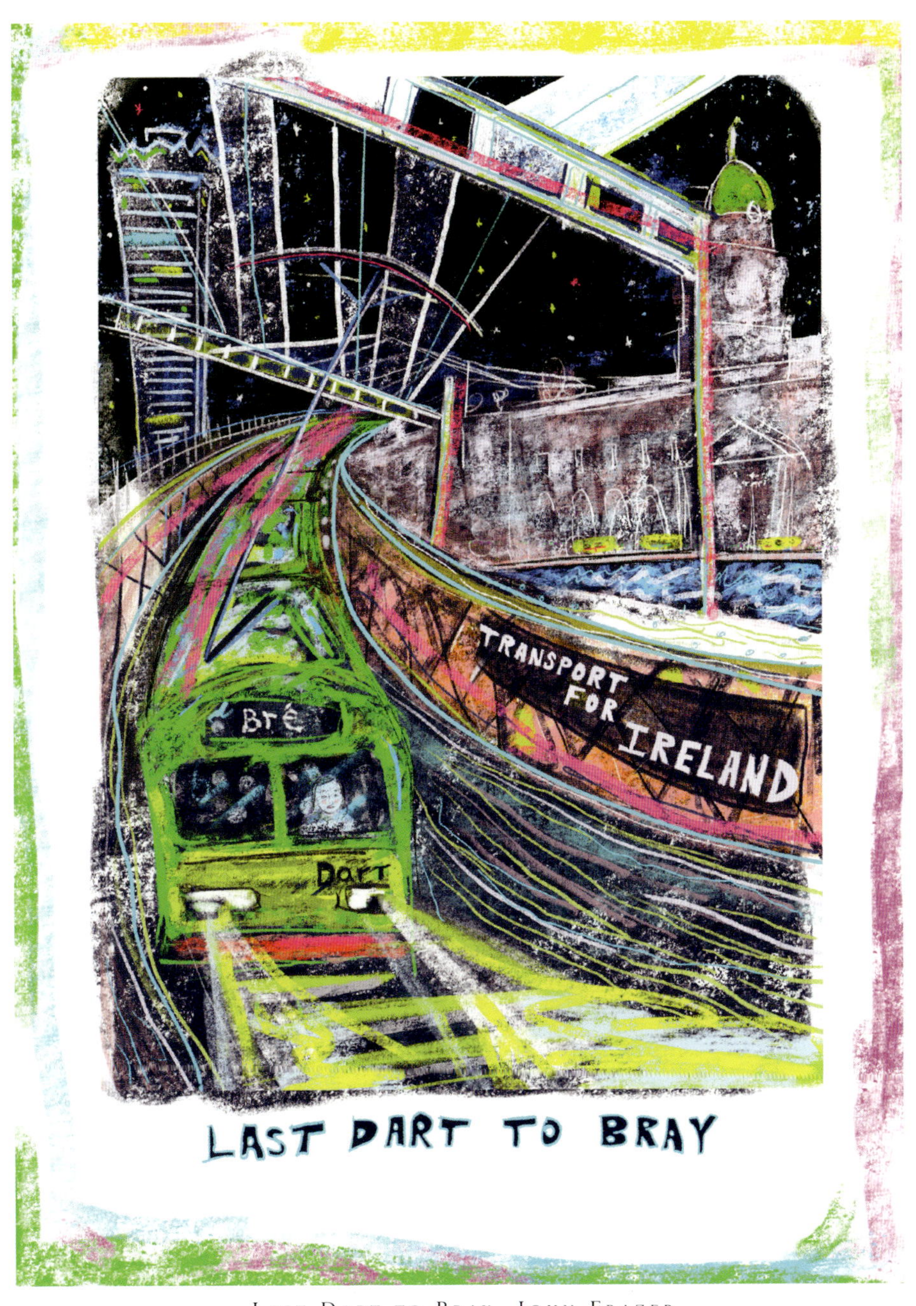

Last Dart to Bray, John Frazer

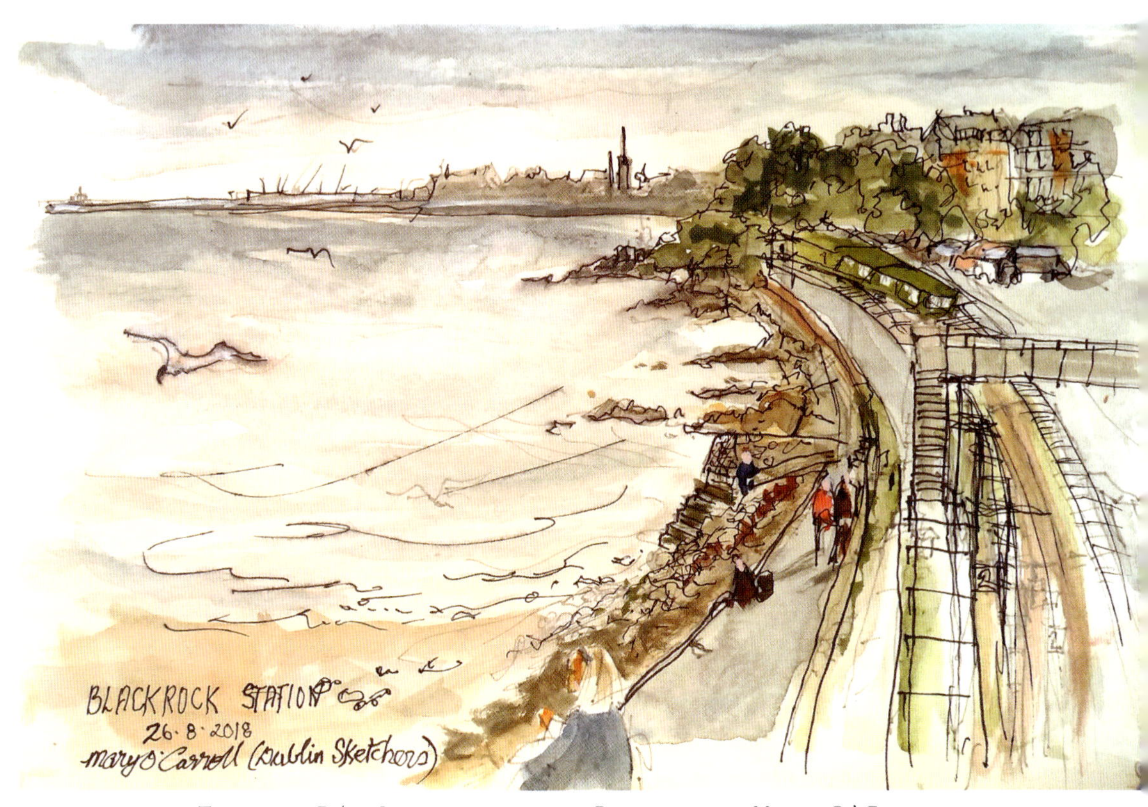

TOWARDS DÚN LAOGHAIRE FROM BLACKROCK, MARY O'CARROLL

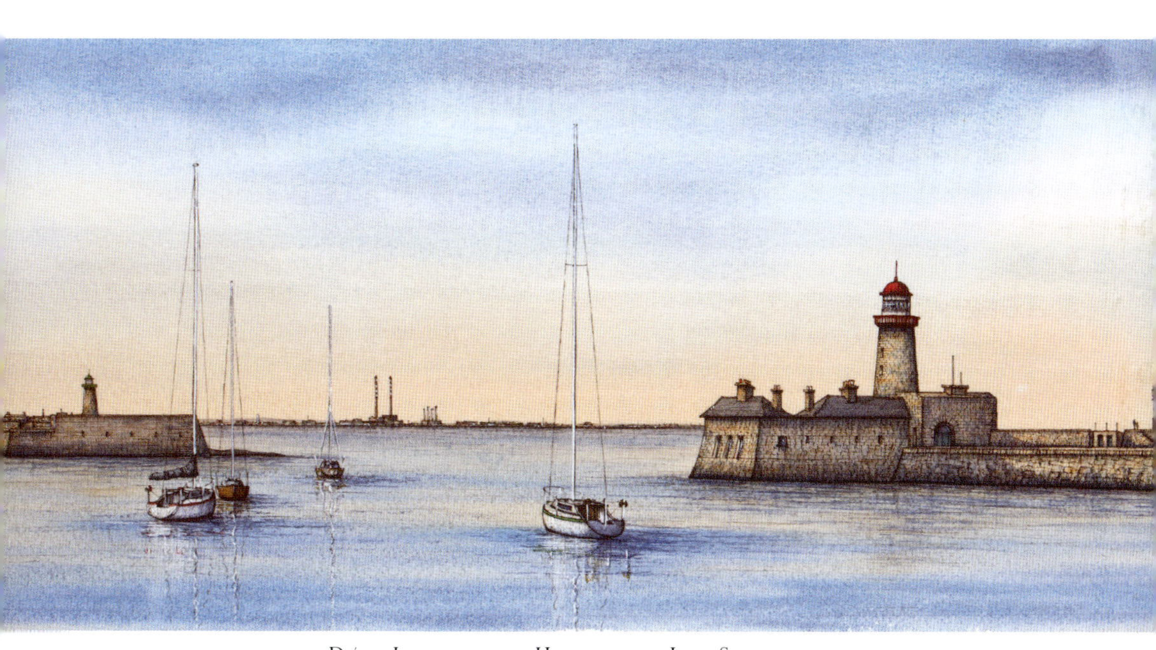

Dún Laoghaire Harbour, Jim Scully

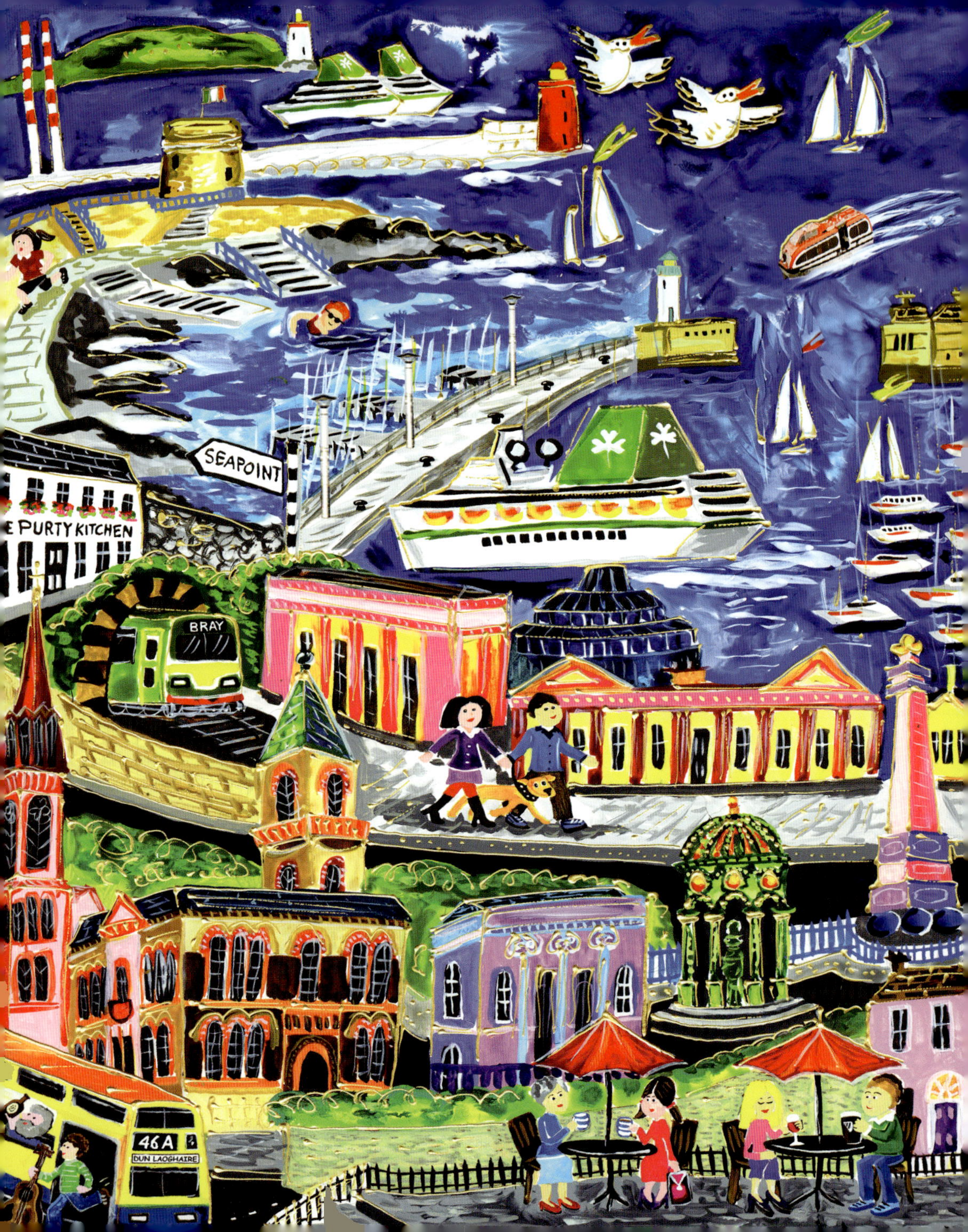
SEAPOINT
E PURTY KITCHEN
BRAY
46 A
DUN LAOGHAIRE

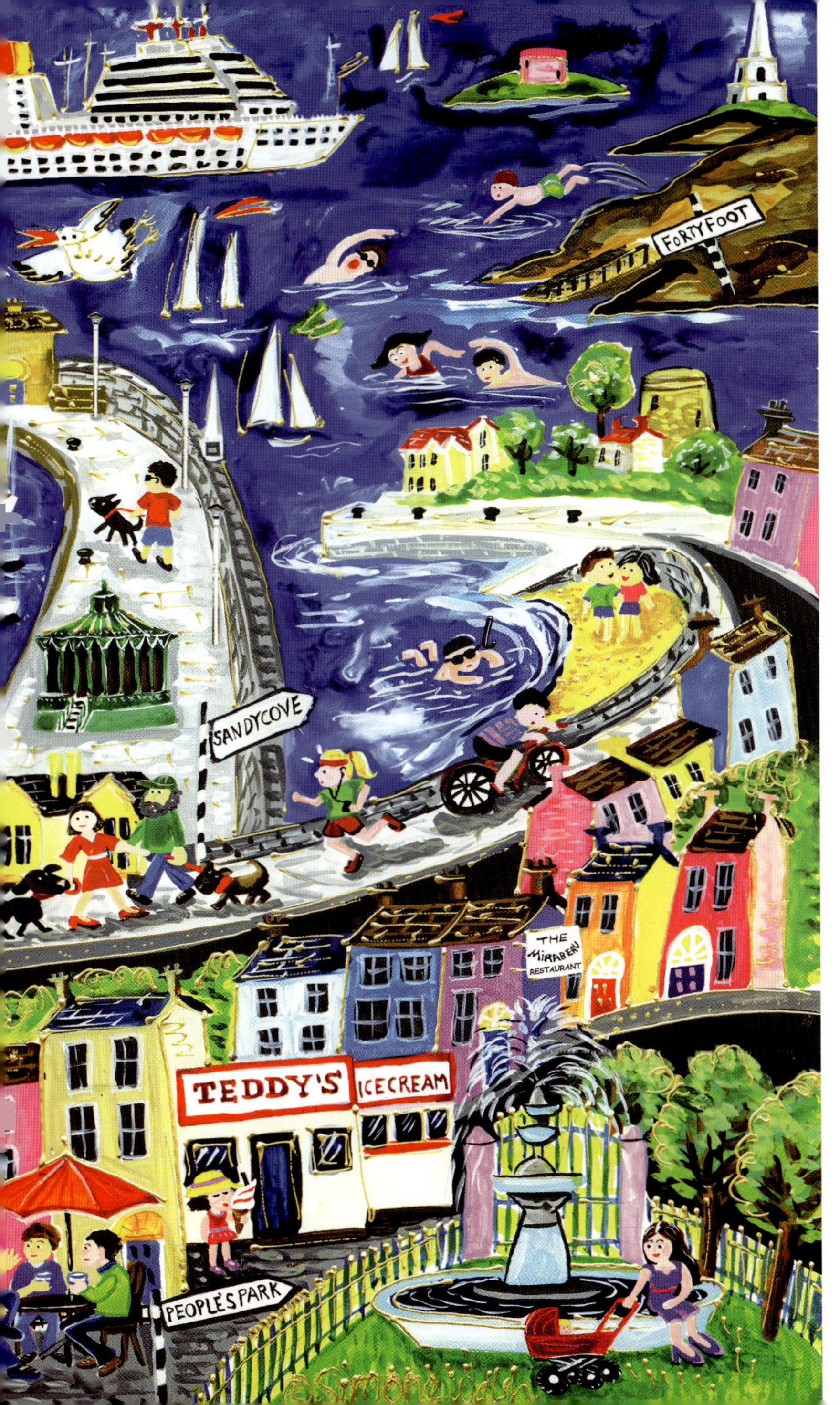

DÚN LAOGHAIRE,
SIMONE WALSH

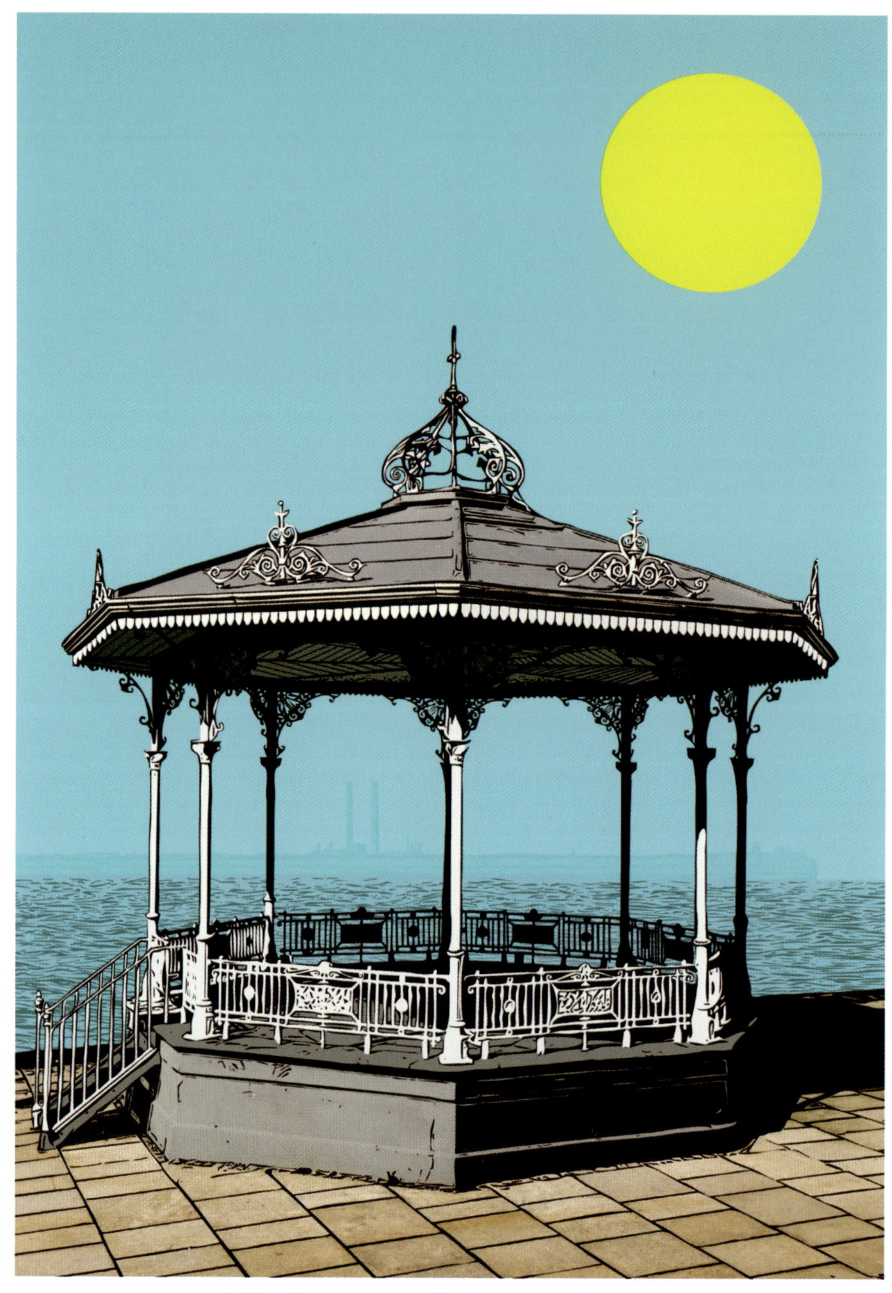

DÚN LAOGHAIRE BANDSTAND, JANDO

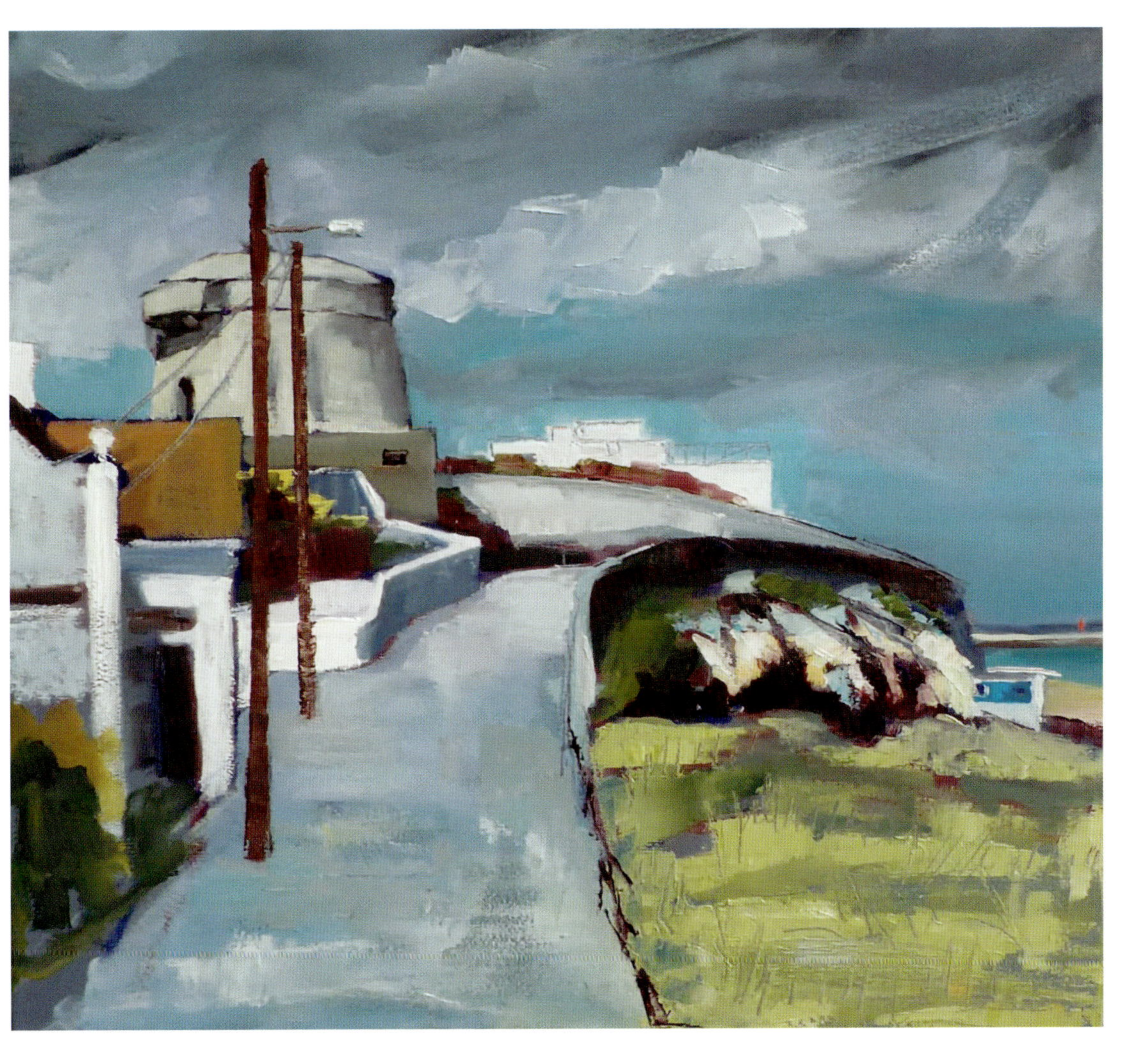

JAMES JOYCE TOWER, SANDYCOVE, ISOBEL HENIHAN

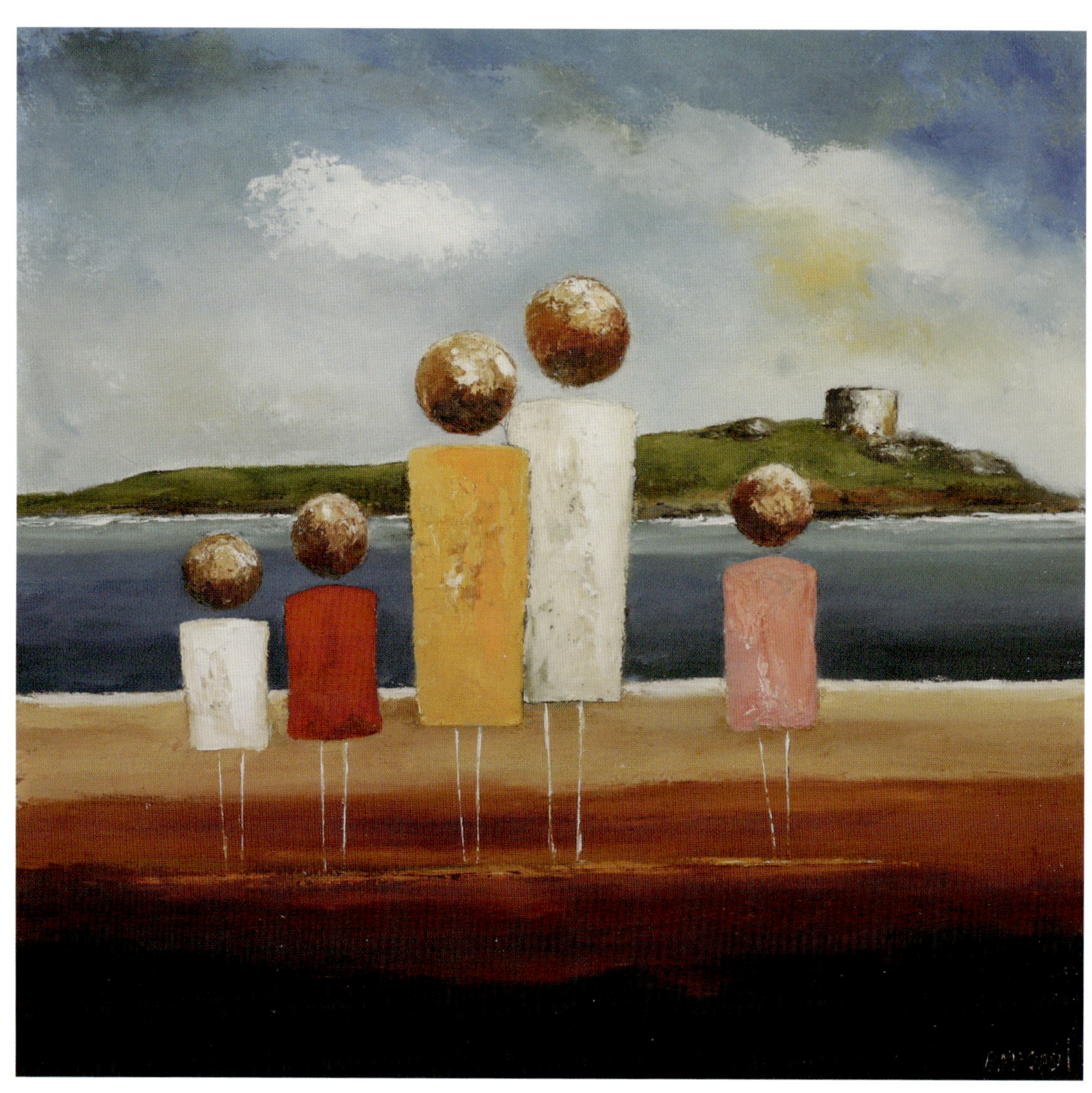

FAMILY AT DALKEY ISLAND, PADRAIG MCCAUL

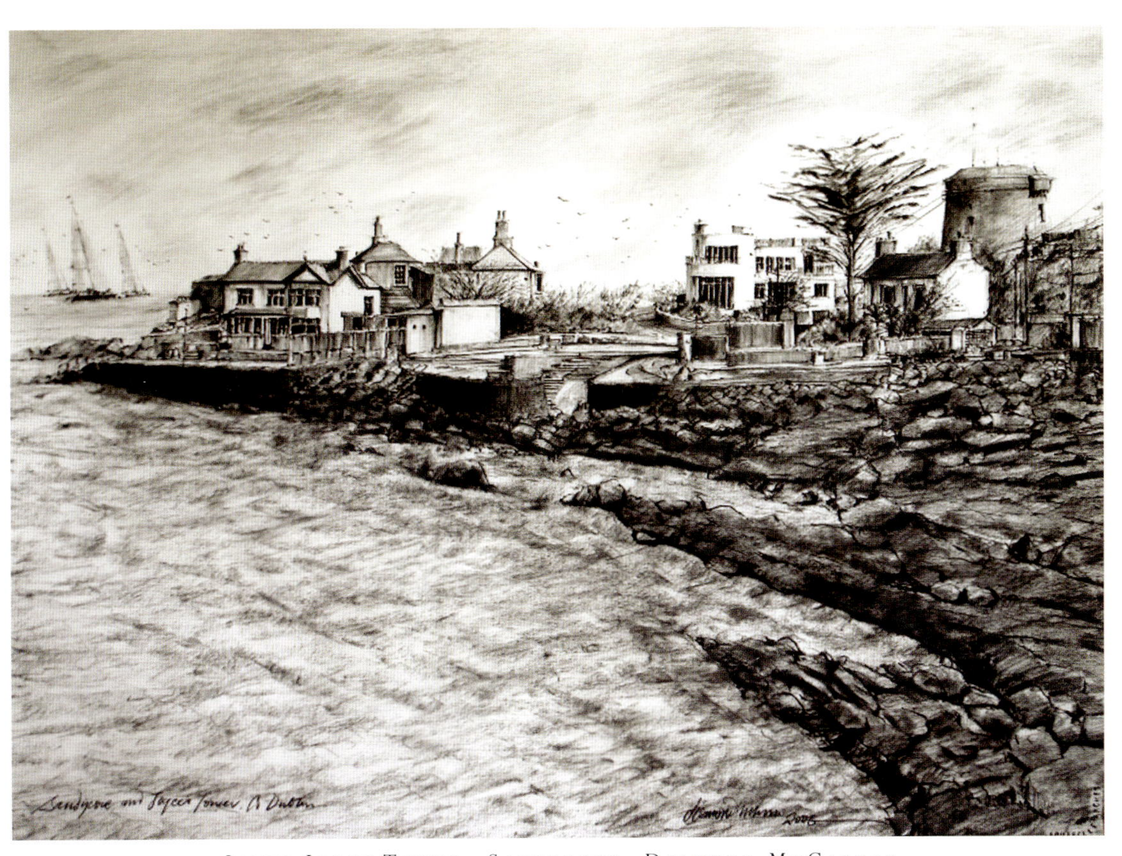

JAMES JOYCE TOWER, SANDYCOVE, DESMOND MCCARTHY

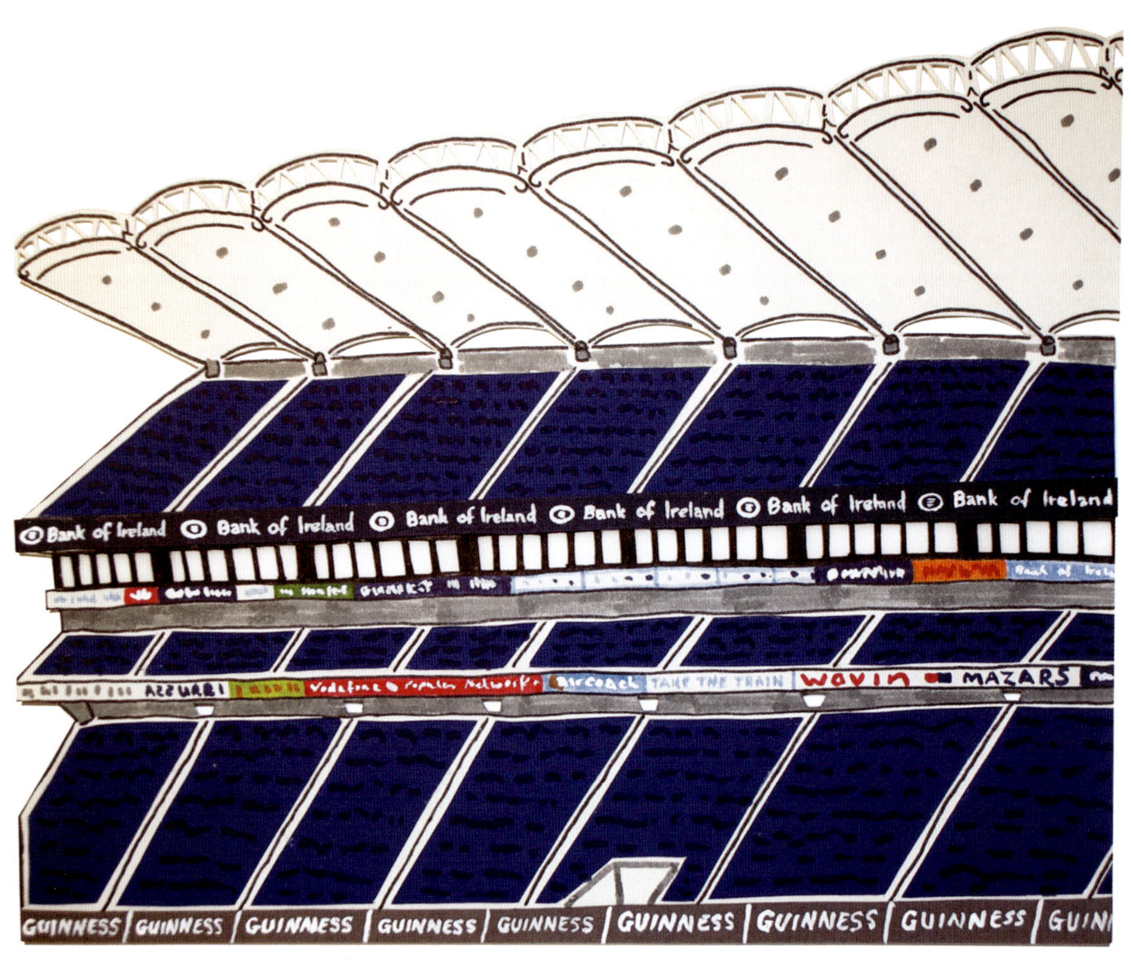

CROKE PARK, JESSICA ROONEY DEANE

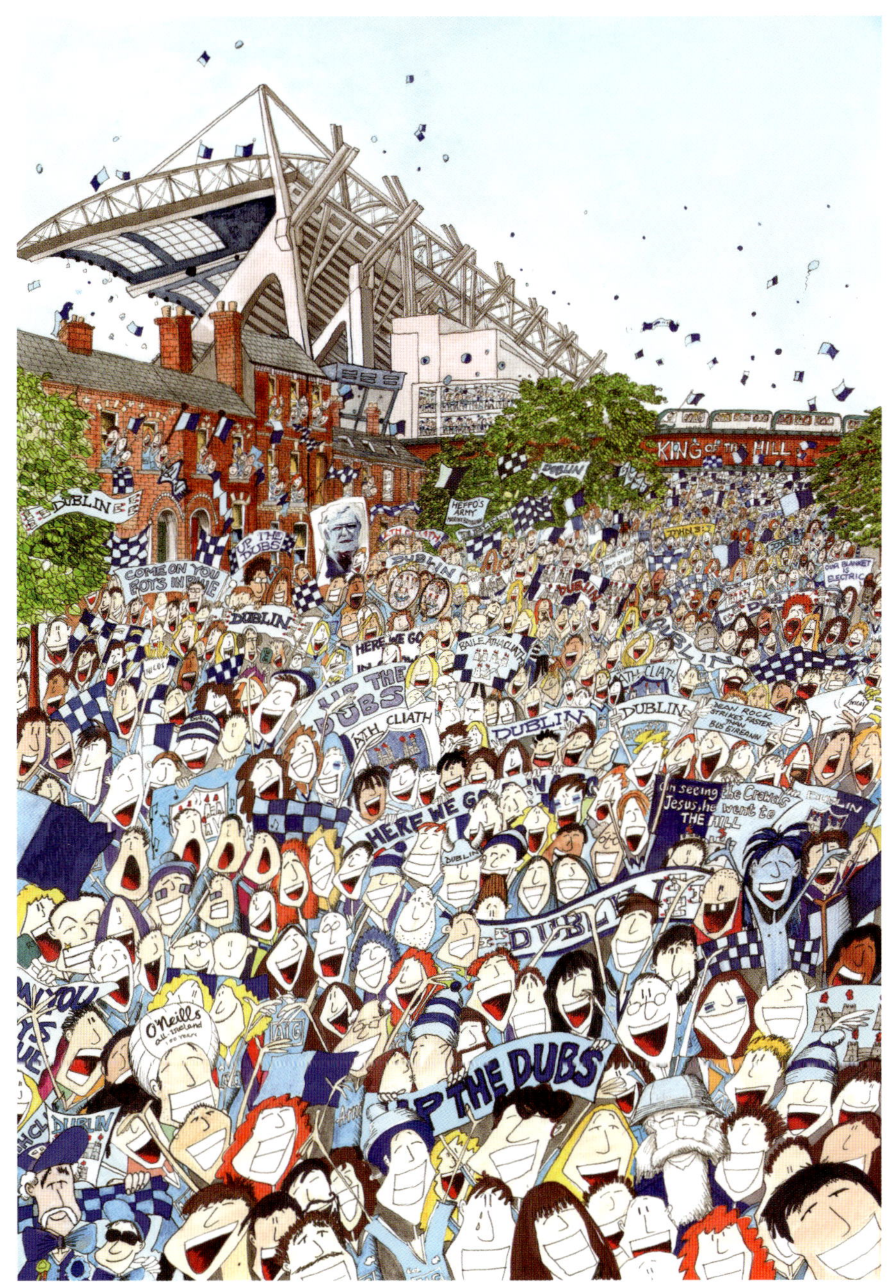

DUBLIN FANS, ANNIE WEST

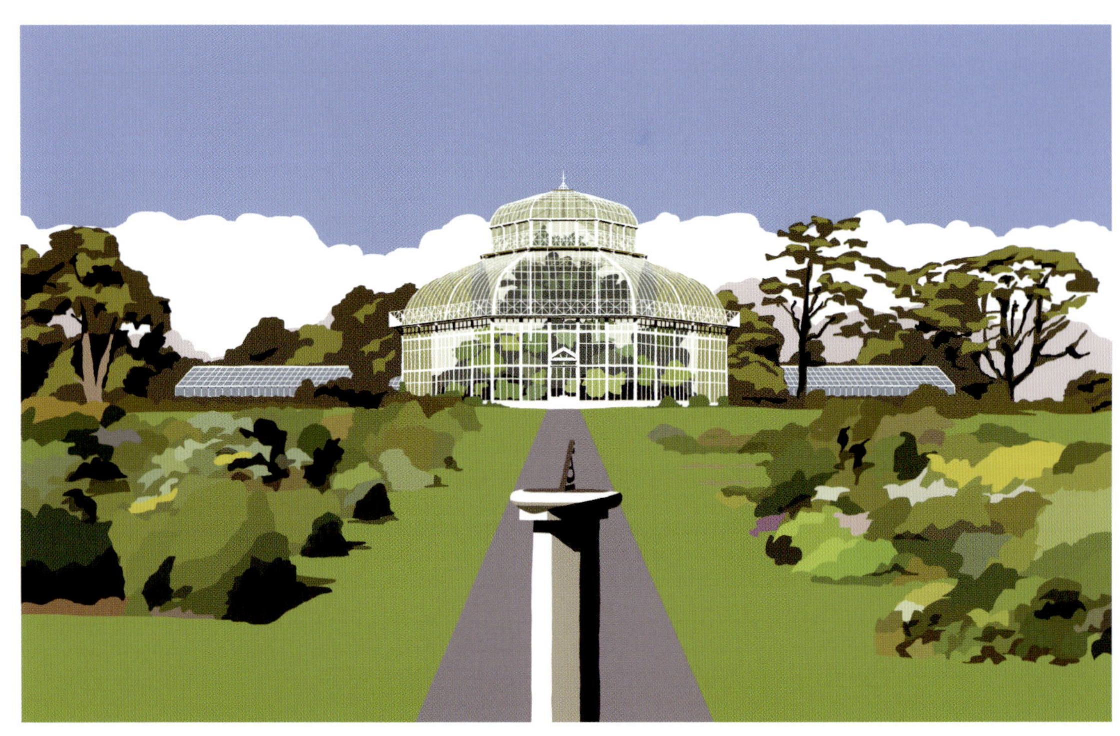

NATIONAL BOTANIC GARDENS, RICHARD O'NEILL

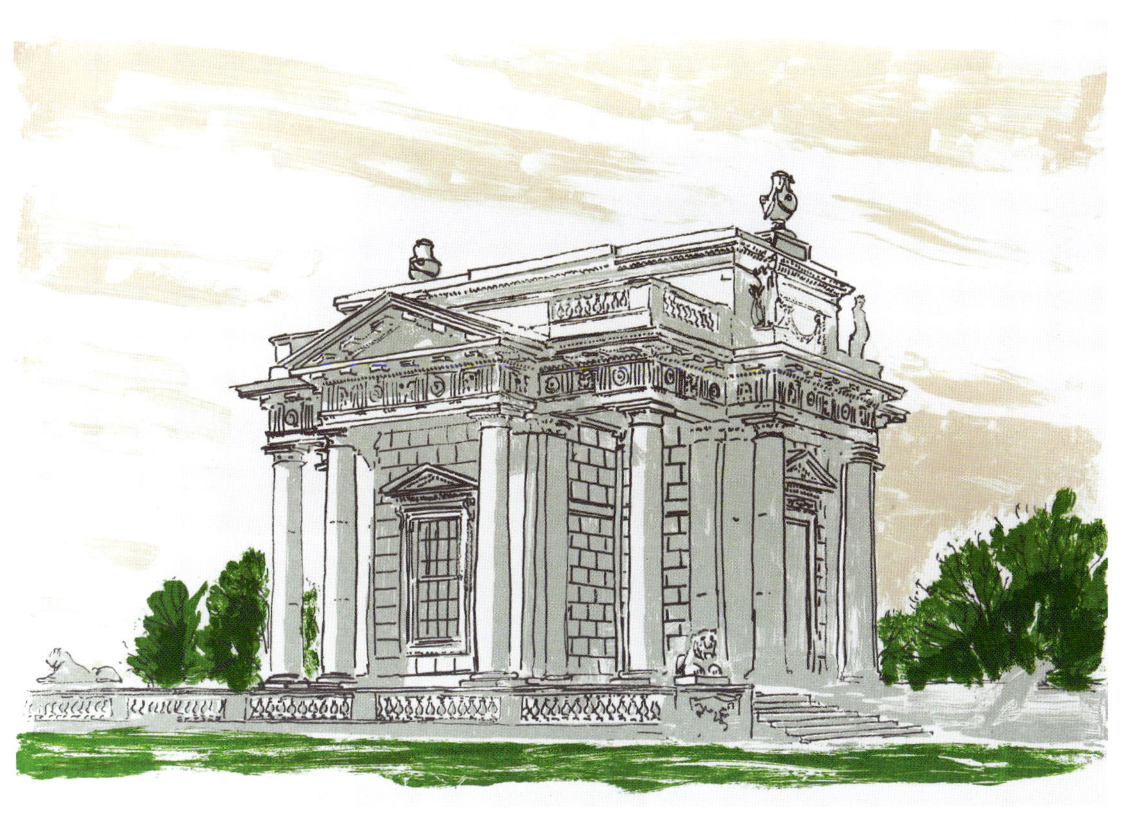

THE CASINO, MARINO, JONATHAN BRENNAN

ARTIST CREDITS

Artists' work can be found on the pages listed in parentheses

Al Power (67)
An Irish based digital illustrator specialising in minimal design
jamartfactory.com/brand/alan-power

Amy Hennesey (19, 63, 76)
Limited edition prints of Ireland; every piece features at least one bird
www.dublinbirdy.com

Anna Gwenllian (98-99)
Colourful illustrations using a combination of traditional and digital media
www.annagwenllian.com

Annie West (10, 139)
Amusing pen and ink illustrations
www.anniewest.com

**Brian O'Neill
(23, 35, 80, 82, 101, 115)**
Works in watercolour, portraiture and ceramic design
brianmoneill@hotmail.com

Caitriona Shaffrey (51, 78-79)
Pen, ink and watercolour sketches looking at living environments, especially those under threat
shafby@gmail.com

**Chris McMorrow
(11, 37, 70, 73, 88, 109)**
Self-taught Dublin artist who paints vibrant romantic street scenes and landscapes
www.chrismcmorrow.net

Claudine O'Sullivan (113)
Coloured pencil drawing of Dublin's Ha'penny Bridge, available as a print
www.claudineosullivan.com

Conor Smyth (22)
A graphic designer and illustrator creating paintings using digital media
www.conorsmythdesigns.com

Dave Thompson (34, 97, 100)
Homage to iconic travel posters rendered digitally in vector flat colour
www.davethompsonillustration.com

Dermot Brennan (49, 50, 124)
Artist painting in watercolour and oils
dermotbrennan670@yahoo.com

Dermot Ryan (16, 32)
Fine Art printmaker of Intaglio, relief and monotype prints
dergeryan@yahoo.co.uk

**Desmond McCarthy
(27, 33, 46, 47, 50, 103, 112, 137)**
International artist/educator, based in Ireland, specialising in commissioned fine art drawings
www.facebook.com/Desmond-McCarthy-308530725974231

Emma Bennett (cover, 40)
Vibrant hand-cut collage using recycled papers and hand-drawn and digital illustration
www.emmabennettcollage.co.uk

Emma Montonen (40, 44)
Watercolour artist and violinist
www.emmamontonen.com

Eva Kelly (17, 21, 25, 74, 116)
Ink and pen drawings combined with digital flat colour and ink washes
www.evakellyillustration.com

Isobel Henihan (60, 135)
Isobel is a Dublin-based artist working mainly in oils on canvas
www.isobelhenihan.com

Jacob Stack (94)
Illustrator, doodler and scribbler,
often found wandering about
instagram.com/jacobstack_art

**James Francis Moore
(64-65, 71)**
Digital artwork using a cartoon
modern approach developed
with At it Again!
www.jamesfrancismoore.com

Jenny Seddon (map of Dublin)
Illustration and screen prints
www.jennyseddon.com

**Jessica Rooney Deane
(84, 123, 138)**
Hand-cut paper and mixed
media illustrations
www.jessrooneydeane.com

Jim Scully (44, 85, 111, 131)
Detailed and vibrant paintings
created using mixed media
of ink and watercolour
www.jimscullyart.ie

John Frazer (28-29, 129)
Hand-drawn images with digital
colour
www.johnfrazerprints.com

John Nolan (59, 106-107)
A celebration of colour
through contemporary, stylized
and abstract painting
www.nolanart.com

John Rooney (96)
Derry-born, Berlin-based illustrator
inspired by wildlife, cult films and
1980s cartoons
www.johnrooneyillustration.com

**Jonathan Brennan
(58, 121, 141)**
Artist, printmaker, photographer,
graphic designer, web developer,
videographer, writer and translator
www.jonathanbrennanart.com

**Julie and Owen Mc Loughlin
(JANDO) (14, 20, 55, 56, 62, 134)**
Original hand-pulled screen prints
and archival pigment prints
www.jando.ie

Kate Kavanagh (72, 125)
A visual recording of what she
observes – always a journalist
katekavart@gmail.com

Kevin McGuinness (57, 69)
Hand-drawn mementos to
capture that special place or
moment for loved ones
www.facebook.com/kevdrawsart

Leo Tierney (72)
Paintings in acrylics using
knife and brush
leom.tierney@gmail.com

Liam Daly (57, 81, 114, 127)
Paintings of landscapes and street
scenes, primarily of Ireland
www.liamdaly.art

Marie O'Callaghan (11)
An artist who paints landscapes
and streetscapes in oils
mcocallaghan52@gmail.com

**Marie-Hélène Brohan Delhaye
(41, 52, 76, 82)**
Marie-Hélène is an urban sketcher.
She loves sketching in pen and
watercolours
www.mhbd.blogspot.com

Marta Wakula-Mac (60, 68)
A fine art printmaker working
in linocut and intaglio printmaking
techniques
Martawakulamac.blogspot.com

**Mary O'Carroll
(25, 54, 124, 130)**
Watercolourist and urban sketcher
maryoc198@gmail.com

Patrick McAfee (53, 122)
Dublin urban sketcher, sketching
on location. Mixed media
mcafee@eircom.net

Padraig McCaul (61, 136)
Palette knife artist working in
oils on canvas
www.padraigmccaul.com

Pete Monaghan (83)
Mixed-media paintings of
vernacular architecture
www.petemonaghan.com

Pol Gallagher (35, 112, 119)
Pol is a Donegal-London
architect exploring locations
through illustration and text
www.zaparchitecture.com

Pico Mac (95)
Black and white watercolour
cityscape art
pico-mac.pixels.com

Rachel Corcoran (45, 118)
Dubliner Rachel is a freelance
illustrator and maker of earth-
kind prints
www.rachelcorcoran.net

**Richard O'Neill (41, 42-43,
120, 121, 125, 140)**
Richard is a digital artist
specialising in hand-drawn,
contemporary landscapes
www.richardoneillart.co.uk

Richard Dalton (8-9)
Richard is an Irish artist
and designer
www.etsy.com/ie/shop/
richardedalton

Rob Torrans (18, 75)
Rob's personal work often
depicts the small everyday
annoyances and silliness
www.robtorrans.com

Ruth Allen (26)
Ruth captures the image
through the use of a delicate
continuous line
www.ruthallenstudio.com

Sean Hillen (12, 26)
Artist /collagist and
photographer; studied
at Slade School
www.seanhillen.com

**Shauna Harrison (89, 90-91
102, 105, 108, 117, 119)**
Illustrator and artist
specialising in hand-drawn
illustration
instagram.com/
shaunaharrisonart

**Simone Walsh
(36, 128, 132-133)**
Acrylic and gold relief
paint on paper
www.simonewalsh.net

Sketchy (24, 31, 101)
With a passion for bright
colour, Sketchy is dedicated to
spreading a positive message
through his work
www.sketchyinc.com

**Terri Kelleher
(15, 30, 48, 69)**
Fine art and illustration
www.terrikelleher.com

**Tetyana Tsaryk
(38-39, 51, 77, 86, 122)**
Oil paintings, watercolours
and ceramics
www.bespokeirishart.ie

Tracey Flynn (87)
Continuous-line mono-print
drawings and mixed media
paintings
traceyflynn.com

Valeri Byrne (92-93)
Valeri can be commissioned
to create your world in
watercolour and ink
www.valeribyrne.com

Véronique Crombé (126)
Watercolours, pastels and
charcoal drawings from many
places around the world
www.artmajeur.com/fr/
veronique-crombe/artworks/
galleries

Victoria Wood (104)
Architecture and landscape
artist, illustrations in ink and
watercolour
www.sketchpadontour.co.uk

**Walter Bernardini
(13, 17, 110)**
Walter works in all mediums
and is always willing to accept
commissions
www.walterbernardini.com

Every effort has been made to correctly credit contributors. In the case of any omissions or
errors we would be pleased to make appropriate corrections in future editions.

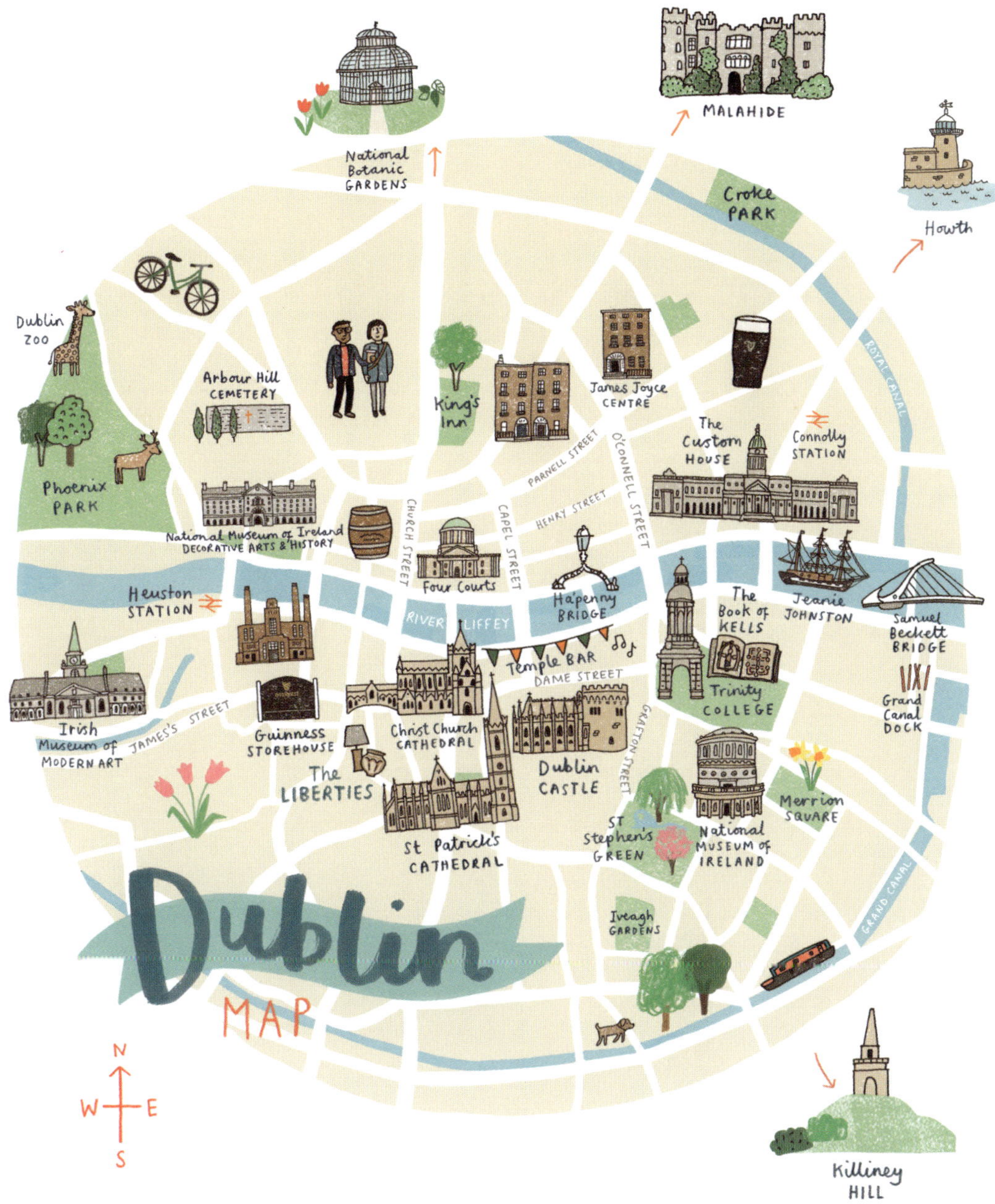

MALAHIDE
Howth
National Botanic GARDENS
Croke PARK
Dublin ZOO
Arbour Hill CEMETERY
King's Inn
James Joyce CENTRE
The Custom HOUSE
Connolly STATION
Phoenix PARK
PARNELL STREET
O'CONNELL STREET
HENRY STREET
National Museum of Ireland DECORATIVE ARTS & HISTORY
CHURCH STREET
CAPEL STREET
Four Courts
Ha'penny BRIDGE
The Book of KELLS
Jeanie JOHNSTON
Samuel Beckett BRIDGE
Heuston STATION
RIVER LIFFEY
Temple BAR
DAME STREET
Trinity COLLEGE
Grand Canal DOCK
Irish Museum of MODERN ART
JAMES'S STREET
Guinness STOREHOUSE
Christ Church CATHEDRAL
Dublin CASTLE
GRAFTON STREET
Merrion SQUARE
The LIBERTIES
St Patrick's CATHEDRAL
St Stephen's GREEN
National Museum of IRELAND
ROYAL CANAL
Dublin MAP
Iveagh GARDENS
GRAND CANAL
N W E S
Killiney HILL

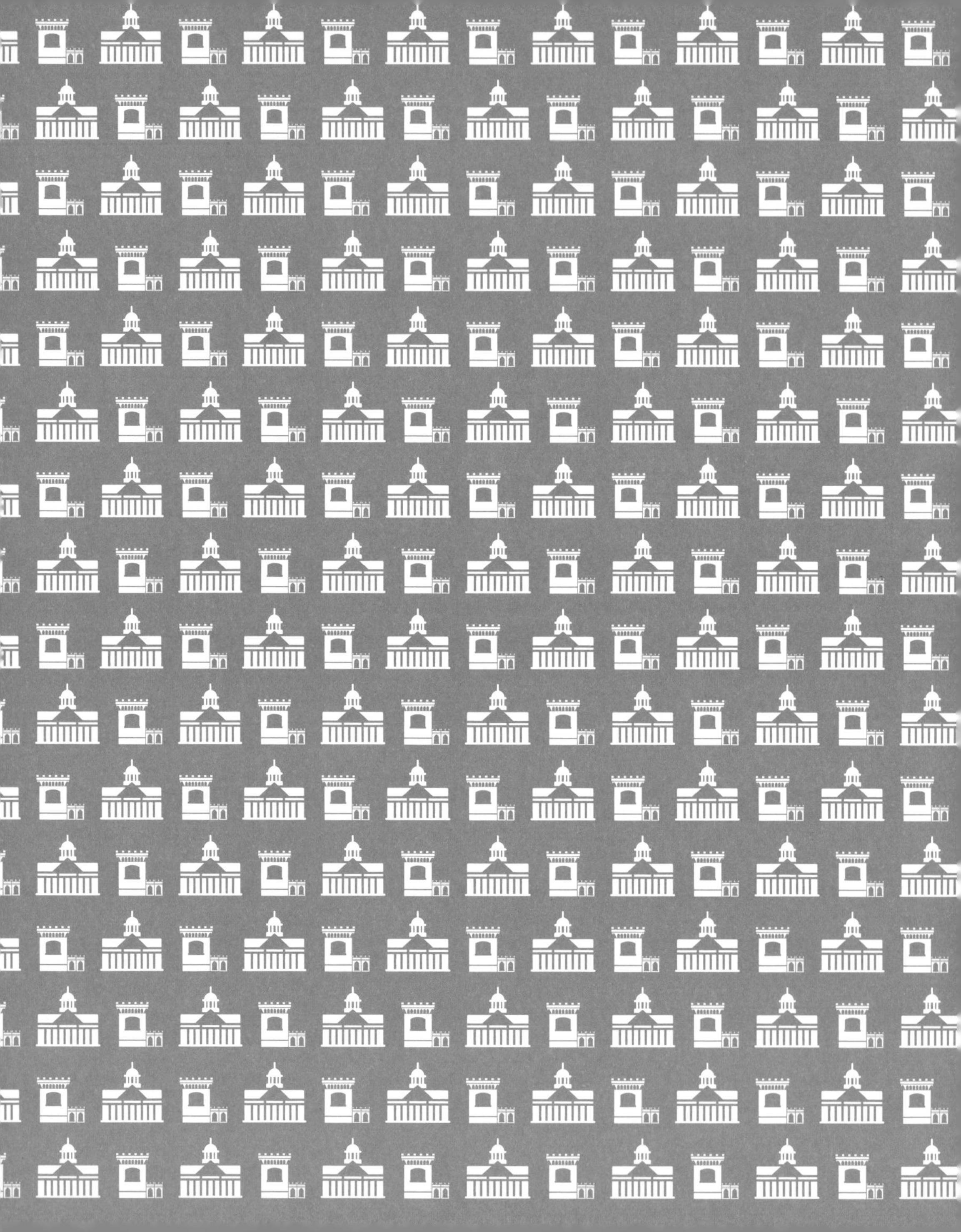